STUDY

REVISION

COLLINS
STUDY & REVISION GUIDE

ENGLISH
National Tests Key Stage 3

▸ Geoff Barton
▸ Laurie Smith

▸ Series Editor: Jayne de Courcy

Collins Educational
An Imprint of HarperCollinsPublishers

Contents

Boosting your National Test score — iii
Your English course – level-by-level — iv

LEVEL 4

1. Reading and Understanding Fiction — 1
2. Reading and Understanding Non-fiction — 4
3. Imaginative Writing — 7
4. Writing to inform and persuade — 10

LEVEL 5

5. Reading and Understanding Fiction — 17
6. Reading and Understanding Non-fiction — 22
7. Imaginative Writing — 26
8. Writing to inform and persuade — 31

LEVEL 6

9. Reading and Understanding Fiction — 39
10. Reading and Understanding Non-fiction — 44
11. Imaginative Writing — 48
12. Writing to inform and persuade — 53

LEVEL 7

13. Reading and Understanding Fiction — 60
14. Reading and Understanding Non-fiction — 65
15. Imaginative Writing — 69
16. Writing to inform and persuade — 73

LEVELS 4–7

17. Reading and Writing about Shakespeare — 83
18. The Essentials of Language — 101

TEST PRACTICE

19. Test Techniques Paper 1 — 119
20. Paper 1 — 123
21. Test Techniques Paper 2 — 130
22. Examiner's Hints Paper 2 — 136
23. Paper 2 — 146

ANSWERS AND EXAMINER'S COMMENTS

24. Paper 1: Section A Narrative — 152
25. Paper 1: Section B Media — 158
26. Paper 1: Section C Writing — 162
27. Paper 2: Macbeth — 181
28. Paper 2: Romeo and Juliet — 188
29. Paper 2: Twelfth Night — 195

Index — 201

Boosting your National Test score

Study and Revise from one book

You may be starting – or part of the way through – your Key Stage 3 English course. You may be in year 9 and getting close to your National Test in English. Wherever you are in your course, this book will help you. It will improve your reading and writing skills in English and your ability to answer Test questions.

The English National Curriculum explained

First, the technical information! The English National Curriculum is divided into three *Attainment Targets*. These are called:

En1 Speaking and listening
En2 Reading
En3 Writing

Each Attainment Target is divided up into *level descriptions*, numbered from level 1 to level 8. (There is also a top level called Exceptional performance.) These level descriptions tell you what you should know and be able to do at each level.

By the end of Key Stage 3, the majority of pupils will be between levels 3 and 7. A typical Key Stage 3 pupil should be around levels 5 and 6.

Exceptional performance •	} considerably better than the expected level
Level 8 •	
Level 7 •	} better than the expected level
Level 6 •	} expected level for 14 year olds
Level 5 •	
Level 4 •	
Level 3 •	} working towards the expected level
Level 2 •	
Level 1 •	
Age • **14 years**	

Typical 14 year olds get a level 5 or 6 in the English National Test. This book will show you where you are and help you move up through the levels.

What's in the English National Test?

The National Test papers for English that you will sit in May of year 9 have questions that cover Reading and Writing. Almost all students sit the same Test papers, but your school may decide that you should sit an Extension paper by which Level 8 and Exceptional performance can be achieved.

There are two Test papers. Paper 1 tests your reading and writing. Paper 2 tests you on the Shakespeare play you have studied in class.

Paper 1
You are required to:
A Read an extract from a novel, short story, biography or autobiography and answer questions on it.
B Read a media text – like a leaflet or a newspaper extract – and answer questions on it.
C Write something about a topic that is related to the texts that you read in the first two sections of the paper.

Paper 2
Paper 2 tests you on the Shakespeare play that you have studied in class.

There is not a separate Test for spelling, punctuation and grammar, but your marks in Paper 1 (section C) and Paper 2 do take account of your spelling, punctuation and grammar.

Your English course – level-by-level

boosting your National Test score

This is the first book to show you, level-by-level, what you need to know for your Tests.

The first 16 chapters in this book are organised by level and skill. At each level – 4, 5, 6 and 7 – there are four sections:

- Reading and understanding fiction
- Reading and understanding non-fiction
- Imaginative writing
- Writing to inform and persuade

These are the skills that you need to develop and practise to do well on Paper 1.

Improving your skill level

The unique structure of this book allows you to build each skill level-by-level, chapter by chapter. You can concentrate on one or two very specific areas at a time, for example:

LEVEL 4 – Reading and Understanding Non-fiction

You need to
- be able to locate ideas and information in texts
- begin to be aware of the purpose of the text

Chapter 2 deals with these two specific areas.

LEVEL 5 – Reading and Understanding Non-fiction

You need to
- be able to locate ideas and information in a text
- begin to be aware of the purpose of the text

plus . . .
- show an overall understanding of the text
- note the effect of some words or phrases
- note the effect of features like layout, if appropriate

Chapter 6 deals with these three additional aspects.

And so on through to Level 7.

You will find this structure makes the book really easy to use. There are two different ways that you can use it...

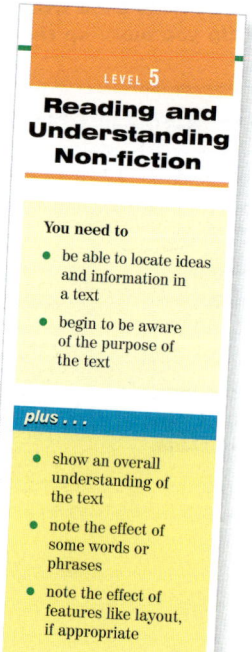

You can work at one Test level

If you are near the start of your Key Stage 3 course, this may be the best way to use the book. You will probably use the chapters at levels 4 and 5 in year 7 and then move onto the other chapters as you move up into years 8 and 9.

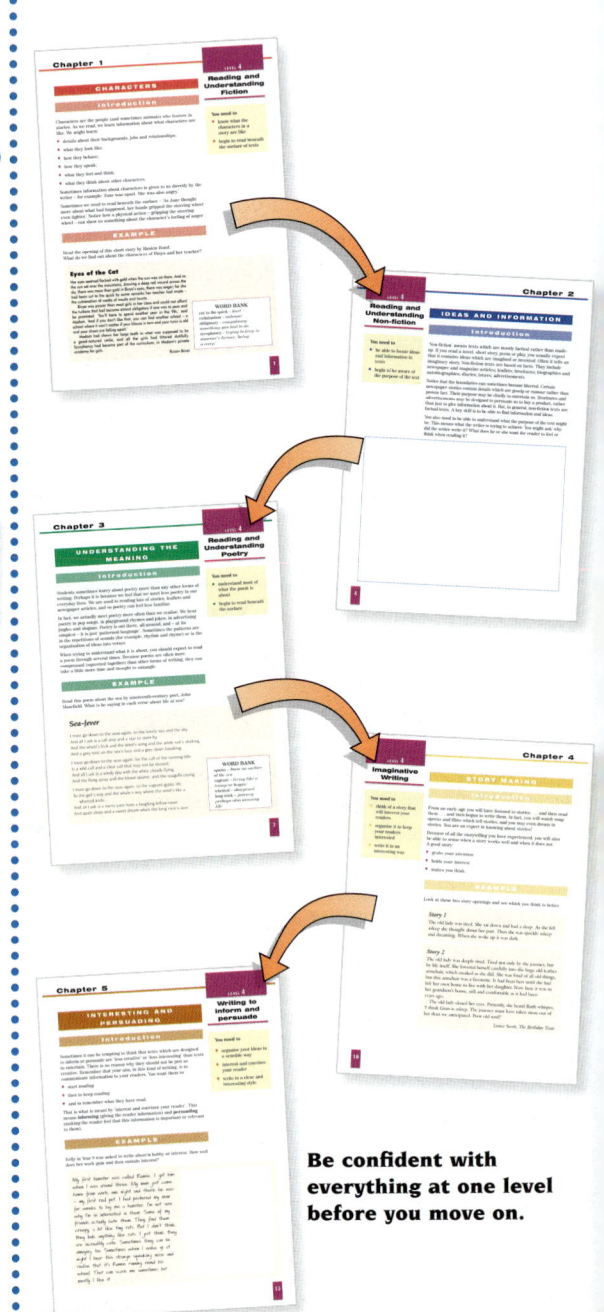

Be confident with everything at one level before you move on.

iv

You can work on one skill across all Test levels

This is a very useful way of improving a skill that you know you need more help with. For example, you can work on Imaginative Writing across four levels.

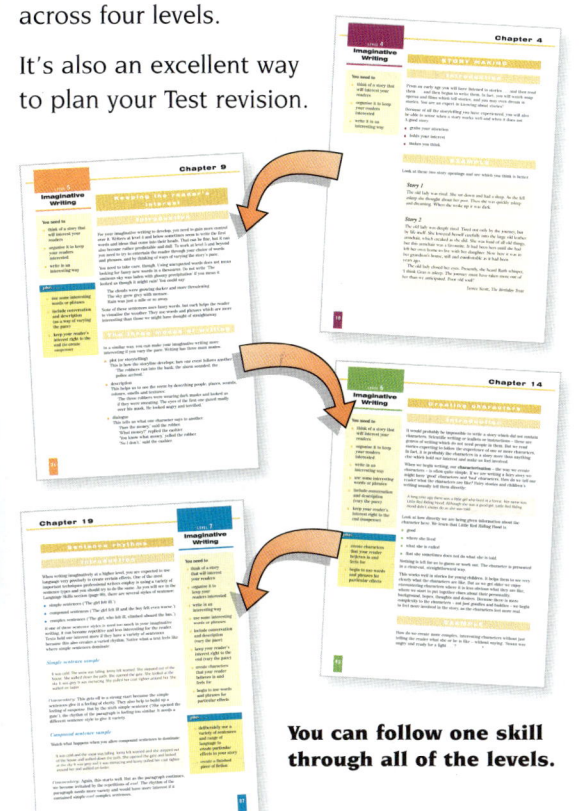

It's also an excellent way to plan your Test revision.

You can follow one skill through all of the levels.

You will find that you can reach a higher level on some skills than others. Don't worry about this – we are all better at some things than at others!

Skills are taught using examples

Every chapter shows you how to go about developing one or two specific skills. The author has carefully chosen a fiction or non-fiction extract or poem and then talks you through it to help you develop your skills in reading or writing.

The author talks you through extracts.

Check yourself

At the end of every chapter there is a *Check yourself* section that consists of several short questions that will show you if you have read and understood the chapter.

Tutorial help – you're never left stranded!

In English, there are many different possible answers to a question. The answer to each of the *Check yourself* questions takes the form of a sample answer that you can compare your answer against. There is also a *Tutorial*. This points out what is good about the answer and shows how it could be improved to get to a higher level. These *Tutorials* have been written by people who mark National Tests so they really do know what they're talking about.

This is the Answer.   This is the Tutorial.

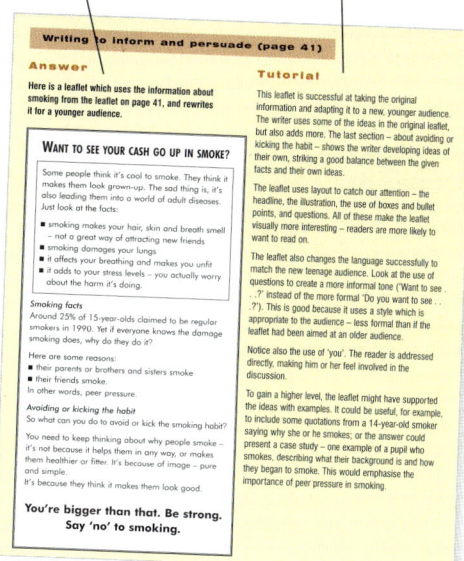

The *Check yourself* questions will test that you have understood the chapter. Every question has help from the examiner in a *Tutorial*.

The Shakespeare chapter

This chapter shows you how to improve your response to Shakespeare, level-by-level. This will give you invaluable help in preparing for Paper 2 of your Test.

Better spelling and grammar

The Essentials of Language chapter helps you build your grammar, spelling, punctuation and vocabulary skills level-by-level.

Practice Test questions

The second part of this book consists of two sample Test papers (Paper 1 and Paper 2) with detailed guidance on how to tackle each Paper. This is your chance to practise the sorts of questions that you will meet in your Test.

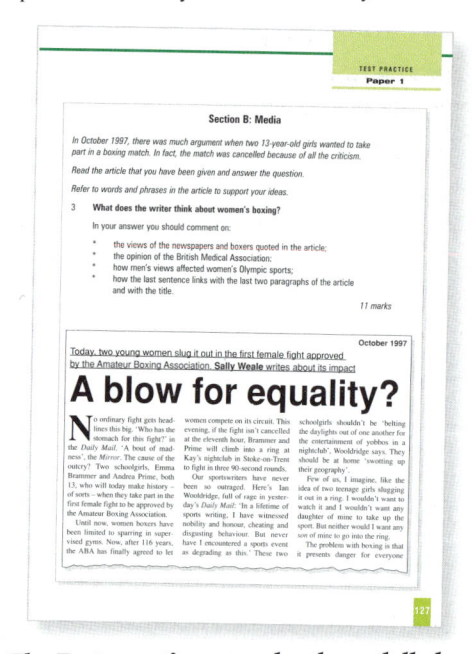

The Test questions are closely modelled on real National Test papers, so you know what to expect.

Help with the Test questions

For each Test question there are two sample students' answers at different levels, ranging from levels 4–7.

There is an examiner's commentary on each answer which points out its strengths and weaknesses. There is also a section which explains 'How you could do better'. This highlights what would upgrade each sample answer to a higher level.

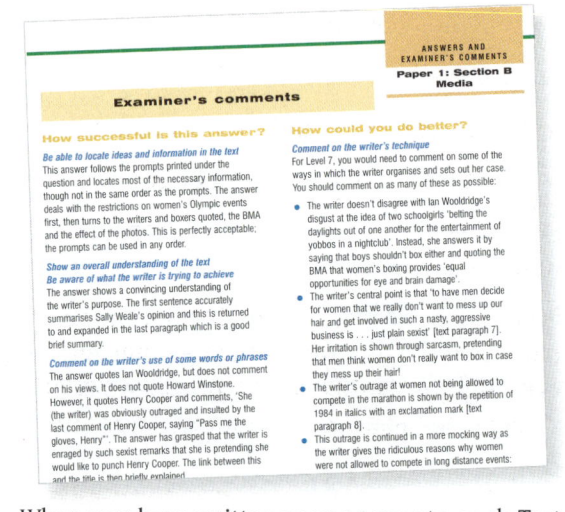

When you have written your answer to each Test question, you can compare it with the sample answers given. You can work out roughly what level your answer would achieve and read about ways that you could improve it.

Boosting your confidence – and your Test level

Using this book will help you to enjoy your Key Stage 3 English course because you will have all the support that you need – at home.

If you use this book throughout your course and in planning your revision, you will have a better chance of achieving the best possible level. Perhaps better than you, your parents or your teacher would ever have thought possible!

Chapter 1

CHARACTERS

Introduction

LEVEL 4

Reading and Understanding Fiction

Characters are the people (and sometimes animals) who feature in stories. As we read, we learn information about what characters are like. We might learn:

- details about their backgrounds, jobs and relationships;
- what they look like;
- how they behave;
- how they speak;
- what they feel and think;
- what they think about other characters.

Sometimes information about characters is given to us directly by the writer – for example: 'Jane was upset. She was also angry.'

Sometimes we need to read beneath the surface – 'As Jane thought more about what had happened, her hands gripped the steering wheel even tighter.' Notice how a physical action – gripping the steering wheel – can show us something about the character's feeling of anger.

You need to
- know what the characters in a story are like
- begin to read beneath the surface of texts

EXAMPLE

Read the opening of this short story by Ruskin Bond.
What do we find out about the characters of Binya and her teacher?

Eyes of the Cat

Her eyes seemed flecked with gold when the sun was on them. And as the sun set over the mountains, drawing a deep red wound across the sky, there was more than gold in Binya's eyes, there was anger; for she had been cut to the quick by some remarks her teacher had made – the culmination of weeks of insults and taunts.

Binya was poorer than most girls in her class and could not afford the tuitions that had become almost obligatory if one was to pass and be promoted. 'You'll have to spend another year in the 9th,' said Madam. 'And if you don't like that, you can find another school – a school where it won't matter if your blouse is torn and your tunic is old and your shoes are falling apart.'

Madam had shown her large teeth in what was supposed to be a good-natured smile, and all the girls had tittered dutifully. Sycophancy had become part of the curriculum, in Madam's private academy for girls.

RUSKIN BOND

WORD BANK
cut to the quick – *hurt*
culmination – *outcome*
obligatory – *compulsory; something you had to do*
sycophancy – *trying to keep in someone's favour; 'being a creep'*

LEVEL 4
Reading and Understanding Fiction

What do we learn about the character of Binya?

The writer tells us a little about what she looks like – 'her eyes seemed flecked with gold . . .'. This suggests that her eyes are bright and special, that she is someone whose looks might catch your attention. The writer also tells us that Binya's eyes reveal feelings of anger because she is constantly criticised by her teacher.

We learn about Binya's background from the teacher's hurtful comments – that she is poor and wears torn clothes. The writer also tells us directly that 'Binya was poorer than most girls in her class'.

We also sense that she is isolated, an outcast. The writer says 'all the girls had tittered dutifully'. This suggests that Binya does not fit in. All the other girls seem to get on well with the teacher, but Binya is victim.

Notice that some of this character information is told to us directly by the writer – 'there was anger'. Some of it is hinted at or implied – such as the feelings that she is an outsider.

What do we learn about the character of the teacher?

We get a quite negative view of the teacher. The writer mentions her weeks of 'insults and taunts'. We are given the words she speaks to Binya, and they are spiteful and unpleasant.

We also gain two other, less direct impressions of the teacher. First, she seems to hold a lot of power over her students, probably because of her sarcasm. The way the girls join in with their teacher when they 'tittered dutifully' – giving her support, rather than being sympathetic to Binya – shows the power the teacher has.

The writer does not give the teacher a name but just refers to her as Madam. This makes us feel rather distant from her. It is easier to have sympathy for a character when we know her or his name – but here the writer keeps us feeling detached because we do not feel we really know the teacher. Think about this: if a story says 'The man walked into the supermarket' it feels different from 'John walked into the supermarket'. Names help us to feel that we are getting to know a character. Without names, they can seem cold or even menacing.

LEVEL 4

Reading and Understanding Fiction

Check yourself

Read this opening of a short story by Roald Dahl. Then answer the character questions which follow. Try to:

- notice direct character clues
- look beneath the surface of the text.

> Anna was in the kitchen washing a head of Boston lettuce for the family supper when the doorbell rang. The bell itself was on the wall directly above the sink, and it never failed to make her jump if it rang when she happened to be near. For this reason, neither her husband nor any of the children ever used it. It seemed to ring extra loud this time, and Anna jumped extra high.
>
> When she opened the door, two policemen were standing outside. They looked at her out of pale waxen faces, and she looked back at them, waiting for them to say something.
>
> She kept looking at them, but they didn't speak or move. They stood so still and so rigid that they were like two wax figures somebody had put on her doorstep as a joke. Each of them was holding his helmet in front of him in his two hands.
>
> 'What is it?' Anna asked.
>
> They were both young, and they were wearing leather gauntlets up to their elbows. She could see their enormous motor-cycles propped up along the edge of the sidewalk behind them, and dead leaves were falling around the motor-cycles and blowing along the sidewalk and the whole of the street was brilliant in the yellow light of a clear, gusty September evening. The taller of the two policemen shifted uneasily on his feet. Then he said quietly, 'Are you Mrs Cooper, ma'am?'
>
> 'Yes, I am.'
>
> The other said, 'Mrs Edmund J. Cooper?'
>
> 'Yes.' And then slowly it began to dawn upon her that these men, neither of whom seemed anxious to explain his presence, would not be behaving as they were unless they had some distasteful duty to perform.
>
> *The Last Act*

QUESTIONS

Q1 What is the character of Anna like?
(Look at her behaviour before the policemen visit. Look at her behaviour after they arrive.)

Q2 What picture of the two policemen does the passage give you?

Try to find clues beneath the surface of the text. You might look at:

- what the characters look like
- how they behave
- what they say
- what they are thinking.

You can find the answers and tutorials on page 13.

Chapter 2

LEVEL 4
Reading and Understanding Non-fiction

IDEAS AND INFORMATION

Introduction

You need to

- be able to locate ideas and information in texts
- begin to be aware of the purpose of the text

'Non-fiction' means texts which are mostly factual rather than made-up. If you read a novel, short story, poem or play, you usually expect that it contains ideas which are imagined or invented. Often it tells an imaginary story. Non-fiction texts are based on facts. They include newspaper and magazine articles; leaflets; brochures; biographies and autobiographies; diaries; letters; advertisements.

Notice that the boundaries can sometimes become blurred. Certain newspaper stories contain details which are gossip or rumour rather than proven fact. Their purpose may be chiefly to entertain us. Brochures and advertisements may be designed to persuade us to buy a product, rather than just to give information about it. But, in general, non-fiction texts are factual texts. A key skill is to be able to find information and ideas.

You also need to be able to understand what the purpose of the text might be. This means what the writer is trying to achieve. You might ask: why did the writer write it? What does he or she want the reader to feel or think when reading it?

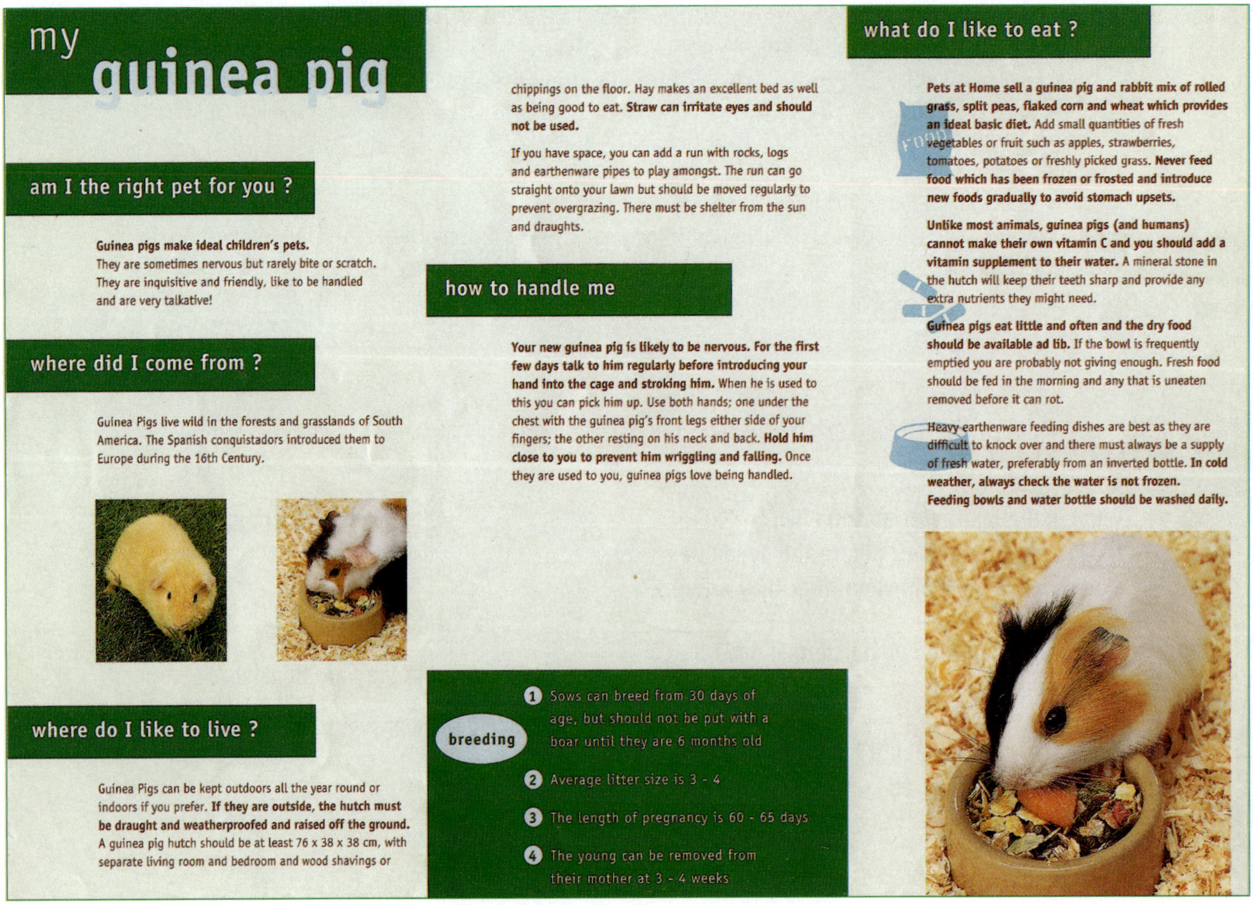

my guinea pig

am I the right pet for you ?

Guinea pigs make ideal children's pets. They are sometimes nervous but rarely bite or scratch. They are inquisitive and friendly, like to be handled and are very talkative!

where did I come from ?

Guinea Pigs live wild in the forests and grasslands of South America. The Spanish conquistadors introduced them to Europe during the 16th Century.

where do I like to live ?

Guinea Pigs can be kept outdoors all the year round or indoors if you prefer. If they are outside, the hutch must be draught and weatherproofed and raised off the ground. A guinea pig hutch should be at least 76 x 38 x 38 cm, with separate living room and bedroom and wood shavings or chippings on the floor. Hay makes an excellent bed as well as being good to eat. Straw can irritate eyes and should not be used.

If you have space, you can add a run with rocks, logs and earthenware pipes to play amongst. The run can go straight onto your lawn but should be moved regularly to prevent overgrazing. There must be shelter from the sun and draughts.

how to handle me

Your new guinea pig is likely to be nervous. For the first few days talk to him regularly before introducing your hand into the cage and stroking him. When he is used to this you can pick him up. Use both hands: one under the chest with the guinea pig's front legs either side of your fingers; the other resting on his neck and back. **Hold him close to you to prevent him wriggling and falling.** Once they are used to you, guinea pigs love being handled.

breeding

1. Sows can breed from 30 days of age, but should not be put with a boar until they are 6 months old
2. Average litter size is 3 - 4
3. The length of pregnancy is 60 - 65 days
4. The young can be removed from their mother at 3 - 4 weeks

what do I like to eat ?

Pets at Home sell a guinea pig and rabbit mix of rolled grass, split peas, flaked corn and wheat which provides an ideal basic diet. Add small quantities of fresh vegetables or fruit such as apples, strawberries, tomatoes, potatoes or freshly picked grass. **Never feed food which has been frozen or frosted and introduce new foods gradually to avoid stomach upsets.**

Unlike most animals, guinea pigs (and humans) cannot make their own vitamin C and you should add a vitamin supplement to their water. A mineral stone in the hutch will keep their teeth sharp and provide any extra nutrients they might need.

Guinea pigs eat little and often and the dry food should be available ad lib. If the bowl is frequently emptied you are probably not giving enough. Fresh food should be fed in the morning and any that is uneaten removed before it can rot.

Heavy earthenware feeding dishes are best as they are difficult to knock over and there must always be a supply of fresh water, preferably from an inverted bottle. **In cold weather, always check the water is not frozen. Feeding bowls and water bottle should be washed daily.**

LEVEL 4

Reading and Understanding Non-Fiction

EXAMPLE

Look at the leaflet opposite which was produced for pet shops. It gives owners advice on looking after guinea pigs. Use the questions below to look at the way information and ideas are presented. Its purpose is chiefly informative, but it is probably also trying to persuade customers to see the people at the pet shop as experts – people who really know and care about animals.

What information does the leaflet give about the behaviour and habits of guinea pigs?

– We learn that they are nervous.
– They rarely bite or scratch.
– They are inquisitive and friendly.
– They can live indoors or outdoors.
– They cannot make their own vitamin C and should therefore receive a vitamin supplement.
– They eat little.
– The sow's pregnancy lasts 60–65 days and she usually produces 3 or 4 babies.

There are probably other points you can spot in the leaflet, but this list is a good one. Notice that the writer looks through the whole leaflet sifting for ideas, rather than just listing information from one section. This is important: to score high marks you need to be able to find information from the whole text, not just the bits you first read.

What facts are given about the origins of guinea pigs?

We learn that they live wild in forest and grasslands of South America. They were introduced to Europe in the sixteenth century.

How clearly is the information in the leaflet presented?

Notice that this is a different style of question. It is not simply asking you to spot facts. It is asking you also to comment on how successful the leaflet is. You might say:

> The layout helps to make the information clear. Headings and sub-headings are clearly set out. Paragraphs are short. The most important pieces of information are printed in **bold type** for emphasis.
>
> The advice is practical and not technical. The writer gives plenty of relevant facts – size of hutch, length of pregnancy, and so on – but does not try to blind the reader with science.
>
> The language is clear. The writer uses questions to get the reader involved ('am I the right pet for you?'). Sentences are usually short, and vocabulary is quite straightforward (except 'conquistadors' – a name for the adventurers from Spain who went to South America in search of money and slaves).

5

LEVEL 4
Reading and Understanding Non-Fiction

Check yourself

Now read this leaflet based on one produced by the Department of the Environment. It aims to make people look at the state of their garden walls and check that they are safe. Use the questions which follow to think about the way information and advice are presented.

YOUR GARDEN WALLS

Garden and boundary walls should be inspected from time to time to see if any repairs are necessary, or whether a wall needs rebuilding.

Such walls are amongst the most common forms of masonry to suffer collapse, and they are unfortunately one of the commonest causes of deaths by falling masonry. Your insurances may not cover you if the wall has been neglected.

Besides the general deterioration and ageing of a masonry wall over the years, walls may be affected by:

- An increase in wind load or driving rain if a nearby building is taken down.
- Felling of nearby mature trees or planting of new trees close to the wall.
- Changes leading to greater risk of damage from traffic.
- Alterations, such as additions to the wall or removal of parts of the wall eg. for a new gateway.

Things to check

1 Is the surface of the brickwork crumbling away? If restricted to a few bricks this may not be serious but walls can be weakened by general crumbling across either face.

2 Is the mortar pointing in good condition? If the hard surface layer can be picked out from the joint, or if the mortar can easily be scraped out with, say, a door key, then this is a good indication that the wall may need repointing.

3 Is there a tree near the wall? As trees mature, there is a risk of the wall being damaged by the roots, and from wind-blown branches. Damaged sections may have to be rebuilt, perhaps with 'bridges' incorporated to carry the wall over the roots. Removal of large trees can also lead to problems because the soil accumulates more moisture and expands.

4 Is the wall upright? Walls lean for a variety of causes, due for example to failure below ground caused by tree roots, a cracked drain, frost damage to the foundations or inadequate foundations. If your wall leans to an extent that could present a danger eg. more than 30mm (half brick wall), 70mm (single brick wall) or 100mm (brick and a half wall) it is recommended that expert advice is sought. This may involve checking of the wall foundations.

5 Is the wall thick enough for its height? The map and tables on the back page give guidance on how high walls should be in different parts of the UK relative to their thickness. Seek expert advice if your wall exceeds the recommended height, or in circumstances whereby this guidance is inapplicable eg. walls incorporating piers, or walls supporting heavy gates or retaining soil.

6 Some climbing plants, like ivy, can damage walls if growth is unchecked. Consider cutting them back and supporting regrowth clear of the wall.

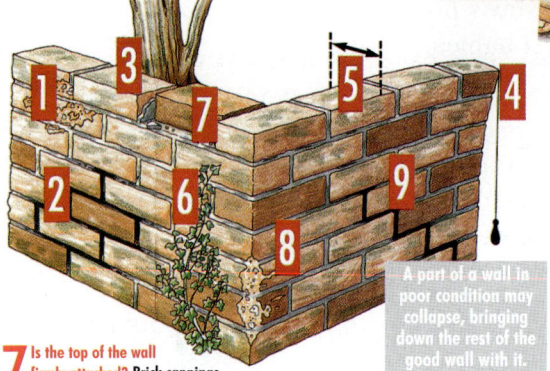

7 Is the top of the wall firmly attached? Brick cappings or concrete copings may be loose or there may be horizontal cracks (frost damage) in the brickwork a few courses down. Loose or damaged masonry near the top of the wall will need to be rebuilt and should include a damp proof course.

8 Has the wall been damaged by traffic? Minor scratch marks or scoring of the surface may obscure more significant cracks. Piers at vehicular entrances may have been dislodged by impact and be unsafe; in such cases they should be rebuilt.

9 Are there any cracks in the wall? Hairline cracks (0–2mm across) are common in walls and may not indicate serious problems. For wider cracks seek expert advice; some may indicate a need for partial or complete rebuilding. Seek advice on any horizontal cracks which pass right through a wall or any cracks close to piers or gates. Repointing of cracks can lead to problems. Do not repoint without establishing the cause of the cracking.

A part of a wall in poor condition may collapse, bringing down the rest of the good wall with it.

QUESTIONS

Q1 What reasons does the leaflet give that walls can become dangerous?

Q2 Write down three pieces of advice the writer gives.

Q3 How successful is the leaflet in presenting information clearly? Do you think it is also intended to persuade us?

You can find the answers and tutorials on page 14.

Chapter 3

STORY MAKING

LEVEL 4
Imaginative Writing

Introduction

From an early age you will have listened to stories . . . and then read them . . . and then begun to write them. In fact, you will watch soap operas and films which tell stories, and you may even dream in stories. You are an expert in knowing about stories!

Because of all the storytelling you have experienced, you will also be able to sense when a story works well and when it does not. A good story:

- grabs your attention
- holds your interest
- makes you think.

You need to
- think of a story that will interest your readers
- organise it to keep your readers interested
- write it in an interesting way

EXAMPLE

Look at these two story openings and see which you think is better.

Story 1

The old lady was tired. She sat down and had a sleep. As she fell asleep she thought about her past. Then she was quickly asleep and dreaming. When she woke up it was dark.

Story 2

The old lady was deeply tired. Tired not only by the journey, but by life itself. She lowered herself carefully into the large old leather armchair, which creaked as she did. She was fond of all old things, but this armchair was a favourite. It had been hers until she had left her own home to live with her daughter. Now here it was in her grandson's house, still and comfortable as it had been years ago.

    The old lady closed her eyes. Presently, she heard Ruth whisper, 'I think Gran is asleep. The journey must have taken more out of her than we anticipated. Poor old soul!'

Janice Scott, The Birthday Treat

LEVEL 4
Imaginative Writing

How much does each story-opening interest the reader?

'Interest' is quite a difficult idea to pin down. What interests one person might bore the next. You might be interested in stories about ghosts or crime; your friend might prefer romance or historical fiction. But a good story will have an idea of who its readers are – their age and background. A story aimed at young children will often be about a small number of characters, with a strong, clear storyline, and perhaps a powerful moral of right and wrong. A story for older readers might be more complicated.

Writers work hard to grab our interest and the first extract does not really catch our attention. It has no sense of tension or suspense to make us want to read on. Its main problem is that we do not feel involved. There is nothing there to draw us into the story.

Look again at story 2. Notice how the writer makes us feel that we are getting to know the old lady. We don't know her name, but we do know that:

- she is tired
- she has been on a journey
- she is also tired of life – suggesting that perhaps she has suffered problems with her family
- she has (or had) a daughter and grandson
- the armchair belongs to her
- she seems to think a lot about the past.

Details like these help us to become involved in a story. They raise questions in the reader's mind: who is this woman? where has she travelled from? what is her relationship with the other people mentioned? and so on.

This is probably the most important way in which writers gain the interest of readers – by raising questions about characters and events that make us want to read on. Crime stories are the best example – the 'whodunit' tale keeps us guessing until the last page, when we finally discover who the murderer was.

LEVEL 4
Imaginative Writing

Check yourself

Look at this story opening and think about how the writer gains the interest of the reader.

That Friday night only three people from Form M noticed anything strange in the sky. Only Annabel Lewis, Timmy Norton and Gerry Moodie were awake, for different reasons.

Annabel was staring despondently out of her window. She'd got up after lying for hours worrying about the forthcoming exams. 'Worrying won't help,' her father was always saying, but that only made Annabel worry about how to stop worrying.

Timmy was looking through a telescope which he had rehabilitated from pieces bought in a junk-shop. He was a dark, rosy-cheeked boy with spectacles, sometimes known as 'Professor', more often as 'Tiny Tim'. Occasionally he wished he could acquire another few inches, but mostly he was too interested in what was going on around him to be bothered by his lack of height.

Gerry was puffing cigarette smoke out of his window and wondering how best to annoy their form teacher, Miss Howarth, next Monday. She'd been picking on him again, calling him a lazy, idle trouble-maker. Right, if that's what she thought, that's what he'd be.

What all three saw was very brief but quite clear. At 2 a.m. precisely the sky towards the west, where Fellfields Comprehensive School lay, turned a brilliant orange. The glow made the three watchers blink, and for moments afterwards the sky looked green. Then, as their vision cleared, they saw a round red light descending slowly at an angle of forty-five degrees. Above the school roof it made an enquiring sort of circle, before resuming its descent and disappearing somewhere behind the school buildings. It was all over in less than two minutes.

At breakfast Annabel said, 'I saw something funny in the sky last night.'

'Oh, Annabel!' wailed her mother, 'couldn't you get to sleep again? You are a worry, dear, really!' That was another thing that worried Annabel; her own worrying got her mother worried too.

When she met her friend Aileen as usual on the way to school she asked her if she'd seen anything, but Aileen began talking about the disco she was going to that night. 'You coming, Annabel?'

'Depends how much homework we get. You know my mum . . .'

Perhaps she'd dreamed it. She did have very vivid dreams.

Anthea Courtenay, *The Alpha-Wave Experiment*

QUESTION

How does the writer organise the story to get the reader interested?

(Look at what we learn about the characters and where the story takes place. What information are we given, and what is held back?)

You can find an answer and tutorial on page 15.

Chapter 4

LEVEL 4

Writing to inform and persuade

INTERESTING AND PERSUADING

Introduction

You need to

- organise your ideas in a sensible way
- interest and convince your reader
- write in a clear and interesting style

Sometimes it can be tempting to think that texts which are designed to inform or persuade are 'less creative' or 'less interesting' than texts to entertain. There is no reason why they should not be just as creative. Remember that your aim, in this kind of writing, is to communicate information to your readers. You want them to:

- start reading
- then to keep reading
- and to remember what they have read.

That is what is meant by 'interest and convince your reader'. This means **informing** (giving the reader information) and **persuading** (making the reader feel that this information is important or relevant to them).

EXAMPLE

Kelly in Year 8 was asked to write about a hobby or interest. How well does her work gain and then sustain interest?

My first hamster was called Ronnie. I got him when I was around three. My mum just came home from work one night and there he was – my first real pet. I had pestered my mum for weeks to buy me a hamster. I'm not sure why I'm so interested in them. Some of my friends actually hate them. They find them creepy, a bit like tiny rats. But I don't think they look anything like rats. I just think they are incredibly cute. Sometimes they can be annoying too. Sometimes when I wake up at night I hear this strange squeaking noise and realise that it's Ronnie running round his wheel. That can scare me sometimes but mostly I like it.

LEVEL 4
Writing to inform and persuade

Is Kelly's assignment sensibly organised and clearly written?

The assignment does not get off to a very exciting start, but it is clear. We can follow all of her ideas fairly well. Journalists are sometimes told that they need to grab their reader's interest from the first sentence, otherwise we will simply move on to the next story. Kelly's opening sentence is hardly likely to fascinate us.

Kelly could have organised those opening sentences differently. It would make more sense to start off with the background information first – like this:

> My mum just came home from work one night and there he was – my first real pet. I had pestered her for weeks to buy me a hamster . . .

Then she could lead into the more specific information about Ronnie.

Does Kelly's account interest us and convince us that we wish to keep reading?

The answer is not really. There is nothing very unusual or original about the writing. It does not make us feel that we have to keep reading. The danger here is that Kelly tries to redraft her work by using fancy vocabulary. She might be tempted to choose words because they sound impressive, perhaps words she finds in a thesaurus, but which do not really fit here. She uses the word 'pestered' for example and it works well. The account would have become false and too complicated if she used 'antagonised' or 'besieged', or another word found in the thesaurus.

The best thing for Kelly to do is to try to make the account come to life by adding detail. She needs to think back to the event and answer the questions:

Who?
Where?
When?

These will lead her to write a more detailed account, and that will make the reader feel more involved because we will actually be able to see, hear and feel what Kelly sees, hears and feels.

LEVEL 4

Writing to inform and persuade

Check yourself

Kelly spent half an hour revising her account. Read the new version below and use the questions to decide how much you think Kelly has improved the original.

> For weeks I had pestered mum about the hamster. I'd go to her in the kitchen, in the garden, even when she was in the bath. 'Mum,' I'd whine, 'please can I have a hamster?'
>
> I don't know what finally made her give in, but one night in November I remember hearing Mum's footsteps outside the backdoor. I heard the key in the lock and went to say hello. I can't have been concentrating because I didn't notice anything different at first. I just started chatting away about my day at school and the things I'd done.
>
> I could see in Mum's face that something was different. She looked at me half serious and half smiling, as if I was a stranger. I suddenly noticed and stopped. There in a tiny cage was Ronnie — my new hamster . . . .

QUESTIONS

Q1 What improvements has Kelly made to her original?

(Look at the vocabulary she uses and the amount of detail she gives.)

Q2 Does the account feel more interesting now?

(Say what you think has improved and which parts make you more likely to read on.)

You can find the answers and tutorials on page 16.

LEVEL 4

Answers and Tutorials to Check Yourself

1 Reading and Understanding Fiction (page 3)

Answers

A1 Anna is married with children. We learn nothing about her physical appearance. There is a hint that she may be nervous. Anna is intelligent – she works out why the policemen have visited before they tell her. There is even a hint that things are not quite as normal for Anna tonight.

A2 The policemen are pale and uneasy. Twice the writer refers to their 'waxen' appearance, suggesting they are not feeling comfortable with their job. The helmets in their hands suggest that they are being formal and polite – a hint perhaps that they are bringing bad news. The description of the gusty evening emphasises how long they pause before giving their news.

Tutorials

T1 The answer starts with the most direct, factual information, and mentions also what we do not learn. The third sentence looks at Anna's behaviour and makes a suggestion (that she is nervous). The final point – that things are not normal – shows good attention to the text.

T2 This is a good answer. Again, it begins with factual information – what we are told about the policemen's appearance. The writer notices details about the atmosphere – the helmets in their hands and the wind – and links these to the characterisation. This is the sign of a promising response to the text.

Both answers could gain higher than level 4 if they were supported by carefully chosen quotations. At the moment they tend to make points without always quoting examples from the story. A higher-level response would also pay more attention to the individual words used by the writer.

LEVEL 4

Answers and Tutorials to Check Yourself

2 Reading and Understanding Non-Fiction (page 6)

Answers

A1 Walls can become dangerous because of the weather; if a local building is removed; if trees are planted nearby; if there is more traffic passing by; if the wall is altered; and as the wall gets older.

A2 You should inspect walls from time to time to see whether they need replacing or rebuilding. For very high walls, seek expert advice. Do not repoint a wall without first finding out what caused the cracking.

A3 The layout of the leaflet helps to make the information clearer. The left-hand side warns of the dangers of ignoring walls, and the picture hints at what might happen. The labelled picture of the wall is also good because it ties in with each of the nine tips. The use of colour – red for the questions – also makes the leaflet easier to follow and more interesting.

The language is not always easy to follow. It uses a number of technical terms ('piers at vehicular entrances' and 'repointing').

The leaflet seems to be designed chiefly to inform the reader – to give information about safety. It might also have a persuasive purpose – to make us feel that this is good, reliable advice. If it did not persuade us of that we would probably ignore the information it contains.

Tutorials

T1 This is a good answer because it covers the points listed in the leaflet. It does not just copy out the points but actually rephrases them a little. It is also good because the writer structures the answer clearly, using semi-colons to separate the different parts of the answer. This makes it a very easy answer to follow. It is also very concise – no words are wasted.

T2 There are several possible answers to this question. This is a good answer because it does exactly what is asked – listing three pieces of advice. The writer could have listed them one beneath the other, perhaps numbering them 1, 2, 3 – to make the answer even clearer.

T3 The answer starts off well. It is true that the layout of the leaflet gives it clarity and makes it more successful at informing the reader. The writer is also right to say that the language level is high. The student could have tied this into the purpose and audience of the leaflet a bit more. It seems to be aimed at a specialist audience (e.g. builders and do-it-yourself fans) who will know these terms. If it is supposed to be aimed at a general audience, it would be more successful if the technical terms were explained.

LEVEL 4

Answers and Tutorials to Check Yourself

3 Imaginative Writing (page 9)

Answer

The story starts with a sentence that grabs our attention. It tells us that there was something 'strange in the sky' but doesn't yet tell us what it is. We have to wait until several paragraphs later before we get the description of strange colours in the sky. The opening therefore immediately gets our interest by creating suspense – what did the three people see? Is it a UFO?

The writer then cuts between the three characters. She has said in her first sentence that three people saw something strange. Now she tells us more about them, with a paragraph on each. This is interesting because we see three very different characters who cannot see each other. We wonder how they will all connect.

We are probably most interested in Gerry because he is a trouble-maker, and we look forward to seeing what he will do in class on Monday.

The description of the strange glow in the sky is quite precise. The writer says a red light descended at 'forty-five degrees'. This makes it feel realistic – as if it has really happened. This kind of detail helps draw a reader into your story and makes it feel believable. It is then a nice twist that Annabel's mother doesn't believe Annabel's story. It makes us interested to see what will happen when Annabel tells someone else.

Tutorial

The commentary on the story shows how skilfully Anthea Courtenay begins her story. She holds back key information after mentioning it in the first sentence. Thriller writers often use this technique – 'Fiona couldn't remember what time she noticed the body …'. You might use it too in your imaginative writing, building the reader's interest by telling them something exciting and then making them wait for any more detail.

You could also use Anthea Courtenay's approach to character and place. She doesn't give us too much description of the people in her story opening, but we can feel how different they all are. This makes them feel real, and we begin to wonder how they will all be brought together. You might try a similar approach – giving some quick pieces of information about a character (Timmy was 'sometimes known as "Professor"') – but not spending more than a few lines creating an impression.

Describing the scene in a detailed way – again without overdoing the descriptive writing – can also bring your story to life. Anthea Courtenay's description of the sky is just precise enough to allow us to visualise it. You need to do the same – create a feeling of a place by giving details of colour, shape and texture, so that the reader feels involved.

LEVEL 4
Answers and Tutorials to Check Yourself

4 Writing to inform and persuade (page 12)

Answers

A1 Kelly has made all kinds of improvements. First, she has changed the order of events so that they start with her earliest memory and then move forward in time. This allows us to get more involved in her story because we see her excitement about getting a hamster before she actually receives it. It also means that she meets the requirement to 'organise your ideas in a sensible way'.

Kelly has also slowed the narrative down. She shows us more about her own feelings and gives us more details – for example, the look on her mother's face, the night-time squeaking of Ronnie's wheel. These really help bring the account to life, making it more believable for the reader. She therefore 'interests and convinces' the reader, as required in the criteria for level 4. Her account does not simply inform us; it also persuades us to keep reading because it is a lively and convincing account. There is more about how to persuade readers in the level 5 section.

Kelly also writes in a greater variety of sentence styles. The first paragraph is a good example. It begins with a short, straightforward statement. The next sentence is then longer, with a different rhythm, and it makes us feel how much she wanted the hamster by hinting at the way she pestered her mother. This variety in her sentence style gives her writing more interest. She writes 'in a clear and interesting way'.

A2 The account is really improved. Kelly's changes to the structure, the focus on details, the greater variety of sentences – all of these make the account much more interesting to the reader. Making use of a word like 'whine' is really effective. It is a simple change to the original, but it perfectly captures the way she pestered her mother.

Tutorials

T1 and T2 Kelly's first account was accurate but rather dull. She had some good material, but it did not catch our interest or make us feel that we had to keep reading. Kelly was working just around level 4. Her changes have made a real impact. Suddenly we feel that here is an interesting person with a lively account to tell. The changes she has made to the story have improved it quite dramatically – in fact, the level of the account is now solidly around level 5.

To improve it further, and to gain a higher level, Kelly would need to work more on the vocabulary, not by using fancy words from a thesaurus but by choosing very precise words to make the reader visualise the scene even more (as she did with the word 'whine'). Her account could show more of her mother's personality and more of her own feelings. It could have more humour. It could benefit from a little more visual detail, so that we see where it is all taking place (e.g. the bedroom, the kitchen), as well as what happened. But Kelly is certainly making good progress.

Chapter 5

Language and understanding

Introduction

LEVEL 5

Reading and Understanding Fiction

As you work through this book you will notice that to achieve higher levels when reading and responding to fiction, you need to be able to focus more and more on the *language* of texts. After all, this is how writers create their effects. The more closely you look at their detailed use of words and phrases, the better you will become at understanding the way the text is constructed.

Students can sometimes misunderstand what using 'language' means. They sometimes judge a text by how complicated the language seems – by how fancy the vocabulary is. It is important not to see the language of texts like this. A writer might write simply or in a very complex style. You need to be able to discuss what effect the writer's style has on your own reading, understanding and enjoyment of the text.

For example, compare these two sentences:

> The man walked along the corridor.
> The old man shuffled along the draughty corridor.

The first sentence gives us some basic information. We know there is a man and we know that there is a corridor. We know that the man is walking, but it leaves out a lot of detail. Who is the man? What does he look like? Why is he walking? Where is the corridor? The writing is simple and direct, but lacks detail, so we do not feel drawn into the story.

The second sentence begins to give a clearer picture of these questions. We learn something about the age of the man. We learn about the way he moved: 'shuffled' rather than 'walked'. The use of the word 'corridor' makes us see him inside, possibly somewhere that is cold and run down – in a home, a hospital, or a prison, perhaps?

In other words, a precise use of vocabulary can allow a writer to give us information about people and places without having to go into lengthy descriptions. The language of the second sentence is not complicated, but it does create a more detailed picture for the reader and so we become more involved in the story.

You need to
- know what the characters in a text are like
- begin to read beneath the surface

plus . . .
- show an overall understanding of the text
- note the effects of words and phrases

EXAMPLE

Now read the opening of this short story by D H Lawrence. Notice in particular the way he uses language to create an impression of the environment – the countryside and the railway that runs through it. Does it seem an attractive, positive picture?

17

LEVEL 5

Reading and Understanding Fiction

Odour of Chrysanthemums

The small locomotive engine, Number 4, came clanking, stumbling down from Selston with seven full waggons. It appeared round the corner with loud threats of speed, but the colt that it startled from among the gorse, which still flickered indistinctly in the raw afternoon, outdistanced it at a canter. A woman, walking up the railway line to Underwood, drew back into the hedge, held her basket aside, and watched the footplate of the engine advancing. The trucks thumped heavily past, one by one, with slow inevitable movement, as she stood insignificantly trapped between the jolting black waggons and the hedge; then they curved away towards the coppice where the withered oak leaves dropped noiselessly, while the birds, pulling at the scarlet hips beside the track, made off into the dusk that had already crept into the spinney. In the open, the smoke from the engine sank and cleaved to the rough grass. The fields were dreary and forsaken, and in the marshy strip that led to the whimsey, a reedy pit-pond, the fowls had already abandoned their run among the alders to roost in the tarred fowl-house. The pit-bank loomed up beyond the pond, flames like red sores licking its ashy sides, in the afternoon's stagnant light. Just beyond rose the tapering chimneys and the clumsy black headstocks of Brinsley Colliery. The two wheels were spinning fast up against the sky, and the winding-engine rapped out its little spasms. The miners were being turned up.

WORD BANK

gorse – *a harsh shrub*
coppice – *small group of trees growing close together*
hips – *red berries*
spinney – *small wood*
cleaved – *stuck*
alders – *type of tree*
tarred – *painted with tar to protect it from rain*
headstocks – *support for revolving parts (e.g. pit-shaft lift)*
winding engine rapped out its little spasms – *the clattering noise made by the wheels which pull the lifts up and down a pit-shaft*
The miners were being turned up – *they are returning to the surface*

LEVEL 5

Reading and Understanding Fiction

How does the writer use words and phrases to create a sense of atmosphere?

D H Lawrence creates a powerful sense of atmosphere chiefly through his use of very precise words and phrases. Look again at the first sentence. Notice what the author tells us about the locomotive engine:

- it is small;
- it is Number 4;
- it makes a clanking sound;
- its movement is 'stumbling' rather than smooth;
- it is coming down from Selston;
- it is pulling seven full waggons.

One sentence has told us all this, with details which are visual ('small', 'Number 4', 'stumbling') and based on sound ('clanking'). Notice also that the author refers to the engine as '*The* small locomotive engine . . .'. How would the story have seemed different if it had begun '*A* small . . .'? The use of the word *the* (technically we call it the definite article) makes the scene seem more precise – this isn't just any locomotive; it is a very specific one.

Yet at the same time as he gives us such precise information, the writer also leaves other questions unanswered. Where is Selston? Why is the locomotive coming from there and where is it going? Why is the narrator watching the engine? Leaving some information out in this way adds interest and makes the reader want to read on.

Look also at the way D H Lawrence presents the contrast between the locomotive and nature. As we have seen, the engine is described in specific terms. It is also shown as disturbing the environment:

> It appeared round the corner with loud threats of speed . . .

Notice the word 'threats' and the use of 'loud' in an environment which is otherwise calm and undisturbed. Look at its effect on the colt, which is 'startled' by the noise. Notice the way the woman reacts: she 'drew back into the hedge,' retreating from the train into nature.

If you look through the rest of that opening paragraph, you will see more examples: nature being disturbed, even scared, by the presence of the train. What might have seemed on the surface like a straightforward description of a locomotive travelling through a field is, in fact, full of feelings of threat and danger.

Lawrence creates the same effect when he describes the colliery. The pit-bank has 'flames like red sores licking its ashy sides'. Notice how visual this description is – the brilliant red of the flames, hinting at danger or even hell, followed by the 'clumsy black headstocks of Brinsley Colliery'. Again, notice how mechanical and industrial elements are described in a negative way – 'clumsy' and 'black'.

LEVEL 5
Reading and Understanding Fiction

Check yourself

Now look at the next few paragraphs of the same story. Make a note of the words and phrases D H Lawrence uses to describe people and places. Look, in particular, for:

- the impression he gives us of nature and of people
- words and phrases which use the senses (colours, textures, sounds, smells)
- the way he uses comparisons (using words like 'as' and 'like').

The engine whistled as it came into the wide bay of railway lines beside the colliery, where rows of trucks stood in harbour.

Miners, single, trailing and in groups, passed like shadows diverging home. At the edge of the ribbed level of sidings squat a low cottage, three steps down from the cinder track. A large bony vine clutched at the house, as if to claw down the tiled roof. Round the bricked yard grew a few wintry primroses. Beyond, the long garden sloped down to a bush-covered brook course. There were some twiggy apple trees, winter-crack trees, and ragged cabbages. Beside the path hung dishevelled pink chrysanthemums, like pink cloths hung on bushes. A woman came stooping out of the felt-covered fowl-house, half-way down the garden. She closed and padlocked the door, then drew herself erect, having brushed some bits from her white apron.

She was a tall woman of imperious mien, handsome, with definite black eyebrows. Her smooth black hair was parted exactly. For a few moments she stood steadily watching the miners as they passed along the railway; then she turned towards the brook course. Her face was calm and set, her mouth was closed with disillusionment. After a moment she called:

'John!' There was no answer. She waited, and then she said distinctly:

'Where are you?'

'Here!' replied a child's sulky voice from among the bushes. The woman looked piercingly through the dusk.

'Are you at that brook?' she asked sternly.

For answer the child showed himself before the raspberry-canes that rose like whips. He was a small, sturdy boy of five. He stood quite still, defiantly.

'Oh!' said the mother, conciliated. 'I thought you were down at that wet brook – and you remember what I told you –'

The boy did not move or answer.

'Come in, come in,' she said gently, 'it's getting dark. There's your grandfather's engine coming down the line!'

The lad advanced slowly, with resentful, taciturn movement. He was dressed in trousers and waistcoat of cloth that was too thick and hard for the size of the garments. They were evidently cut down from a man's clothes.

As they went towards the house he tore at the ragged wisps of chrysanthemums and dropped the petals in handfuls along the path.

from *Odour of Chrysanthemums*

LEVEL 5

Reading and Understanding Fiction

QUESTIONS

Q1 What words and phrases does D H Lawrence use to describe nature?

Q2 How does he use words and phrases to describe the characters of the mother and son?

Answers and tutorials can be found on page 34.

> **WORD BANK**
> squat – *close to the ground*
> dishevelled – *untidy; unkempt*
> imperious mien – *formal appearance*
> disillusionment – *disappointment*
> conciliated – *pleased that things were not as you thought*
> taciturn – *silent*

Chapter 6

LEVEL 5

Reading and Understanding Non-fiction

You need to

- be able to locate ideas and information in a text
- begin to be aware of the purpose of the text

plus . . .

- show an overall understanding of the text
- note the effect of some words or phrases
- note the effect of features like layout, if appropriate

Autobiography

Introduction

We saw in the level 4 section that non-fiction can include a wide range of categories or 'genres'. One of these is autobiography. Look at the Greek origin of the word to see exactly what it means:

auto = self
bio = life
graphy [Latin out of Greek] = writing

Autobiography means writing about your own life. Biography is writing about someone else's life.

Both genres are highly popular. After novels, autobiography and biography are the biggest selling category of books. They share a number of features with fiction writing. They:

- have characters (often, in the case of autobiography, including a narrator – 'I');
- are usually chronological (starting at the beginning of a person's life and moving to their most recent years);
- move from one scene to another, using description and detail to bring people and places to life.

For this reason, it can sometimes be easy to treat autobiography and biography as if it is made up, or fictional. Remember though that when we read extracts like these we are given a rare chance to look inside the mind of a real person, and to relive events through their eyes.

Notice, once again, that a level 5 response needs to show sensitivity to some of the words and phrases used by the writer – just getting the general feeling of a text is not enough.

EXAMPLE

In the extract below Marcel Mariën, a writer from Belgium, recalls his childhood during the Second World War. From his home he was sent to a concentration camp in Nuremberg and then on to the Gorlitz camp in Upper Silesia. He writes about a memory of being searched for forbidden items by the Nazi soldiers – knowing that he has a suitcase filled with forbidden books.

LEVEL 5
Reading and Understanding Non-fiction

One Sunday morning we were ordered to assemble in the yard with all our luggage. The time had arrived for the dreaded inspection that I had avoided so successfully until then. We took down our suitcases. The dormitories were to be searched simultaneously to examine all our belongings and anything we might have left or hidden there.

In the building opposite, open to all the winds that blew, was a little corridor leading to the kitchen. At meal times we queued up there with our mess tins. And that was where two of our jailers had put the table on which our bags were going to be inspected.

They lined us up in alphabetical order, to make things easier for them. Then the search began. It was so slow and so meticulous that I suffered agonies. I was carrying my two suitcases, the one with the forbidden books and the other containing various objects, my linen, and my more innocuous books.

As I was nearing the search table I suddenly noticed that, due to the obscure yet straightforward composition of the alphabet, Mabe, the navvy I had been talking to the other day, had just gone through the inspection and was about to turn round and come back. There was only one man between us, who was preparing to take his place. My forbidden suitcase was in my left hand. Mabe had only a small bag, which he was carrying in his right. As he turned I moved forward. Without thinking, without even looking at him, I unhesitatingly thrust my suitcase into his free hand which, amazingly, obeyed. Unless someone had been keeping on eye on us, no one could have detected this substitution. The narrow corridor hemmed us in on both sides. In front of us the guards had their noses stuck into the belongings of our brother who, according to the laws of the alphabet, came between us. There was virtually no risk that anyone behind me in the queue could have spotted this sleight of hand, which was all the more rapid in that I had in no way prepared for it. I realised later that I probably wouldn't even have tried it on if I hadn't broken the ice with Mabe a few days earlier. No doubt it was the modicum of fellow-feeling born of our one conversation that had guided my hand before my brain had had time to weigh up the pros and cons and hold it back. It is also very likely that anyone else would either have refused me his complicity or, out of pure cowardice, denounced me.

I passed the inspection without incident. Mabe, whose dormitory was on the first floor, brought the heavy suitcase of his own accord to the second floor where I slept. He was full of suppressed anger, because nothing could either justify or recompense the risk I had made him run. But all he could do was mutter. In return I mumbled a few apologies and, as needs must, the incident was forgotten and things went back to normal . . .

from Marcel Mariën *Brought to Books*

WORD BANK
dormitories – *rooms for sleeping*
mess tins – *metal dishes in which food was served*
innocuous – *harmless*
navvy – *labourer*
substitution – *switch of one item with another*
sleight of hand – *rapid movement, as used in magic tricks*
modicum – *small amount*
complicity – *support*
denounced – *reported*
recompense – *repay*

23

LEVEL 5

Reading and Understanding Non-fiction

What is the text about?

The extract describes a dangerously uncomfortable moment as Marcel Mariën waits to be searched by German soldiers. The writer knows that he has some forbidden books and suffers 'agonies' as he sees the jailers approaching. He then, without planning the incident, manages to switch his suitcase with someone who has already been searched – thus saving himself.

What impression do we get of the writer and his environment?

We do not get any visual details of the writer – it is difficult to imagine what he looks like. But we do sense that he is worried by the inspection that is about to take place – chiefly because he refers to the 'dreaded inspection' and the fact that he had 'avoided' it so successfully.

We learn that the writer is kept in dormitories along with other people. It sounds very cramped and regimented with people obviously expected to keep all of their possessions there, ready at any time for inspection. The writer often uses the word 'forbidden' – a sign that people have little freedom. They are treated as if they are in a prison or army barracks – we note, for example, the reference to 'mess tins' and the way they are expected to queue up. Apart from Mabe, the navvy, no one else is mentioned by name. This emphasises the feeling of people being herded together and treated as a group rather than individuals.

Check yourself

Now re-read the extract and answer the questions below. Wherever possible, refer to particular words and phrases in your answers to show your understanding of how the writer uses language for particular effects.

QUESTIONS

Q1 What impression do you get of the character of the writer during this incident?

Q2 How do you explain Mabe's reaction to what happens?

Q3 How does the environment help the writer to swap the bags?

Answers and tutorials can be found on page 35.

Looking at layout

LEVEL 5
Reading and Understanding Non-fiction

Introduction

To achieve level 5 you need also to be able to comment on the writer's use of layout. For some texts this will be more important than others. In the extract from Marcel Mariën's autobiography (page 23), for example, the layout is exactly what we would expect: sentences organised into paragraphs and set out like a novel or book of travel writing. But other non-fiction texts use layout more directly to create their effects – leaflets, posters, letters and advertisements, for example.

EXAMPLE

Look at the leaflet about getting fit on page 31.

What effect does the layout of the leaflet have?

The leaflet aims to make the reader feel that exercise can be easy and straightforward. The layout is therefore designed to be reassuring. The pink strip across the top contains the headline – 'it's never too late *TO START*'. This captures the main message of these two pages of the leaflet. Underneath, there is a cartoon image of two elderly women. One is roller-skating with her shopping basket. The idea here is to suggest that keeping fit can be done while you are doing other jobs. It also suggests that it is fun.

The print is also designed to make the reader feel reassured. The 'G' for Grown up and phrases like 'Take it Easy' are printed in a handwritten style. This makes them feel more comforting and less threatening than if they were typed.

The leaflet uses bullet points to organise information on the right-hand page. This makes each point easy to spot, adding to the sense that the information is clear, straightforward and manageable.

Check yourself

Look at the leaflet about keeping guinea pigs on page 4. What effect does the layout of the leaflet have?

Answer and tutorial can be found on page 36.

Chapter 7

LEVEL 5
Imaginative Writing

You need to
- think of a story that will interest your readers
- organise it to keep your readers interested
- write in an interesting way

plus ...
- use some interesting words or phrases
- include conversation and description (as a way of varying the pace)
- keep your reader's interest right to the end (to create suspense)

Keeping the reader's interest

Introduction

For your imaginative writing to develop, you need to gain more control over it. Writers at level 4 and below sometimes seem to write the first words and ideas that come into their heads. That can be fine, but it can also become rather predictable and dull. To work at level 5 and beyond you need to try to entertain the reader through your choice of words and phrases, and by thinking of ways of varying the story's pace.

You need to take care, though. Using unexpected words does not mean looking for fancy new words in a thesaurus. Do not write 'The ominous sky was laden with gloomy precipitation' if you mean it looked as though it might rain! You could say:

> The clouds were growing darker and more threatening.
> The sky grew grey with menace.
> Rain was just a mile or so away.

None of these sentences uses fancy words, but each helps the reader to visualise the weather. They use words and phrases which are more interesting than those we might have thought of straightaway.

The three modes of writing

In a similar way, you can make your imaginative writing more interesting if you vary the pace. Writing has three main modes:

- plot (or storytelling)
  This is how the storyline develops; how one event follows another:
  > 'The robbers ran into the bank; the alarm sounded; the police arrived.'

- description
  This helps us to see the scene by describing people, places, sounds, colours, smells and textures:
  > 'The three robbers were wearing dark masks and looked as if they were sweating. The eyes of the first one gazed madly over his mask. He looked angry and terrified.'

- dialogue
  This tells us what one character says to another:
  > 'Pass the money,' said the robber.
  > 'What money?' replied the cashier.
  > 'You know what money,' yelled the robber.
  > 'No I don't,' said the cashier.

LEVEL 5
Imaginative Writing

If you allow one of these modes to dominate, then your story could become dull. The best writing usually uses a variety of these techniques to vary the pace and keep the reader's interest right to the end.

Writers also learn to keep the reader guessing about what will happen next. We call this 'suspense' and tend to think it is used only in thrillers and ghost stories. In fact, suspense is used in most good writing – it means making the reader want to read on. Getting a reader involved in the story is the chief way of creating suspense because they will want to keep reading.

EXAMPLE

Look at these brief extracts from the opening of a short story by Welsh writer, Leslie Norris. Look at the way he starts with description and plot, and then – later – introduces dialogue. (See Word Bank on next page.)

Prey

When the cold weather came, the sky was suddenly full of hawks. Not great flocks of them, as with communal birds, but hawks were suddenly more plentiful; wherever I went, when I looked up, somewhere, at the corner of eyesight, there would be a still point in the moving sky. A hawk, a kestrel, hovering.

In the spring a motorway was completed north of the village, two straight wide roads cut parallel through the brown dirt. For months huge earth-shifters and diggers churned through the land, but in spring all was done. The soft banks of little severed hills made easy burrowing, and in moved colonies of rats and voles and rabbits. Hawks hang on a rope of high air above the scurrying traffic, stationed at intervals along the road. I understand this. I know just where the favoured vantage points are on that highway. Often the birds, still as porcelain, keep unceasing watch above a crossroads or an intersection, or hammer into the grass for prey invisible to me as I drive past. They claim, too, the small bodies of creatures freshly killed on the roads. I know why the hawks watch there.

But with the frost, the hawks, the autumn-coloured birds, seemed to be more numerous. I saw a kestrel high over Ernie Foster's big field where I'd never seen one before, not in twenty years. I saw it there, intent, hanging, a machine for looking and killing. I put the glasses on him so that I could watch him make his sudden little shifts as he changed his wing-tip hold on the wind, the swift flutter of tail and finger-ends as he adjusted his view of the upturned world. That morning I counted ten of them, hawks, high and solitary, as I drove the dozen miles to town. Then, in the evening, one was mercilessly beating the hedge at the side of the house.

Years ago, one swooped almost into my windscreen as I drove under the downs. He came late out of his dive, wings and legs braced in front of the glass. I saw the open hook of his beak, his furious yellow eye.
. . .
On Sunday Dennis came to see me. He comes seldom to my house, for he is a busy man, active in public causes, forever attending committees and meetings. He talks incessantly, the soft words grow about him. I cannot imagine that he is ever alone. He was in bountiful form, expansive, telling me of a jungle of small injustices, urging me to support this or that community action.

27

LEVEL 5
Imaginative Writing

'All together,' he said. 'That's the answer. We should all pull together.'

I rarely answer Dennis. For all his kindness and endless patience, I am indifferent to him. Leaning back in the chair, away from his optimistic voice, I saw the kestrel, a female, hovering outside my window. She was so near I felt I could almost touch her. I saw the clear outline of her every feather . . .

from Lesley Norris *Sliding: Short Stories*

> **WORD BANK**
> communal birds – *birds which tend to stay in groups*
> severed – *shortened*
> vantage – *lookout*
> expansive – *talking a lot*

What words and phrases does Leslie Norris use to interest the reader?

The writer starts with a well-balanced sentence: 'When the cold weather came, the sky was full of hawks.' (You can find out about this type of complex sentence on page 103.) It is a strong opening sentence because it seems to get us straight into the world of the story. Imagine another writer placing greater emphasis on description. The opening might have read:

> There is a small valley in Surrey where the sun often shines and the birds often sing – a valley where the trees grow green and strong . . .

This feels repetitive and wasteful of words. We don't seem to have started the story properly. It has no suspense, and the repetition of 'valley', 'where' and 'often' make it feel very laboured.

Leslie Norris's story, in contrast, builds a feeling of tension. In the first paragraph we are not sure:

- where we are
- who the narrator is
- what is going to happen.

This makes us want to read on to find out answers to these uncertainties.

Lesley Norris also uses language in a powerful way. The first paragraph focuses just on the hawks and makes them seem quite menacing. This is partly because they appear so 'suddenly' (he uses the word twice in quite a short paragraph). This hints that the birds are not behaving in their normal way. The fact that they are there 'wherever I went' gives a feeling that the birds are gathering menacingly, as if the writer cannot escape them.

LEVEL 5

Imaginative Writing

In the next paragraph he describes the hawks as 'still as porcelain' and then, later in the same sentence, he says that they 'hammer into the grass'. This suggests that they are unpredictable – one second delicate and calm, the next violent and aggressive. The language gives us a strong feeling that something unpleasant is going to happen – that the hawks are gathering for a purpose.

How does he vary the pace by using plot, description and dialogue?

The first two paragraphs combine description and plot. An obvious plot sentence tells us 'In the spring a motorway was completed north of the village . . .'. An obvious descriptive phrase is 'the birds, still as porcelain . . .'. These opening paragraphs work because neither plot nor description dominate. There is enough storyline to keep us interested and enough description to help us visualise the scene.

Watch what happens when a story is all plot:

> The man walked into the station and got on the train and read his newspaper and looked out of the window. Then he read until the train stopped, got off the train, and walked home.

That is not a story that holds our interest because we feel no involvement with the man and his journey.

What if the story had been dominated by description?

> The old, grey-haired man in the tatty duffel-coat shuffled along the long, wind-swept platform of the dark railway station. A piece of paper flapped on the tracks. Some signals clattered in the wind. A woman in the buffet laughed loudly. A train on a distant platform started revving up. The old man was sweating and tired.

Most people would agree that this is more interesting than the first example because it includes some description. It gains our interest with some well-chosen words – like 'flapped' and 'clattered' – and it presents quite a strong picture of the man and his environment. But if it went on for too long without something happening (i.e. some plot) we would begin to lose interest.

Dialogue is another way of changing the texture of your story. Look at the way Leslie Norris's brief, simple use of dialogue changes the feel of the story:

> 'All together,' he said. 'That's the answer. We should all pull together.'
> I rarely answer Dennis . . .

LEVEL 5
Imaginative Writing

Dialogue is useful here for a number of reasons:

- It tells us something about the character of Dennis (he is very positive about life).
- It tells us something about the narrator (he gets impatient with Dennis).
- It changes the texture of the story, adding variety to the written style and, therefore, helping to hold the reader's interest.

Check yourself

Read this opening sequence of a ghost story. Then try to continue the story for two more paragraphs. Try to put into practice what you have learned about using plot, description and dialogue. Include them all but don't let any one of them dominate your writing.

> I knew it was time to leave the party, but I didn't want to go. There was something safe and comforting about the laughter-filled house, with its bright lights and smiling people. Yet I knew I couldn't stay all night. Finally I said my goodbyes and slipped out into the dark night.
>
> There were two routes home – one longer but street-lit, the other quicker but darker. 'You're being a fool,' I said to myself. 'All that business about hauntings – it's just a kids' story.' And trying to make myself feel older and braver, I set off down the long passage past the churchyard.

What happens next? Describe the narrator's journey down the passageway.

- Use description to create a feeling of tension as the person notices sights, sounds or smells on the way. Perhaps they hear something move – footsteps ahead, the wind moving the branch of an old tree.
- Use plot to move the story forward.
- Use dialogue to show how the narrator tries to persuade her/himself that this is all a result of imagination. Build up the tension by showing the narrator's fear in detail.
- Make your choice of words and phrases as interesting as possible.

Answer and tutorial can be found on page 37.

Chapter 8

LEVEL 5

Writing to inform and persuade

Leaflets

Introduction

We saw in the level 4 section that writing can be informative – that is, it gives people facts and advice. Writing can often have a persuasive purpose too. It may be intended to:

- change your mind about an issue (think of party political leaflets given out during an election campaign)
- make you believe that someone is being fair or unfair
- persuade you to buy one company's product.

Writing to inform requires certain skills: being able to organise ideas and present them in a clear, straightforward way which the reader will understand. **Writing to persuade** involves these skills – and more. You need also to be able to present the information so that it convinces your readers to change their mind about something.

You need to
- organise your ideas in a sensible way
- interest and convince your reader
- write in a clear and interesting way

plus . . .
- develop some of your ideas more fully
- use a more formal style
- give examples to support your case

EXAMPLE

Look at this leaflet produced by the Health Education Authority. It aims to encourage readers to get a more active lifestyle, so that they become fitter. It is aimed at older readers.

it's never too late TO START

Grown up children and retirement bring a new freedom. Now you have the time to do the things you really enjoy and the opportunity to try out new activities.

You may be interested in taking up exercise, but feel that you're a little too old for that sort of thing.

The simple answer is that you're never too old. Taking part in physical activities is a great way to stay healthy, mobile and independent – living an active life.

Steady progress is the key to success. Once you feel comfortable with gentle exercise, you may want to try other activities such as swimming, walking or cycling. Why not try them all, and see which you enjoy the most?

If you do have any serious health worries, consult your doctor before you start. Otherwise, increasing your level of activity can only be of benefit (see p.1).

Take it Easy

The key to exercising safely is to take things at a suitable pace.

- Always warm up thoroughly.
- Gradually ease your body into exercise or activity for the first few minutes.
- Be careful to increase the length and intensity of your exercise slowly: pain or uncomfortable stiffness following activity are a sign that you have overdone things – ease off next time.

And if you're being a bit more active – exercising or playing sports – remember:

- Stretch out your muscles, holding each stretch for about six seconds.
- To finish, ease down gradually and stretch again, this time holding each stretch for up to 30 seconds.
- Never force your body to stretch further than is comfortable and never bounce during a stretch.

  ▪ "Don't try to fit all your activities into one day. It is far better to do less on each day, but to be active on most days of the week."

31

LEVEL 5

Writing to inform and persuade

How well does the leaflet persuade readers to follow its advice?

The leaflet is good at addressing its target audience directly – 'Now you have the time to do the things you really enjoy . . .'. The reference to grown up children and retirement shows that it is clearly aimed at an older audience, and this means it will be more likely to persuade them to follow the advice.

The leaflet is reassuring – it is careful not to scare its readers: 'Once you feel comfortable with gentle exercise . . .'. Words like 'comfortable' and 'gentle' are important in making the reader feel that the suggestions are realistic and will not do any harm.

The leaflet gives plenty of solid, practical advice in the bullet points. These are again reassuring, but also give specific ideas to the reader of what she or he might do: 'Stretch out your muscles, holding each stretch for about six seconds.'

The leaflet is good at persuading its readers because it makes exercise sound so manageable, with plenty of reassuring words and phrases. The layout is clear and straightforward, and the cartoon images make the subject seem light-hearted. Once again, this will probably appeal to readers who are nervous about the idea of taking exercise.

Does it develop ideas in more detail, use a formal style and support its case?

- *Detail*
  The leaflet is a mixture of general advice on the left and more detailed suggestions on the right. Even on the left, though, it lists possible activities – 'swimming, walking or cycling' – rather than just making a vague statement about exercise. The right page could go into more detail – what to wear, where to exercise, and so on – but that is not really necessary. It gets the level of detail right, showing readers what practical steps they could take to get fitter.

- *Formal style*
  The leaflet uses a style which is neither very informal nor very formal. A more informal, chatty style might be used for a younger audience: 'So you want to get fit? Why don't you start with this . . .?'. The question and the word 'don't' instead of 'do not' give it a more casual tone. That would not be appropriate for an older audience.

  But the leaflet is not too formal either. If it said 'It has been estimated that more frequent exercise can benefit people in a variety of ways . . .' then the reader would not feel involved. It would feel remote and not really addressed at us. The key to the tone of this leaflet is the way it addresses readers as 'you' and then addresses them in a clear, straightforward style.

LEVEL 5

Writing to inform and persuade

- *Using examples*
  The leaflet gives examples of the kinds of activities readers might try (the right page is a brief exercise plan which readers can try for themselves). It also uses a quotation at the bottom of the page ('Don't try to fit . . .') which is giving further detailed advice.

Check yourself

Look at the anti-smoking leaflet below. It aims to show the harm smoking can do to young people. At present it is written *about* young people, but does not really seem to talk directly to them. How would you use the information from this leaflet to make one more directly aimed at 12–16 year olds?

Put together your own leaflet on one side of A4 paper. Use the information below to create a persuasive leaflet which persuades teenage readers that smoking is harmful. Try to:

- develop your ideas
- use a style that is appropriate for a young audience
- give specific examples.

YOUNG PEOPLE AND SMOKING

Smoking is associated with adulthood. As long as young people see adults smoking and are exposed to tobacco advertising and promotion, there will always be some who experiment with cigarettes and risk becoming addicted to smoking.

In England in 1990, 25 per cent of girls and 25 per cent of boys were regular smokers by the age of 15. Children who smoke are twice as likely to have parents or brothers and sisters who smoke. Parental attitude plays a role in children's smoking behaviour, whether or not parents smoke themselves. Children who think their parents won't mind about them smoking are more likely to be smokers than those whose parents disapprove of them smoking. Having friends who smoke, and being susceptible to peer group pressure, increases the likelihood of smoking among teenagers.

THE BENEFITS OF GIVING UP

Giving up smoking is probably the greatest single thing smokers can do to improve their health.

When the daily assault of nicotine, carbon monoxide, tar and other poisons has stopped, the body begins to repair the damage. Body systems start to return to normal, resulting in the following benefits, many of which can be experienced within a few weeks:

- hair, skin and breath no longer smell of tobacco smoke
- the natural decline in the efficiency of the lungs slows down to a rate similar to the non-smoker
- sense of taste and smell improves
- breathing improves
- more able to cope with sudden exertion
- reduction in phlegm and loss of smoker's cough
- lack of worry over damage smoking is doing to health
- feeling good about yourself for having stopped
- reduction in risk of smoking related diseases.

Answer and tutorial can be found on page 38.

LEVEL 5

Answers and Tutorials to Check Yourself

5 Reading and Understanding Fiction (page 20-21)

Answers

A1 Nature is presented in quite a negative way. D H Lawrence uses adjectives which make the plants seem far from perfect: a 'bony vine', 'wintry primroses', 'twiggy apple trees', 'ragged cabbages'. All of these words create an impression of things which are withering away or perhaps struggling to survive. Towards the end of the extract, the chrysanthemums are in 'ragged wisps', as if they are unlikely to survive. Lawrence also writes that the child 'tore' at them. This gives a strong impression that nature is under attack by human beings.

A2 D H Lawrence gives us quite a lot of visual detail about the woman – her way of walking ('erect'), her clothes (a 'white apron'), her face ('imperious mien, handsome, with definite black eyebrows').

The child is described as 'small' and 'sturdy', and we get an impression of the way he is dressed: 'trousers and waistcoat of cloth that was too thick and hard for the size of garments'. These are important details because they tell us something about the background of the two characters – that they are poor. We know this because the boy's clothes are 'cut down from a man's clothes'. This suggests that they cannot afford clothes for the child.

Tutorials

T1 This is a very good answer because it gives exactly the information required by the question. The writer picks out all the key examples of the way language is used about nature and, importantly, quotes them directly. This means that the answer feels very detailed and accurate.

The final point, about the child tearing at the nettles, is also well made. It shows the reader has noticed that nature is under attack. To achieve an even higher level, the writer might have written a bit more about this, linking it to the way the train (a machine created by humans) is damaging and disturbing nature, just as the child is doing the same.

T2 This answer pays good, close attention to the writer's language. It answers systematically, too – starting with the mother and then moving on to the child. It is a solid level 5 answer.

To gain a higher level, the student might have noticed that D H Lawrence also hints at the woman's feelings. He says that her 'mouth was closed with disillusionment'. We do not know much about her feelings from this, but we do know that the woman is unhappy with her life, and it leads us to start thinking about why. For a higher level the answer might also have noticed the stern way the woman speaks to the child – it seems quite a cold relationship.

LEVEL 5

Answers and Tutorials to Check Yourself

6 Reading and Understanding Non-fiction (page 24)

Answers

A1 At the beginning the writer is very worried. He says he 'suffered agonies'. Then when he sees an opportunity to change over the bags, he seizes it 'without thinking'. We get the impression that he is very decisive because he acts 'unhesitatingly'. He also does not seem to feel much fear because he says 'there was virtually no risk that anyone behind me in the queue could have spotted this sleight of hand . . .'. At the end of the extract the writer 'mumbled a few apologies' to Mabe – for putting him in such a dangerous position – but he does not really feel sorry because he has possibly saved his own life.

A2 Mabe's reaction is 'suppressed anger'. He keeps himself under control but is privately furious at the danger in which the writer has placed him. It is clear from what the writer says at the end of the extract that the incident was soon forgotten.

A3 The writer's environment is cramped and dark. He says 'the narrow corridor hemmed us in on both sides'. While this would make uncomfortable living conditions, it makes the hiding of the bag much easier. The writer says it would have been hard for anyone to see 'this sleight of hand'.

Tutorials

T1 to T3 These are really good, solid level 5 answers. If your answers were the same or similar then they would also achieve level 5.

Each question is answered clearly and in a sensible order, and all the points are supported with well-chosen quotations. The answers show awareness of the writer's use of words and phrases and the quotations are integrated into the sentences, giving a smooth, easy-to-follow effect.

To move to a higher level your answers would need to comment in more detail on the language the writer uses – not just noticing effects, but actually commenting on them in greater depth. A level 6 answer, for example, might comment on the way the writer varies long and short sentences. The short sentences – such as 'the narrow corridor hemmed us in on both sides' – build up a feeling of suspense and state very directly the difficult circumstances in which the writer finds himself.

LEVEL 5

Answers and Tutorials to Check Yourself

Reading and Understanding Non-fiction (page 25)

Looking at layout

Answer

The leaflet about keeping guinea pigs uses questions, set in green panels, followed by short answers. The layout is clear and straightforward. The questions are in a larger print size, so they stand out more, but parts of some answers are printed in bold text to emphasise them – for example: 'Straw can irritate eyes and should not be used.'

The leaflet uses illustrations to add variety. It has three photographs of guinea pigs, and shows bowls of food. This helps to emphasise what the paragraphs are about.

The headings are quite unusual because they are all in small letters – there aren't even capitals at the start of the headings. This may be to give it a more modern feel. The main heading – 'my guinea pig' – is also printed in lower case letters and it overlaps the bottom of the green box. This may again be to make it look less formal and so encourage young people, possibly even children, to read it.

Tutorial

This is a good, sharp-eyed commentary. It notices the details of the layout (use of coloured panels, lower case lettering, photographs, and so on) and goes on to discuss the effect of this. Most importantly of all, it links the layout of the leaflet to the people who are likely to read it – in this instance, young people.

To gain a higher level, the answer could be more critical. That means it could make more of a judgement about the layout. The leaflet is designed to inform, and yet the layout is quite distracting. The main heading actually looks quite messy, as if the words haven't printed correctly in the box. Also, the text size of the answers is probably too small for young people to read quickly and easily.

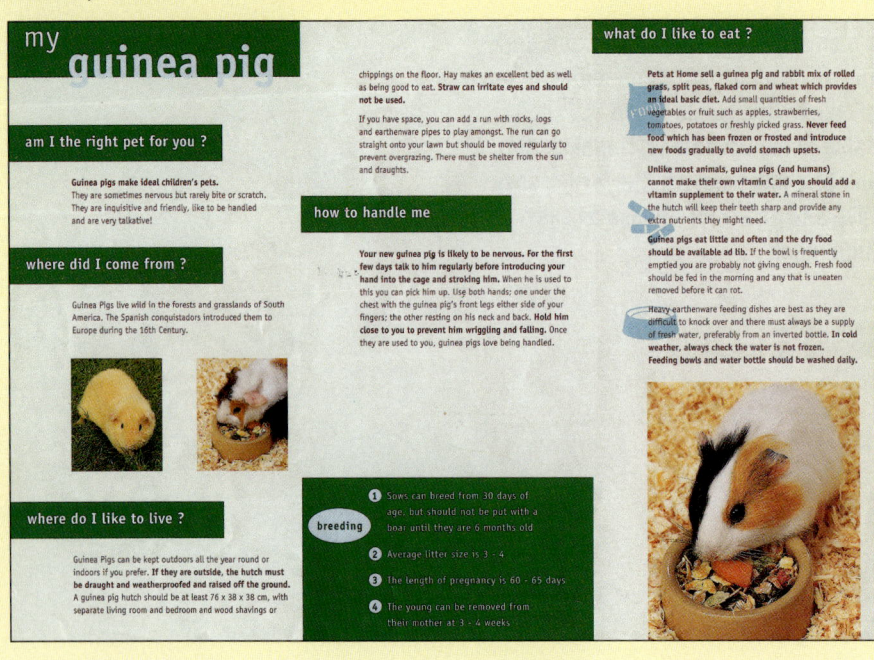

LEVEL 5

Answers and Tutorials to Check Yourself

7 Imaginative Writing (page 30)

Answer

Here is how the story might be continued, using plot, description and dialogue:

> The passageway led towards the church and it was darker than I remembered it. I could hardly see a thing, but smelt a strong scent of damp moss on the walls. I walked slowly, and tried hard to keep my nerve. 'You're fourteen for heaven's sake,' I said to myself, 'and yet you're behaving like a baby.' I wished I was a baby, tucked up in a cot safe and warm.
>
> Then I heard something ahead of me. It was a sound at the end of the passageway. At first it sounded like footsteps. Perhaps it was something else. Perhaps the wind was scraping some old branch along the wall. I stopped to listen. There it was again – the definite sound of shoes on gravel. Someone was down there, waiting. 'So?' I thought. 'Other people have a right to be out, don't they? Pull yourself together.' But it was hard to pull myself together when the sound of my beating heart was starting to blank out all the sound from outside. I began to fear that I was going to collapse. I needed to keep moving, to get out of here. Should I return or keep going . . . be brave or be a coward?

Tutorial

This is a strong, atmospheric piece of writing. It uses the three modes of plot, description and dialogue to vary the pace, and it manages to hold our interest successfully by creating suspense. Because it is chiefly about the narrator's fears, there is less plot than in other kinds of story – a children's story, for example, would probably have less description and more plot – but the mix is right.

To move beyond level 5, the writing could contain more interesting words and phrases. At the moment it uses fairly ordinary vocabulary – *dark, cold, long, old*, and so on. These words do not really capture our interest. The writer's next step should be to make the language more unexpected and more visual, perhaps using comparisons in places to help us to see what she or he sees – for example, 'the tree branch scraped along the wall like bony fingers down a blackboard . . .'. Notice how the word 'bony' creates a powerful, uncomfortable effect, helping us to imagine what the tree branch looks like.

LEVEL 5

Answers and Tutorials to Check Yourself

8 Writing to inform and persuade (page 33)

Answer

Here is a leaflet which uses the information about smoking from the leaflet on page 33, and rewrites it for a younger audience.

WANT TO SEE YOUR CASH GO UP IN SMOKE?

> Some people think it's cool to smoke. They think it makes them look grown-up. The sad thing is, it's also leading them into a world of adult diseases. Just look at the facts:
> - smoking makes your hair, skin and breath smell – not a great way of attracting new friends
> - smoking damages your lungs
> - it affects your breathing and makes you unfit
> - it adds to your stress levels – you actually worry about the harm it's doing.

Smoking facts
Around 25% of 15-year-olds claimed to be regular smokers in 1990. Yet if everyone knows the damage smoking does, why do they do it?

Here are some reasons:
- their parents or brothers and sisters smoke
- their friends smoke.

In other words, peer pressure.

Avoiding or kicking the habit
So what can you do to avoid or kick the smoking habit?

You need to keep thinking about why people smoke – it's not because it helps them in any way, or makes them healthier or fitter. It's because of image – pure and simple.
It's because they think it makes them look good.

You're bigger than that. Be strong. Say 'no' to smoking.

Tutorial

This leaflet is successful at taking the original information and adapting it to a new, younger audience. The writer uses some of the ideas in the original leaflet, but also adds more. The last section – about avoiding or kicking the habit – shows the writer developing ideas of their own, striking a good balance between the given facts and their own ideas.

The leaflet uses layout to catch our attention – the headline, the illustration, the use of boxes and bullet points, and questions. All of these make the leaflet visually more interesting – readers are more likely to want to read on.

The leaflet also changes the language successfully to match the new teenage audience. Look at the use of questions to create a more informal tone ('Want to see . . .?' instead of the more formal 'Do you want to see . . .?'). This is good because it uses a style which is appropriate to the audience – less formal than if the leaflet had been aimed at an older audience.

Notice also the use of 'you'. The reader is addressed directly, making him or her feel involved in the discussion.

To gain a higher level, the leaflet might have supported the ideas with examples. It could be useful, for example, to include some quotations from a 14-year-old smoker saying why she or he smokes; or the answer could present a case study – one example of a pupil who smokes, describing what their background is and how they began to smoke. This would emphasise the importance of peer pressure in smoking.

Chapter 9

A fiction writer's aims

LEVEL 6
Reading and Understanding Fiction

Introduction

Writers may try to achieve a variety of aims in their work. A writer of children's stories may aim chiefly to entertain. A ghost story writer may want to thrill or scare us. Someone writing about a place may want to draw us into the world of the text so that we feel we are there. The key to what a writer is trying to achieve will be in the use of language – the specific words and phrases she or he uses.

At level 6, you are asked to start making judgements about writing – 'What is this writer trying to do? Look closely at the use of language and comment on the use of words and phrases.' You need now to do more than *notice* particular effects in a text; you need also to *comment* on them – to find something to say about the writer's style. This means being able to look closely at the detail of the language and then drawing back to discuss what you see.

You need to
- know what the characters in a text are like
- begin to read beneath the surface
- show an overall understanding of the text
- note the effects of words and phrases

EXAMPLE

Look at the opening of this short story by Irish writer Brian Friel. As you read, pay particular attention to his careful use of language to create a strong sense of people and places. Start to think about what the writer may be trying to achieve.

plus . . .
- be aware of what the writer is trying to achieve
- comment on the writer's use of some words or phrases

November frost had starched the flat countryside into silent rigidity. The 'rat-tat-tat' of the tractor's exhaust drilled into the clean, hard air but did not penetrate it; each staccato sound broke off as if it had been nipped. Hunched over the driver's wheel sat Kelly, the owner, a rock of a man with a huge head and broken fingernails, and in the trailer behind were his four potato gatherers – two young men, permanent farm hands, and the two boys he had hired for the day. At six o'clock in the morning, they were the only living things in that part of County Tyrone.

    The boys chatted incessantly. They stood at the front of the trailer, legs apart, hands in their pockets, their faces pressed forward into the icy rush of air, their senses edged for perception. Joe, the elder of the two – he was thirteen and had worked for Kelly on two previous occasions – might have been

LEVEL 6
Reading and Understanding Fiction

WORD BANK
staccato – *abrupt, sudden*
perception – *feeling things*
infectious – *catching*

quieter, but his brother's excitement was infectious. For this was Philly's first job, his first opportunity to prove that he was a man at twelve years of age. His energy was a burden to him. Behind them, on the floor of the trailer, the two farm hands lay sprawled in half sleep.

Twice the boys had to cheer. The first time was when they were passing Dicey O'Connell's house, and Philly, who was in the same class as Dicey, called across to the thatched, smokeless building, 'Remember me to all the boys, Dicey!' The second time was when they came to the school itself. It was then that Kelly turned to them and growled to them to shut up.

'Do you want the whole country to know you're taking the day off?' he said. 'Save your breath for your work.'

When Kelly faced back to the road ahead, Philly stuck his thumbs in his ears, put out his tongue, and wriggled his fingers at the back of Kelly's head.

The Potato Gatherers

What do you think the writer is trying to achieve in this extract?

Firstly, Brian Friel is trying to achieve a powerful *sense of place*. He wants us to feel strongly involved in the world of the story – to see the place and to imagine that we are there. He gives us a picture of the 'flat', 'silent' countryside, with the tractor moving across its hard surface. He also makes us strongly aware of the weather. The air is 'clear and hard' and there has been a severe frost.

Secondly, he wants the reader to understand immediately the nature of the relationship between the characters. Although he gives little description of the man or the boys, we gain a strong sense of the relationship between them. The boys are lively, chattering and noisy. Kelly is calm, silent, wanting some peace. We get a clear sense of the gulf between them – between age and youth.

Throughout the extract this gulf develops. The boys get louder – 'twice they had to cheer' – and this provokes Kelly to turn on them: he 'growled to them to shut up'. Brian Friel then makes the distance between the boys and the older man even clearer when one of the boys, Philly, 'stuck his thumbs in his ears, put out his tongue, and wriggled his fingers at the back of Kelly's head'.

Brian Friel intends to show us a relationship, and what is most skilful is that he does this through *showing* rather than *telling*. Some writers – especially young writers – feel that you have to tell the reader information directly:

> Kelly was an old man.
> Kelly was bad-tempered.
> Kelly felt a gulf between himself and the boys.

LEVEL 6

Reading and Understanding Fiction

Brian Friel does not do this. He shows us the behaviour of the boys and the behaviour of Kelly, but leaves it to us to sense what the relationship is like. This makes reading more active, and probably more interesting, because we are expected to pick up the clues about the relationship rather than just be told about it directly. This is what is meant by 'reading beneath the surface of a text'.

Brian Friel, then, successfully achieves both of his aims:

- he conveys a sense of place
- he shows the relationship between the characters.

Comment on some of the words and phrases he uses

Brian Friel uses language that is mostly simple but visual. He creates images in our mind – pictures of what he is describing – by choosing words and phrases that have echoes and associations.

You may have heard of the term 'images' in connection with poetry. There are three kinds: simile, metaphor and personification. This is what they mean:

- **Simile** This is when a writer compares one thing with another to create an effect. The comparison will use the word 'like' or the word 'as'. We use plenty of similes in everyday speech:

> I'm fit as a fiddle.
> He has a face like the back-end of a bus.
> She ran as fast as lightning.

Notice the words 'like' and 'as' in each example – these are your clues that you are dealing with similes.

- **Metaphor** This is again when a writer compares one thing with another to create an effect. This time there will be no obvious comparing word – no 'like' or 'as'.

> The footballer was a terrier on the wing.
> The car was a jewel.

Metaphors can be more difficult to spot, but notice that both examples are really comparisons: to show the speed and cunning of the footballer, he is compared to a terrier; to show how expensive and attractive the car is, we compare it to a jewel.

- **Personification** This technique is much less common, and we come across it most in poetry. It means giving human qualities to something which is not alive:

> Death stalked the village.
> Hope deserted them.
> Summer brought her bounty to the people.

41

LEVEL 6

Reading and Understanding Fiction

Notice how the abstract ideas – death, hope and summer – are presented as if they are alive: they are 'personified'.

Now look at 'The Potato Gatherers' extract again.

Brian Friel's first sentence describes the landscape: 'November frosts had starched the flat countryside into silent rigidity.' The most striking word in this is 'starched'. It conjures up in our mind all the right images for frost – whiteness, stiffness, something that has been made clean. It is followed by the phrase 'silent rigidity', which gives a strong impression of the effect the frost has had on the landscape, making it completely still and hard. Together, the images give an impression about the November frost: they suggest its power to make the landscape submit, to change the way things are. Usually we imagine that people starch things to make them clean and pure. Here the November frost is doing the same. It is therefore an example of personification. The comparison of the landscape to the process of being starched is a metaphor.

You do not necessarily need to know these terms: you will not be expected to look at a text and spot the similes, metaphors and personification. But you will need to be able to look as closely as this at the writer's use of language because you need to comment on what you notice.

There are other comments you could make on the way Brian Friel uses language in the first paragraph of 'The Potato Gatherers'. Look at the second sentence, which describes the sound of the tractor's exhaust. The writer creates a powerful effect by saying that the 'rat-tat-tat' sound 'drilled into the clean, hard air'. The 'rat-tat-tat' helps us to hear what the sound was like. The word 'drilled' gives an impression of the harshness of the sound, and its insistence – that is, it just keeps on going. The sentence also hints at the hardness of the landscape and the power of the November frost because the drilling sound 'did not penetrate it'. It is as if the power of nature is being shown as stronger than the power of the human world because each sound 'broke off as if it had been nipped'. This is an image of plants being nipped by the frost. It suggests that the power of the frost defeats the power of the engine noise.

The writer then describes the tractor driver, Kelly, with some details about his way of sitting, his head and his 'broken fingernails'. These last words hint at someone who works hard and whose body is being damaged by all of his labour. Brian Friel also describes him as 'a rock of a man'. The metaphor is a powerful way of showing how big and solid Kelly must be.

Overall, the particular words and phrases Brian Friel has chosen to use in this opening paragraph draw us into the story by creating a striking visual impression of the landscape and the people in it.

LEVEL **6**

Reading and Understanding Fiction

Check yourself

Now look at the rest of the extract. Look in particular at the presentation of the other characters and the way the writer uses language to create his effects.

QUESTIONS

Q1 What ideas about the relationship between the characters is Brian Friel trying to show in these paragraphs?

Q2 Comment on his use of language, picking out words and phrases which help him to achieve his aim.

Answers and tutorials can be found on page 56.

Chapter 10

LEVEL 6
Reading and Understanding Non-fiction

Reading newspapers

Introduction

You need to

- be able to locate ideas and information in a text
- begin to be aware of the purpose of the text
- show an overall understanding of the text
- note the effect of some words or phrases
- note the effect of features like layout, if appropriate

plus . . .

- be aware of what the writer is trying to achieve
- comment on the writer's use of some words or phrases
- comment on the effect of features like layout, if appropriate

Newspapers in Britain sell millions of copies each day. It is easy to assume that they are intended just to inform us – to tell us about events that have happened. But newspapers also try to persuade and entertain. The opinion or 'leader' page in a newspaper will give the editor's views on a subject: she or he will try to convince us that we should believe the same thing. Increasingly, newspapers are also full of articles which have little to do with the news. Instead there are feature articles – pieces of writing about lifestyle issues, such as health, showbiz or gossip. The feature article writers are trying to capture the reader's attention. This is why they put eye-catching headlines; use stunning photographs and artwork; and place the most important information in the first paragraph.

Newspaper reporting tries to tell a story as briefly as possible. A typical news report contains certain key features:

1. *A headline:* this catches the reader's eye and should make you want to find out more about the story.

2. *A topic sentence:* this is the first sentence of the story. It will usually tell you who, what, when and where something happened.

3. *Short paragraphs:* often a newspaper story will have paragraphs which are just one sentence long. This is important because newspapers are usually laid out in columns – so long blocks of text could look off-putting. Short paragraphs help readers to read quickly by keeping our eyes skimming down the page.

4. *Subheadings:* the topic of a group of paragraphs may be summarised in a subheading, like 'crisis' or 'scandal' – again as a way of making our reading more efficient.

5. *Labelling:* people are labelled by job, age and attitude. For example: 'Local policewoman Sarah Smythe, 27, . . .'.

6. *Quotations:* newspapers will often quote people's words because it adds more detail to the story.

EXAMPLE

LEVEL 6
Reading and Understanding Non-fiction

Look closely at this newspaper article from the *East Anglian Daily Times*.

East Anglian Daily Times   18 June 1997

White line rage of roadworker as paint smudged

by CAHAL MILMO

A ROADWORKER who flew into a blind fury after a Suffolk couple accidentally drove over his freshly painted white lines was yesterday put on probation.

Burly Terry Davison, 28, screamed abuse at the husband and wife after they inadvertently smudged his neat paintwork on the A143 near Haverhill before denting their car with a volley of kicks.

St Edmundsbury magistrates yesterday gave Davison a 12-month probation order after hearing "he completely lost control" on a hot summer's day last year – terrifying his astonished victims.

Gareth Davies, prosecuting, said: "The defendant totally lost his sense of proportion. He became very aggressive, shouting at the couple and kicking and banging at the car.

"He was using a great deal of offensive language and left the couple in a state of deep alarm. He repeatedly attacked the car." Staff nurse Margaret Thomas, 62, was being taken to work by her husband Alan, 60, from their home in Hundon, near Haverhill, when they came across the volatile roadworker at nearby Stradishall.

Davison, who comes from Durham, had travelled south after the firm he was working for, JFC Roadmarkings, was sub-contracted to paint lines by Suffolk County Council.

The court heard the couple had been trying to find what was causing a sudden traffic jam. Mr Davies said: "They came across a queue of vehicles and were trying to see what was happening.

"As they were doing so Mr Thomas inadvertently pulled the wheels across the fresh white lines. The next thing they knew they were being screamed at by the completely out-of-control defendant."

Father-of-two Davison, who admitted charges of criminal damage and causing distress on August 1 last year, was ordered to pay a £258 repair bill to the Thomas' car.

The court heard the roadworker, who has since had to give up the job after suffering severe burns six months ago, was "deeply remorseful" for his actions.

Helen Cleaver, mitigating, said: "He is ashamed of what happened and has himself referred to his behaviour as stupid. He recognises the need to learn to control his temper."

Davison also admitted a public order offence after being caught brawling with a soldier in the car park of the Regal Cinema at Stowmarket in February. No separate penalty was imposed.

---

1   What do you think the writer is trying to achieve?

2   What do you notice about the writer's use of language?

3   Comment on the use of layout.

LEVEL 6

Reading and Understanding Non-fiction

1. The writer is reporting an event – aiming chiefly to inform readers about what happened. The tone is therefore quite factual. The topic sentence, for example, tells us who (a roadworker), when (yesterday) and what he did.

2. The use of language contains some typical newspaper terms: 'blind fury', 'screamed abuse', 'astonished', and so on. This is quite dramatic language designed to make the event sound exciting and sensational. The headline contains similarly dramatic words (such as 'rage') and leaves out a verb to create a more compressed feel ('. . . as paint smudged' rather than 'as paint is smudged').

    The writer labels the people involved in the incident: 'Burly Terry Davison, 28 . . .' and 'staff nurse Margaret Thomas, 62'.

    The sentences are fairly short, within short paragraphs, so that they are easy to take in. The writer directly quotes some of the people involved – 'He is ashamed of what happened . . .'. Quotations are 'dramatic' – like dialogue in a novel. They present evidence that readers can judge for themselves.

3. The layout is typical of newspapers – a headline of compressed language (the missing verb); short paragraphs, text organised into columns. This makes it instantly recognisable as newspaper text rather than, say, a novel. The text does not, however, use subheadings which is a feature of some newspaper and magazine layouts.

LEVEL 6
Reading and Understanding Non-fiction

Check yourself

Now read the following newspaper article from *The Daily Mirror*.
Use it to look at the writer's aims, language and layout.

TWISTER (IN BURY ST EDMUNDS)

WORKERS FLEE 100MPH TORNADO

TORNADOES usually devastate towns in the US but yesterday it was the turn of sleepy Bury St Edmunds to be in the frontline.

A twister with winds of up to 100mph hit the Suffolk town as thunderstorms swept across the country.

Terrified workers ran for their lives as the winds ripped through an industrial estate.

Cars were lifted into the air and buildings were damaged.

Bernard Sutcliffe told yesterday how a wooden pallet was sent crashing through a roof.

Mr Sutcliffe, of Rougham Motor Company, said: "The pallet, which must have been eight feet by four feet, was lifted at least 40 feet off the ground.

"We shut all the windows and doors and tried to shelter."

Malcolm Burroughs, manager of a neighbouring firm on the Rougham estate which lost part of its roof, said: "At first we thought we had been struck by a bolt of lightning. We were terrified.

"The workers just dived for cover in all directions. We could see the roof panels being sucked away. The whole thing only lasted five minutes but it seemed a lot longer."

A Met Office spokesman said mini-tornadoes were rare in Britain.

He added: "Most people would go through their lives without seeing one."

BLITZED: Wreckage left by the mini-tornado

WIND POWER: Worker Bernard Sutcliffe captured force of twister on film

No-one was injured when the twister struck around 6pm on Wednesday but firms were left without electricity when plywood was blown into a power cable.

Overnight downpours brought flooding to other parts of the country.

Some areas had more than an inch of rain in just an hour.

By Matthew Hudson

QUESTIONS

Q1 What is the purpose of this story?
- to inform?
- to persuade?
- to invoke the reader's sympathy?

Q2 What do you notice about the writer's use of language?

Q3 Comment on the use of layout.

Answers and tutorials can be found on page 57.

47

Chapter 11

LEVEL 6

Imaginative Writing

You need to

- think of a story that will interest your readers
- organise it to keep your readers interested
- write in an interesting way
- use some interesting words or phrases
- include conversation and description (vary the pace)
- keep your reader's interest right to the end (suspense)

plus . . .

- create characters that your reader believes in and feels for
- begin to use words and phrases for particular effects

Creating characters

Introduction

It would probably be impossible to write a story which did not contain characters. Scientific writing or leaflets or instructions – these are genres of writing which do not need people in them. But we read stories expecting to follow the experience of one or more characters. In fact, it is probably the characters in a story more than anything else which hold our interest and make us feel involved.

When we begin writing, our **characterisation** – the way we create characters – is often quite simple. If we are writing a fairy story we might have 'good' characters and 'bad' characters. How do we tell our reader what the characters are like? Fairy stories and children's writing usually tell them directly:

> A long time ago there was a little girl who lived in a forest. Her name was Little Red Riding Hood. Although she was a good girl, Little Red Riding Hood didn't always do as she was told . . .

Look at how directly we are being given information about the character here. We learn that Little Red Riding Hood is:

- good
- where she lived
- what she is called
- that she sometimes does not do what she is told.

Nothing is left for us to guess or work out. The character is presented in a clear-cut, straightforward way.

This works well in stories for young children. It helps them to see very clearly what the characters are like. But as we get older we enjoy encountering characters where it is less obvious what they are like, where we start to put together clues about their personality, background, hopes, thoughts and desires. Because there is more complexity to the characters – not just goodies and baddies – we begin to feel more involved in the story, as the characters feel more real.

EXAMPLE

How do we create more complex, interesting characters without just telling the reader what she or he is like – without saying, 'Susan was angry and ready for a fight . . .'?

LEVEL 6
Imaginative Writing

The answer is to use language to give clues to the reader about characters, but to leave the reader to put the clues together. This is called 'implying' rather than telling.

Look at this example from the opening of a powerful short story by northern writer Stan Barstow. In this opening sequence he establishes the character of Mrs Fletcher – sometimes by telling us about her, sometimes by giving hints. The extract has been annotated (notes added in the margins) to show the difference between direct and implied character information.

WORD BANK
Angoras – *long-haired rabbits*

▶ *direct information*

There were times when Mrs Fletcher was sure her husband thought more of his rabbits than anything else in the world: more than meat and drink, more than tobacco and comfort, more than her – or the other woman. And this was one of those times, this Saturday morning as she looked out from the kitchen where she was preparing the dinner to where she could see Fletcher working absorbedly, cleaning out the hutches, feeding the animals, and grooming his two favourite Angoras for the afternoon's show in Cressley.

▶ *direct information*

She was a passionate woman who clung single-mindedly to what was hers, and was prepared to defend her rights with vigour. While courting Fletcher she had drawn blood on an erstwhile rival who had threatened to reassert her claims. Since then she had had worse things to contend with. Always, it seemed to her, there was something between her and her rightful possession of Fletcher. At the moment it was the rabbits. The big shed had been full of hutches at one time, but now Fletcher concentrated his attention on a handful of animals in which he had a steady faith. But there were still too many for Mrs Fletcher, who resented sharing him with anything or anybody, and the sight of his absorption now stirred feelings which brought unnecessary force to bear on the sharp knife with which she sliced potatoes for the pan.

▶ *implied information*

'Got a special class for Angoras today,' Fletcher said later, at the table. He was in a hurry to be off and he shovelled loaded spoons of jam sponge into his mouth between the short sentences. 'Might do summat for a change. Time I had a bit o' luck.' He was washed and clean now, his square, ruddily handsome face close-shaven, the railway porter's uniform discarded for his best grey worsted. The carrying-case with the rabbits in it stood by the door.

Mrs Fletcher gave no sign of interest. She said, 'D'you think you'll be back in time for t'pictures?'

Fletcher gulped water. He had a way of drinking water which showed his fine teeth. 'Should be,' he answered between swallows. 'Anyway, if you're so keen to go why don't you fix up with Mrs Sykes?'

'I should be able to go out with you, Saturday nights,' Mrs Fletcher said. 'Mrs Sykes has a husband of her own to keep her company.'

'Fat lot o' company he is Saturday night,' Fletcher said dryly. 'Or Sunday, for that matter . . . Anyway, I'll try me best. Can't say fairer than that, can I?'

'Not as long as you get back in time.'

Fletcher pushed back his chair and stood up. 'I don't see why not. It shouldn't be a long job today. It isn't a big show. I should be back by half-past seven at latest.'

'Well, just see 'at you are,' she said.

She stood by the window and watched him go down the road in the pale sunshine, carrying-case, slung from one shoulder, prevented from jogging by a careful hand. He cut a handsome, well-set-up figure when he was dressed up, she thought. Often too handsome, too well-set-up for her peace of mind.

By half-past seven she was washed, dressed, and lightly made-up ready for the evening out. But Fletcher had not returned. And when the clock on the mantelshelf chimed eight there was still no sign of him. It was after ten when he came. She was sitting by the fire, the wireless blaring unheard, her knitting needles flashing with silent fury.

◀ *direct information*

◀ *implied information*

The Fury

49

LEVEL 6
Imaginative Writing

How does Stan Barstow use language to create a character we believe in?

What Stan Barstow does . . .

Stan Barstow begins by telling us directly about Mrs Fletcher's thoughts. Notice how *he allows the reader to see what is in her mind*, and this immediately begins the process of helping us to understand the character. The opening sentence hints at the bitterness Mrs Fletcher feels, as she thinks about her husband who 'thought more of his rabbits than anything else in the world'. It also hints at reasons for her bitterness – 'the other woman'.

You could try it too . . .

When you are creating a character in a story, try to use this writing technique: let the reader into the thoughts of your character at certain moments of the story. It will help the reader believe in – and feel for – your character.

What Stan Barstow does . . .

Stan Barstow then makes us look through Mrs Fletcher's eyes at her husband working contentedly outside with his rabbits. This writing technique of *looking at a scene through a character's eyes* again brings the reader closer to the character. In this case it seems to emphasise the divide between Mrs Fletcher alone in her kitchen and her husband surrounded by his animals.

You could try it too . . .

When you are writing a story try to think when it would be better to describe what is going on through one of your character's eyes, rather than just describing the scene as you, the narrator, see it. Look at this example:

> Shut up alone in his stuffy room, Daniel looked out of his window and saw the children racing up and down the street.

This gives a much more powerful impression of how cooped up Daniel feels than if you write:

> Daniel was shut up in his room. The children were playing in the street.

What Stan Barstow does . . .

Stan Barstow uses his second paragraph to build up our impression of Mrs Fletcher's character with some *direct information*. He calls her a 'passionate woman' and writes that she 'resented sharing him with anything or anybody'.

50

LEVEL 6
Imaginative Writing

You could try it too . . .

There are times in a story when you will want to give your readers some direct information about your characters. It will help people reading your story find out information about them quickly.

What Stan Barstow does . . .

Read this passage from the second paragraph again:

> . . . the sight of his absorption now stirred feelings which brought unnecessary force to bear on the sharp knife with which she sliced potatoes for the pan.

This is *implied information* about Mrs Fletcher. Stan Barstow doesn't state that the 'stirred feelings' are feelings of anger, but he implies this with his choice of words: 'unnecessary force', 'sharp knife', 'sliced'.

You could try it too . . .

When writing a story, try to look for moments when you can give the readers information about your characters' feelings through *what they do* and *how they do it* rather than describing these feelings directly.

What Stan Barstow does . . .

Remember how important it is to vary the pace of your writing – changing from plot to description to dialogue (see page 37). Stan Barstow changes the pace of his story by moving next into dialogue. The dialogue lets him develop Mrs Fletcher's character further through *what she says*: feelings about him – she may be jealous that other women are looking at him.

> 'I should be able to go out with you, Saturday nights . . .'
> 'Not as long as you get back in time.'
> 'Well, just see 'at you are . . .'

Stan Barstow uses dialogue here to let the reader know Mrs Fletcher is demanding and resentful.

You could try it too . . .

When you are writing a story, you will want to include some dialogue. Think about what you want this dialogue to reveal about your characters. Think hard about the actual words you put into their mouths, not just how they speak them (e.g. 'she shouted', 'she moaned', 'she whispered'). The words your characters speak can tell the reader as much about them as their actions or your direct description of them.

LEVEL 6
Imaginative Writing

Check yourself

Imagine a character at a party. Her name is Emma. She is not enjoying the party at all – she feels lost and isolated, with no one to talk to. Then someone she knows from school, called Kevin, comes over and starts chatting. He has a reputation for being a real bore, and everyone has been avoiding him. Emma cannot stand him, and lets him do most of the talking. Inside, however, she is just wishing he would go away.

Now write this scene as the opening to a short story. Your reader knows none of the above, so you need to convey Emma's character through your writing. Try to use both *direct* and *implied* information about Emma.

Use this opening sentence to get you started, if you wish:

> The party dragged on and Emma gazed around the dark room looking for someone – anyone – she knew . . .

Answer and tutorial can be found on page 58.

Chapter 12

Speeches

LEVEL 6

Writing to inform and persuade

Introduction

Sometimes you might be asked to write a speech persuading your audience about an issue. Speeches are still important in our society. Despite television, film, the Internet and other information sources, speeches are still used in running the country: government in Britain is built around a system of speeches and debates to decide upon policy.

You need to

- organise your ideas in a sensible way
- interest and convince your reader
- write in a clear and interesting way
- develop some of your ideas more fully
- use a more formal style
- give examples to support your case

EXAMPLE

Speeches can be powerful ways of persuading your listeners to change their views. Robert was asked to take part in a school debate about the state of Britain's prisons. His task was to write and deliver a short speech to persuade people that prison life is not harsh enough.

Look at his speech.

plus . . .

- begin to use words and phrases for particular effects
- structure your piece of writing to create an effect on the reader

> In Britain we have never had more prisoners locked up in jail than there are now. There is a crowding crisis which means that our prison population is overflowing. Why? One reason has to be that prison doesn't work. These people who get sent to prison obviously weren't deterred by the threat of prison. It didn't worry them enough to prevent them from offending. In fact, there are probably some people who like the idea of prison because they can escape their own problems and get looked after.
>
> People in prisons must sometimes think they're at a holiday camp. They get their three meals a day cooked and served. They have televisions and newspapers. They can play snooker or cards. They have a laugh with the prison guards. How can this be punishment? How can this be a serious deterrent to crime? Little wonder that such a high number of people sent to prison re-offend within a year of being released.
>
> It's time to say 'enough is enough'. Time to say we want prisons as places of punishment, not holiday camps. Time to stop molly-coddling these criminals and give them a taste of the real price they should pay for committing crime. All the rewards and luxuries should go. Then prison will become the last place you want to be sent – not a soft-option you look forward to.

LEVEL 6

Writing to inform and persuade

How does the writer use language and structure to persuade us?

Language

Robert's speech uses some key techniques. It uses **emotive words** – words that are likely to provoke a response in readers and listeners: calling prisons 'soft-options' and 'holiday camps'; saying that we should 'stop molly-coddling' people. Notice how prisoners are called 'these people who get sent to prison': this sounds much stronger than the neutral word 'prisoners'. Think how different the speech would be if the writer called them 'victims'.

Robert's speech also uses **repetition**. This is one of the most powerful techniques in speeches because it creates a kind of rhythm which carries the reader or audience along:

> They have televisions and newspapers. They can play snooker or cards. They have a laugh with the prison guards.

Each sentence starts off with the word 'They', building up the rhythm of the sentence. Within the first two sentences there is also a pattern: 'televisions and newspapers . . . snooker or cards'. Here the writer is listing things that prisoners do. The speech might have said: 'They have televisions, newspapers, snooker and cards'. Breaking the ideas down into two shorter sentences makes the idea more powerful.

Robert's speech also uses **rhetorical questions**. These are questions you ask to the audience to get them thinking: for example, 'How can this be punishment?' The writer does not expect an answer to this. Instead the question is being used to persuade us that this is not a real form of punishment.

Structure

Robert's speech is organised in a logical way. The first paragraph describes the 'crisis' in Britain's prisons. It starts off as informative rather than persuasive, and gives the impression that the writer can be trusted as someone who knows the facts. It is quite a general paragraph, stating the topic.

The next paragraph is much more specific. It selectively describes the conditions in prisons – snooker and cards, and so on. This is where the writer really begins to persuade us that prison life is not tough enough. He chooses to describe all the comforts of prison. He deliberately omits to mention all the drawbacks – locked doors, warders, restricted contact with the outside world.

The third paragraph is the most persuasive. The writer here is aiming to conclude the argument and get our agreement. There are no facts here, just a strong sense of the writer's opinions:

> It's time to say 'enough is enough'. Time to say we want prisons as places of punishment, not holiday camps. Time to stop molly-coddling these criminals.

Robert reserves the most emotive language and repetition for this paragraph because it is designed to round the argument off.

LEVEL 6
Writing to inform and persuade

Check yourself

Imagine you have been asked to take part in a debate about the rights and wrongs of sending people to prison. Write a speech which will persuade your listeners that 'too many people are being sent to prison for minor offences'.

You might make the following points:

- prisons *are* overcrowded – but many people are sent to prison who should receive other sentences; for example, vagrants and beggars;
- prisons have a negative effect on people who are sent there because they end up mixing with other criminals and learn new crime techniques;
- prison isn't a comfortable option – many prisoners are locked up in cells 23 hours a day;
- if we treat people like animals, we should expect them to behave like animals – therefore we should be teaching prisoners how to live better lives, how to get on with other people, how to be responsible, and so on.

You might use these sentences to get you started:

> Everyone agrees that prisons are overcrowded. But this isn't because prisons are a soft-option. It's because we don't seem to have many other ways of punishing petty criminals.

A sample answer and tutorial can be found on page 59.

55

LEVEL 6

Answers and Tutorials to Check Yourself

9 Reading and Understanding Fiction (page 43)

Answers

A1 Brian Friel wants to create a strong impression of the boys – their liveliness, energy and chatter. He shows how they contrast with Kelly and the older helpers. Kelly in the first paragraph is hunched over and his fingernails are broken. He seems to be cowering from the harshness. The boys, in contrast, are standing 'legs apart, hands in their pockets, their faces pressed forward into the icy rush of air, their senses edged for perception'. This description suggests that they are feeling excited about the day's work – rather than cowering from nature, they are facing it, standing in a kind of challenging stance (legs apart, hands in pockets). The phrase 'their senses edged for perception' hints at their excitement about what will be happening – they are waiting to experience the day.

This contrasts not only with Kelly, but also with the two farm hands who are 'sprawled in half sleep'. Later one of the boys makes fun of Kelly. All of this shows how Brian Friel achieves a sense of the difference between the younger and older generation – the boys keen, excited, lively; the older characters gloomy, lifeless, showing no enthusiasm.

A2 The writer creates a strong sense of the boys' enthusiasm. He says, for example, that 'his brother's excitement was infectious'. This metaphor describes enthusiasm like an illness, showing how the high-spirits of one boy are caught by the next. His phrase to describe Philly – 'His energy was a burden to him' – shows someone who actually has too much energy, so much that he finds it difficult to cope with. The writer is suggesting that this is a boy who is actually dissatisfied with himself: he wants to 'prove that he is a man at twelve years old', but what stops him is his overflowing boyish energy.

The writer shows the energy of the boys in the cheering they do. The second time, Kelly 'growled to them to shut up'. The use of the word 'growled' makes Kelly seem menacing – perhaps, like an animal; or it may be a hint that he has not the energy to speak any louder. This contrasts with the eager enthusiasm of the boys.

Tutorials

T1 and T2 These are both good, observant answers. They are detailed, clearly expressed, and support their points with quotations. Most importantly, the answers do more than just spot language features: they *comment* on them. This means that by the end of reading the answers, we feel that our own understanding of the text has increased – the answers have actually taught us things about the story which perhaps we had not spotted. These answers easily achieve level 6.

To achieve level 7, the answers would need to look more at the writer's *technique*. This might involve analysing his use of sentences, for example – the rhythm of his writing and the effect this has. The answers would also need to begin making judgements about the success of the writing: which parts worked best and which were less successful – and why.

LEVEL 6

Answers and Tutorials to Check Yourself

10 Reading and Understanding Non-fiction (page 47)

Answers

A1 The writer is describing an unusual event. He emphasises the unlikely nature of what happens by comparing the usual sites of twisters (towns in the US) with Bury St Edmunds, which he describes as 'sleepy'. The writer is aiming chiefly to inform us, but he also wishes to entertain readers. We can tell this by the slightly joky style of his language, in particular the headline, which emphasises the unlikely place where the twister occurs.

A2 The writer begins with a topic sentence which tells us what happens (twister), where (Bury St Edmunds) and when (yesterday). He uses labelling to give information about people – for example, 'Malcolm Burroughs, manager of a neighbouring firm . . .'. The writer uses some dramatic language to tell the story; for example, 'flee', 'crashing', 'devastate'. He also uses quotations to make it more factual; for example, quoting the words of Mr Sutcliffe, Mr Burroughs and a Met Office spokesman.

A3 The layout is typical of newspaper style. It uses a headline, followed by a subheading ('workers flee 100mph tornado'). There are captions beneath each photograph to add drama: 'WIND POWER' and 'BLITZED'. These are in capital letters for emphasis. The paragraphs are short to hold the reader's attention. It is also striking that the first paragraph is printed in bold type to grab our attention.

Tutorials

These are solid answers. They respond to the questions in a very direct way, and support their points with quotations.

T1 Writers may often be trying to achieve more than one thing with their writing. Try to remember this when reading texts, whether fiction or non-fiction. When you read a piece through the first time, you may feel you are sure of one thing the writer is trying to achieve; for example, inform the reader.

But don't leave it there and assume you have got to the bottom of the writer's intentions. Read the piece through again and see whether you can spot clues that indicate that the writer may also be trying to do something – in the case of this article, entertain.

This answer correctly says that the writer's intention is to inform *and* entertain.

T2 The impressive thing with this answer is that it refers to a 'topic sentence'. The answer could have said 'the first sentence' but the use of the technical term 'topic sentence' shows that the student is familiar with the way newspapers are constructed. Be careful though – if you want to identify different language features by their technical terms, make sure that you use them correctly.

T3 The references to paragraphing, capital letters and bold print are the kind of detailed references needed by level 6.

If your answers are similar to these then you would gain level 6. To move to a higher level, your answers would need to be more critical – to say whether the writer's style completely worked or not. You might, for example, say more about the joky tone the writer uses. Is it appropriate? Does it trivialise the story?

57

LEVEL 6
Answers and Tutorials to Check Yourself

11 Imaginative Writing (page 52)

Answer

You might have written something like this:

> The party dragged on and Emma gazed around the dark room looking for someone – anyone – she knew. She couldn't recognise anyone. 'Why did I come here?' she asked herself. She wasn't a party-type in any case. She should have stayed at home.
>
> She heard the autumn wind howling outside and, above the background throb of the music, a branch scraped at the window. Emma clutched tighter at the plastic cup containing her drink. She wondered if she should get up and go into the kitchen . . . or would that seem a sign of desperation?
>
> Emma was suddenly aware of someone coming in behind her. Perhaps a new crowd was arriving – people she knew or people she'd like to know. But it wasn't a crowd, it was one person – and he was coming to sit down next to her.
>
> 'Hello,' he said.
>
> Emma turned her head. 'Hi.' With horror she realised who this was: Kevin 'class-nerd' Sykes. He was grinning madly at her. 'What a brilliant surprise. We haven't talked for ages. How are things?'
>
> Across the room some people were laughing loudly. A couple got up to dance. Emma could see people chatting in the brighter lights of the kitchen.
>
> 'Fine,' she said, 'I'm fine.'
>
> 'That's great,' said Kevin. 'It's great to have chance to talk again, isn't it?'
>
> 'Yes,' replied Emma, her voice flat, 'yes, it's great' and a heavy weight of boredom settled on her shoulders.

Tutorial

This opening works well. We pick up plenty of information about Emma's character. Much of the information is direct – feeling horror, feeling bored, feeling lost and isolated. There is implied information, too. Those details about the weather (autumn wind and scratching branch) echo her feelings of coldness and loneliness. The way she tightens her grip on her cup is a sign that she is far from relaxed. We look through her eyes at other people – laughing, dancing, chatting: these details are especially important because they show that she notices everyone else having a much better time than she is. Notice also the 'flat' tone of her voice and, importantly, the way she repeats Kevin's word 'great' rather than say anything original or personal.

The language of the story is straightforward and this is appropriate for the subject-matter. We would not expect heavily descriptive language in this genre (type of writing). But there is sufficient detail to make us feel that the party is real – mention of rooms and people.

Overall, the story establishes the character of Emma well – through direct statement, implied information and use of dialogue. It might draw us in even more if we were to learn more of Emma's appearance, or her background, or who invited her to the party – but these are details which the writer could move on to next.

LEVEL 6
Answers and Tutorials to Check Yourself

12 Writing to inform and persuade (page 55)

Answer

Everyone agrees that prisons are overcrowded. But this isn't because prisons are a soft-option. It's because we don't seem to have many other ways of punishing petty criminals. The result? Bursting prisons full of people who aren't serious criminals . . . but who are learning fast how to be.

This is one of the main arguments against prisons: they don't actually teach anyone not to offend again. Someone sent to prison for a minor crime – vagrancy or debt – ends up learning from hardened cases and comes out a much greater threat to society. Wouldn't it be far better if these people had never been sent in the first place?

Some people claim that prisons are a deterrent. Some people say we should have unpleasant prisons to scare people off crime. But this argument doesn't stand up. In the Victorian age prisons were appalling places of filth and disease – and yet more and more people kept getting sent there because there was nowhere else to go.

We certainly won't improve our crime figures today if we carry on sending petty criminals to prison where they mix with hardened criminals. Prison isn't cushy either. It's not a hotel. Most prisoners are locked in cramped cells for 23 hours a day. 'They deserve it,' you might be thinking, but remember this: if we treat humans like animals, they will start to behave like animals. But if we can show them that there's a better future – with education, care, and thinking about others – then we might just begin to change their attitudes and turn them into more successful members of society.

This isn't the soft-option. The soft-option is to do nothing. The brave decision is to try and work out better ways to punish people who have committed minor crimes.

Tutorial

This speech uses some of the techniques needed for an effective persuasive piece. It uses:

- repetition quite well: 'This isn't the soft-option. The soft-option is to do nothing.' 'Some people claim . . . Some people say . . .'.

- emotive language: for example, 'bursting prisons'; 'if we treat humans like animals'. In the last paragraph the phrase 'the brave decision . . .' makes us feel that any other opinion is weak.

- rhetorical questions: 'The result?'; 'Wouldn't it be far better . . .?' This holds the reader's interest.

The speech also has a good balance of different lengths of sentences, which again give it a kind of variety to hold our interest.

To gain a higher level, it could use a more daring structure. At present it feels a bit repetitive. A better speech would seem to move logically from one topic to the next. It might also use more memorable language – instead of well-known phrases like 'soft-option' – the writer might try to use more creative ideas, perhaps using metaphors, similes and personification (as explained on page 41). This could make it a little more 'unexpected' to read.

Chapter 13

LEVEL 7

Reading and Understanding Fiction

Writers' techniques

Introduction

You need to

- know what the characters in a text are like
- begin to read beneath the surface
- show an overall understanding of the text
- note the effects of words and phrases
- be aware of what the writer is trying to achieve
- comment on the writer's use of some words or phrases

plus . . .

- comment on the writer's techniques
- say how successful you think the writer has been

You might have noticed that the skills you are expected to have in reading and understanding fiction develop very clearly as you move up through the levels. To progress you need to be able to spot features (for example, what characters are like); then pay closer attention to language (for example, the writer's use of words and phrases); then comment on the use of language; and now, at the higher level, comment on the writer's technique and judge how successful it is.

What do we mean by a writer's technique? We mean looking beyond the use of individual words and phrases and examining how the writer's use of plot, characterisation and language works throughout a text. Here are some techniques which different fiction writers use:

- Jane Austen (eighteenth-century novelist) closely describes relationships between people. She is famous for her ability to show the reader the weaknesses and odd features of her characters by letting them say one thing but showing us that they mean another. This technique is known as *irony*.

- Charles Dickens (nineteenth-century novelist) creates a huge range of characters in many of his novels. One of his techniques is to make his characters quirky and memorable, giving them funny speech patterns (for example, a woman who never finishes her sentences, or a man who never gets to the point) and highly individual behaviour.

- James Joyce (twentieth-century novelist) writes about characters from the inside, as if the reader is listening into their random, unstructured thoughts. This technique is known as *stream of consciousness*.

Some authors write in the first person ('I'); some in the third person ('she' or 'he'); a few in the second person ('you'). Some writers are highly descriptive. Some are interested in showing what a main character is like. Others want to use characters to highlight the way of life of a community or society. Some authors write poetically. Others write in a style which seems transparent – as if we are looking through the words and phrases at the characters and events, hardly noticing the language itself.

None of these techniques is better than another. The point is they are all techniques, and at the higher levels you need to be able to comment upon them.

LEVEL 7
Reading and Understanding Fiction

Success

Commenting on 'success' is always a difficult business because you are being asked to make a judgement about the text, and then to justify your ideas.

You should start by thinking about what 'successful' means. For a leaflet, it might be how efficiently the reader is given precise information. In a novel, it might be how involved we feel with the characters and storyline. In a ghost story, it is probably to do with the sense of atmosphere and suspense.

The easiest way of thinking about success is:

- What has the writer set out to achieve?
- Has she or he achieved it?

Remember that this is a chance to give your own opinion, to say what you think. But beware: you also need to support your judgement with examples from the text.

EXAMPLE

Look at the opening of this ghost story by H G Wells. He was writing at the turn of the twentieth century and is probably best known for his science fiction stories – such as *The Time Machine* and *The War of the Worlds*.

The Red Room

'I assure you,' said I, 'that it will take a very tangible ghost to frighten me.' And I stood up before the fire with my glass in my hand.
　'It is your own choosing,' said the man with the withered arm …
　'Eight-and-twenty years,' said I, 'I have lived, and never a ghost have I seen as yet.'
　The old woman sat staring hard into the fire, her pale eyes wide open. 'Ah,' she broke in: 'and eight-and-twenty years you have lived and never seen the likes of this house, I reckon. There's a many things to see, when one's still but eight-and-twenty.' She swayed her head slowly from side to side. 'A many things to see and sorrow for.'
　I half suspected the old people were trying to enhance the spiritual terrors of their house by their droning insistence. I put down my empty glass on the table and looked about the room, and caught a glimpse of myself . . . in the queer old mirror at the end of the room. 'Well,' I said, 'if I see anything tonight, I shall be so much the wiser. For I come to the business with an open mind.'
　'It's your own choosing,' said the man with the withered arm once more.
　I heard the sound of a stick and a shambling step on the flags in the passage outside, and the door creaked on its hinges as a second old man entered, more bent, more wrinkled, more aged even than the first. He supported himself by a single crutch, his eyes were covered by a shade, and his lower lip, half averted, hung pale and pink from his decaying yellow teeth. He made straight for an armchair on the opposite side of the table, sat down clumsily, and began to cough. The man with the withered arm gave this newcomer a short glance of positive dislike; the old woman

WORD BANK
tangible – *real*
enhance the spiritual terrors – *exaggerate the stories about ghosts*
insistence – *repetition*
averted – *hidden*

61

LEVEL 7

Reading and Understanding Fiction

took no notice of his arrival, but remained with her eyes fixed steadily on the fire.

'I said – it's your own choosing,' said the man with the withered arm, when the coughing had ceased for a while.

'It's my own choosing,' I answered.

The man with the shade became aware of my presence for the first time, and threw his head back for a moment and sideways, to see me. I caught a momentary glimpse of his eyes, small and bright and inflamed. Then he began to cough and splutter again.

What techniques does Wells use to create suspense?

H G Wells creates a strong impression of the characters and setting, even though we learn none of the characters' names. We learn that the narrator (the person telling the story) is quite confident. He starts by saying that it would take a 'very tangible ghost to frighten me'. If anything, he seems over-confident, even arrogant. This is highlighted by the way he describes the people. He is quite rude about them, commenting on their 'droning insistence', as if they are exaggerating the stories about ghosts in their house in a rather boring manner.

H G Wells creates a vivid picture of the other characters, using memorable details. The old man's 'withered arm' is referred to several times, and the appearance of the mysterious visitor is described in some detail: crutch, covered eyes, hanging lip and 'decaying yellow teeth'. It is a fairly grotesque picture.

The writer uses two main techniques to create suspense:

- Firstly, he creates an opening sequence which hints at trouble to come. He presents people and places that the reader feels uncomfortable with. The confidence of the narrator actually builds up the suspense, because we sense from his cocky certainty that if there are ghosts they will not last long. The details of the other characters – especially the withered arm and decaying yellow teeth – also build the tension, making us wonder who these people are and what might happen.

- Secondly, he deliberately holds back much of the basic information of the story – who these people are and where they are. This forces the reader to make guesses and predictions, getting us immediately more involved with the storyline.

How successful is this opening to a ghost story?

H G Wells' writing techniques are successful at creating suspense because they make us want to read on. He raises all kinds of questions: Why is the text called the Red Room? Is there going to be a sighting of a ghost there? Where are we? Who are these strange characters? Who is the narrator and what is he expecting to see that night? Why does the man with the withered arm say 'It's your own choosing' three times? Who is the mysterious visitor?

The writer is also successful at creating suspense – his use of language is very atmospheric. The formal, old-fashioned nature of the language makes the world of the story feel very real. The pompous style of the narrator – 'I can assure you . . .' – gives a powerful impression of him without H G Wells needing to say directly what he is like. When he says things like 'eight-and-twenty', rather than twenty-eight and 'never a ghost have I seen', we get a further impression of the narrator as someone who is formal, self-confident and probably arrogant. Because of this, we may even start to hope that he will see a ghost and be terrified.

LEVEL 7
Reading and Understanding Fiction

Check yourself

Read the opening of a ghost story by Lance Salway.

The Darkness under the Stair

As soon as he stepped into the hall, Andrew knew at once that something was wrong. He couldn't tell what it was; he was simply aware of a dark wave of dread that rose to meet him the minute the front door was opened.

'Ah, there you are,' the woman said. 'You must be Andrew. We were wondering where you'd got to. I'm Carol Sharman.'

Andrew blinked at her, dazzled by the light in the hall. He wanted to turn and run, he wanted to get away from the house, but he couldn't. He had to stay.

'Your parents are in the sitting room,' Mrs Sharman went on. Then, as he hesitated still, 'Well, are you coming in or aren't you? I'm not going to hold the door open all night.'

'Sorry,' he muttered, and edged past her into the light, towards the darkness. He blinked again, and shuddered. Fear settled round him like a dark stifling blanket.

Ahead of him, a wide wooden staircase rose into shadows. To the left, he could hear voices, his mother's loud among them, behind a half-open door. He pushed it open and walked into the room.

'Ah, here he is at last,' his mother said, smiling at him from the sofa where she was sitting with his father.

'Sorry,' Andrew muttered again. 'I had some homework to finish.' He stared down at his feet and wished with all his heart that he'd stayed at home. He hadn't wanted to come in the first place. He could have met the new neighbours at any other time. But no, his mother had insisted that they all go next door together. The Sharmans had been kind enough to invite them all in for a drink so the very least he could do was accept graciously. And anyway, she said, just think how interesting it will be to see inside the house at last. After all these years.

'This is Mr Sharman, Andrew,' his mother said.

Andrew looked up into the pleasant face of a dark middle-aged man in glasses who nodded at him and said, 'Good to meet you, Andrew.'

LEVEL 7

Reading and Understanding Fiction

'You've met *Mrs* Sharman, of course,' his mother went on. 'And then there's – it's Danny, isn't it? – yes, Danny.'

Andrew noticed for the first time a boy of about his own age sitting in a corner by the window. He had spiky red hair and pale blue eyes. 'Hi,' the boy said.

Andrew mumbled something and sat down abruptly on a chair by the door.

'I've just been telling Mr and Mrs Sharman about the house,' his mother went on brightly. 'How this is the first time we've ever been inside it. I've explained about old Mrs Bromley.'

Andrew nodded. He glanced across at Danny, and the boy stared back, his eyes as cold as stone. Andrew looked quickly away. He wanted to go home. How soon could he get up and leave? He didn't like the Sharmans. He didn't like the house. And besides, he still had some maths to finish . . .

QUESTIONS

Q1 What do you notice about the writer's technique?

Q2 How successful is this as the opening of a ghost story?

Answers and tutorials can be found on page 77–78.

To move beyond level 7 you would also need to:

- read a variety of texts, some of them complex and demanding works from other centuries;
- gain an ability to get involved with what you are reading and to be able to stand back and comment on: structure, characters, themes and use of language;
- express your response to fiction in thoughtful, well-organised writing.

Chapter 14

Writers' techniques

LEVEL 7

Reading and Understanding Non-fiction

Introduction

We have seen earlier in this book that newspapers have a variety of aims – for example, to entertain and persuade, as well as to inform us about the news. People sometimes make a distinction between two kinds of newspaper journalism: news and features.

News reporting is what we expect in newspapers – it tells us about events that have happened.

Features writing has a different purpose. Sometimes it is giving us background information to events – for example, an interview with someone who is in the news. Sometimes it is unconnected to the news of the day. It might be a review, an article about someone, a light-hearted piece about fashion, a serious commentary on marriage, film violence, money matters . . . anything.

Features writing often has similarities to the assignments and essays you are asked to write in school. They enable a journalist to explore issues, to compare different views, and to say what they themselves think.

One of the key skills of features writing is to make us keep reading about something we did not think we were interested in. The headline will try to get us started; the first paragraph will try to grab our attention; the rest of the piece will try to hold our interest. Features writers therefore use a variety of techniques to entertain, persuade and inform us.

EXAMPLE

Read the article on page 64 which is from an issue of *Early Times*, a newspaper which was aimed at young readers. In it, the reporter (aged 12) presents his interview with someone who opposes physical punishment of children. Notice how he structures his writing: the interview is not presented directly as an interview. If it was, it might read like this:

Interviewer: *Why do you oppose smacking?*

Interviewee: *Because it's wrong . . .*

In some instances this might be a useful format. It would allow the reader to read the exact conversation that the two people had. But over a whole page or two it might not make interesting reading. Look then at the way the writer ('press ganger') uses the interview as the basis for an article. See if you can tell what his own views are on the subject.

You need to

- be able to locate ideas and information in a text
- begin to be aware of the purpose of the text
- show an overall understanding of the text
- note the effect of some words or phrases
- note the effect of features like layout, if appropriate
- be aware of what the writer is trying to achieve
- comment on the writer's use of some words or phrases
- comment on the effect of features like layout, if appropriate

plus . . .

- comment on the writer's techniques
- say how successful you think the writer has been

LEVEL 7

Reading and Understanding Non-fiction

Check yourself

Read this article about the day in the life of a local policeman. It was printed in the *Daily Telegraph* at a time when the performance of the UK police force was being reviewed.

All in a day's work for Pc Bob Murray

PC BOB MURRAY, 34, is one of 12 officers in Plymouth's St Peter's Ward team, patrolling some of the city's toughest streets.

They investigate minor offences and make routine follow-up inquiries on more serious incidents. They are often stopped in the street by the public, who recognise them and sometimes pass on information.

Pc – acting Sgt – Murray and his colleagues claim success in the role, with reported crime down 10 per cent and detection rates up. This is a day in his duties:

0800: Starts day at Charles Cross police station covering rundown area close to Plymouth city centre and including Union Street, with its reputation for seedy night life and drunken punch-ups involving sailors and Royal Marines.

0800–0815: Review overnight logs recording details of alleged shop robbery by two teenage girls in Millbay and re-arrest of prisoner who escaped earlier this month from magistrates' court hearing.

0815–0930: Paperwork, mainly concerning criminal damage and firework-throwing by boy in the car park of Toys R Us store the previous day. Contact social services regarding 14-year-old suspect "so that we can do something short of prosecution with this lad before he gets on to the slippery slope of crime".

0930–0945: Attend inspectors briefing on joint police–council campaign on unlicensed, unroadworthy cabs.

0945–1200: On patrol in steady downpour, joining council officials for checks on 18 taxis and four taxi offices. One vehicle ordered off road after examination reveals defective tyres and no insurance; three others given tickets for illegal parking.

1200–1230: More paperwork at Charles Cross, submit report on morning duties and inquiries.

1230–1315: Meal break – "a bit rushed".

1315–1530: Patrol on foot to leisure centre. Consult shopkeepers about shoplifting and nuisances associated with schools' half-term and run-up to Guy Fawkes Night.

1530–1600: Check Toys R Us car park in case of more children playing with fireworks.

1600–1630: Return to station, help colleague with paperwork on nuisance phone calls. Dry out after day on beat in heavy rain.

QUESTIONS

Q1 What techniques does the writer use?

Q2 How successful is the article?

Answers and tutorials can be found on pages 79–80.

To move beyond level 7 you would also need to:

- be quick at spotting the main ideas in a text, and confident about analysing the way the writer has used language to inform and persuade;
- be quite critical in your reading – willing to say what works and does not work;
- pay close attention to layout, ideas and language;
- express your own ideas with precisely-chosen vocabulary.

Chapter 14

Writers' techniques

Introduction

LEVEL 7

Reading and Understanding Non-fiction

We have seen earlier in this book that newspapers have a variety of aims – for example, to entertain and persuade, as well as to inform us about the news. People sometimes make a distinction between two kinds of newspaper journalism: news and features.

News reporting is what we expect in newspapers – it tells us about events that have happened.

Features writing has a different purpose. Sometimes it is giving us background information to events – for example, an interview with someone who is in the news. Sometimes it is unconnected to the news of the day. It might be a review, an article about someone, a light-hearted piece about fashion, a serious commentary on marriage, film violence, money matters . . . anything.

Features writing often has similarities to the assignments and essays you are asked to write in school. They enable a journalist to explore issues, to compare different views, and to say what they themselves think.

One of the key skills of features writing is to make us keep reading about something we did not think we were interested in. The headline will try to get us started; the first paragraph will try to grab our attention; the rest of the piece will try to hold our interest. Features writers therefore use a variety of techniques to entertain, persuade and inform us.

EXAMPLE

Read the article on page 84 which is from an issue of *Early Times*, a newspaper which was aimed at young readers. In it, the reporter (aged 12) presents his interview with someone who opposes physical punishment of children. Notice how he structures his writing: the interview is not presented directly as an interview. If it was, it might read like this:

Interviewer: *Why do you oppose smacking?*

Interviewee: *Because it's wrong . . .*

In some instances this might be a useful format. It would allow the reader to read the exact conversation that the two people had. But over a whole page or two it might not make interesting reading. Look then at the way the writer ('press ganger') uses the interview as the basis for an article. See if you can tell what his own views are on the subject.

You need to

- be able to locate ideas and information in a text
- begin to be aware of the purpose of the text
- show an overall understanding of the text
- note the effect of some words or phrases
- note the effect of features like layout, if appropriate
- be aware of what the writer is trying to achieve
- comment on the writer's use of some words or phrases
- comment on the effect of features like layout, if appropriate

plus . . .

- comment on the writer's techniques
- say how successful you think the writer has been

LEVEL 7
Reading and Understanding Non-fiction

EARLY TIMES   August 24th to August 30th, 1989

Cracking down on smacking

Press Ganger Jonathan Shapiro, 12, from Hertfordshire, interviews Peter Newell, director of the new charity EPOCH campaigning for an end to grown-ups physically punishing their children.

COULD it be that in the very near future the dreaded 'smacked bottom' will be a thing of the past? This is what Peter Newell who runs the national organisation EPOCH (End Physical Punishment of Children) hopes.

I met Mr Peter Newell at his offices in London recently and discussed his views on smacking children. He has worked for a long time in children's rights societies, but in April decided to start his own campaign and has also written a book on the subject. The reason he feels so strongly about smacking children is that, 'it seems illogical that children cannot hit adults but adults can hit children'.

HITTING CHILDREN

I asked him whether he had suffered physical punishment himself as a child, to dreadful consequences, but this was not so:

'The only time I was ever physically punished by my parents was when I stood in wet paint and trampled all over the house,' replied Peter.

'My mother pulled my hair, although they did not think spanking was a good thing to do.'

I then asked out of sheer curiosity what effect smacking has on children. He knew this question was coming, and tried to answer it briefly!

VIOLENCE

'The odd smack here and there has little effect. The only lesson the children learn is to use smacking on their younger relations or own children later on. Children who are smacked tend to have a violent attitude.'

I wanted to know whether children who became delinquents had been smacked frequently in their early years, and he thought they probably had.

Most parents think that if they smack their children they will not misbehave again, but is this so? 'Not really,' Peter responded. 'Two-thirds of mothers hit their children who are under one years old and they are just as likely to do what they are smacked for again.'

I thought that corporal punishment in schools had stopped ages ago, but I learnt the facts from Peter Newell. Corporal punishment has only been banned in state schools since 1987, and teachers in private schools are still able to cane their pupils. In Scotland instead of using the cane, they use a leather strap.

What techniques does the article use?

There is an eye-catching headline, using 'cracking' to rhyme with 'smacking'. It is quite informal – for example, it might have been expressed more formally as 'eliminating corporal punishment'. This would be far less likely to appeal to readers, and the informal tone draws the reader into the article.

The article opens with a question as a way of further gaining our attention. The writer poses a question which he then aims to answer through his interview with Peter Newell. The writer's next paragraph is biographical – that is, it gives us information about Peter Newell. It tells us who he is and what he does. The article then continues by presenting the interview with Peter Newell, quoting some of the words directly ('The only time I was ever physically punished . . .') and reporting some of them indirectly ('he thought they probably had'). The writer, in other words, uses some variety here, not simply quoting everything that the interviewee said.

The journalist sometimes uses a chatty tone. At one point he says: 'I then asked out of sheer curiosity . . .'. This is telling us more about the writer himself than the interviewee. It might be argued that this adds to our interest in the interview because we learn more about the person asking the questions.

At the end of the extract the writer quotes the facts about corporal punishment in English state and private schools and in Scotland. This gives an impression that the writer agrees with Peter Newell that this form of punishment is wrong.

How successful is the article overall?

The headline succeeds in catching our attention, as does the opening sentence. But some of the writing feels unexciting – for example: 'I met Mr Peter Newell at his offices in London recently and discussed his views on smacking children.' This could have been more direct and more interesting if it said: 'Peter Newell sat in his London office and gave me his views.' This feels less like an autobiography: Mr Newell (the centre of the article) is placed first, rather than the writer ('I').

The informal tone of the article does not always work. You feel as if the interviewer could have asked more demanding questions – for example, what should parents do with children who are out of control? It perhaps feels too much like a cosy chat rather than a probing interview.

LEVEL 7
Reading and Understanding Non-fiction

LEVEL 7

Reading and Understanding Non-fiction

Check yourself

Read this article about the day in the life of a local policeman. It was printed in the *Daily Telegraph* at a time when the performance of the UK police force was being reviewed.

All in a day's work for Pc Bob Murray

PC BOB MURRAY, 34, is one of 12 officers in Plymouth's St Peter's Ward team, patrolling some of the city's toughest streets.

They investigate minor offences and make routine follow-up inquiries on more serious incidents. They are often stopped in the street by the public, who recognise them and sometimes pass on information.

Pc – acting Sgt – Murray and his colleagues claim success in the role, with reported crime down 10 per cent and detection rates up. This is a day in his duties:

0800: Starts day at Charles Cross police station covering rundown area close to Plymouth city centre and including Union Street, with its reputation for seedy night life and drunken punch-ups involving sailors and Royal Marines.

0800–0815: Review overnight logs recording details of alleged shop robbery by two teenage girls in Millbay and re-arrest of prisoner who escaped earlier this month from magistrates' court hearing.

0815–0930: Paperwork, mainly concerning criminal damage and firework-throwing by boy in the car park of Toys R Us store the previous day. Contact social services regarding 14-year-old suspect "so that we can do something short of prosecution with this lad before he gets on to the slippery slope of crime".

0930–0945: Attend inspectors briefing on joint police–council campaign on unlicensed, unroadworthy cabs.

0945–1200: On patrol in steady downpour, joining council officials for checks on 18 taxis and four taxi offices. One vehicle ordered off road after examination reveals defective tyres and no insurance; three others given tickets for illegal parking.

1200–1230: More paperwork at Charles Cross, submit report on morning duties and inquiries.

1230–1315: Meal break – "a bit rushed".

1315–1530: Patrol on foot to leisure centre. Consult shopkeepers about shoplifting and nuisances associated with schools' half-term and run-up to Guy Fawkes Night.

1530–1600: Check Toys R Us car park in case of more children playing with fireworks.

1600–1630: Return to station, help colleague with paperwork on nuisance phone calls. Dry out after day on beat in heavy rain.

QUESTIONS

Q1 What techniques does the writer use?

Q2 How successful is the article?

Answers and tutorials can be found on pages 79–80.

To move beyond level 7 you would also need to:

- be quick at spotting the main ideas in a text, and confident about analysing the way the writer has used language to inform and persuade;

- be quite critical in your reading – willing to say what works and does not work;

- pay close attention to layout, ideas and language;

- express your own ideas with precisely-chosen vocabulary.

Chapter 15

Sentence rhythms

Introduction

When writing imaginatively at a higher level, you are expected to use language very precisely to create certain effects. One of the most important techniques professional writers employ is using a variety of sentence types and you should try to do the same. As you will see in the Essentials of Language section (pages 102–104), there are several styles of sentence:

- simple sentences ('The girl felt ill.')
- compound sentences ('The girl felt ill and the boy felt even worse.')
- complex sentences ('The girl, who felt ill, climbed aboard the bus.')

If one of these sentence styles is used too much in your imaginative writing, it can become repetitive and less interesting for the reader. Texts hold our interest more if they have a variety of sentences because this also creates a varied rhythm. Notice what a text feels like where simple sentences dominate:

Simple sentence sample

> It was cold. The snow was falling. Jenny felt worried. She stepped out of the house. She walked down the path. She opened the gate. She looked at the sky. It was grey. It was menacing. She pulled her coat tighter around her. She walked on faster.

Commentary: This gets off to a strong start because the simple sentences give it a feeling of clarity. They also help to build up a feeling of suspense. But by the sixth simple sentence ('She opened the gate'), the rhythm of the paragraph is feeling too similar. It needs a different sentence style to give it variety.

Compound sentence sample

Watch what happens when you allow compound sentences to dominate:

> It was cold and the snow was falling. Jenny felt worried and she stepped out of the house and walked down the path. She opened the gate and looked at the sky. It was grey and it was menacing and Jenny pulled her coat tighter around her and walked on faster.

Commentary: Again, this starts well. But as the paragraph continues, we become irritated by the repetitions of *and*. The rhythm of the paragraph needs more variety and would have more interest if it contained simple *and* complex sentences.

LEVEL 7

Imaginative Writing

You need to

- think of a story that will interest your readers
- organise it to keep your readers interested
- write in an interesting way
- use some interesting words or phrases
- include conversation and description (vary the pace)
- keep your reader's interest right to the end (vary the pace)
- create characters that your reader believes in and feels for
- begin to use words and phrases for particular effects

plus . . .

- deliberately use a variety of sentences and range of language to create particular effects in your story
- create a finished piece of fiction

LEVEL 7
Imaginative Writing

Complex sentence sample

> It was cold and the snow was falling. Jenny, who felt worried, stepped out of the house. After she had walked down the path, she opened the gate. Looking at the sky, she saw that it was grey. Because it also felt menacing, Jenny pulled her coat tighter around her and walked on faster.

Commentary: The first couple of sentences work here, but then the text begins to feel laboured and unnatural. We become distracted by the style and cannot clearly follow the storyline.

Varied sentence sample

Each of the sample texts you've looked at so far suffers from using one sentence style too much. Lively writing will usually contain a variety of sentence styles and lengths: perhaps a simple sentence at the start and end of a paragraph, to give it clarity; then compound and complex sentences within the paragraph to maintain a more interesting variety of sentence rhythms.

> It was cold and the snow was falling. Jenny felt worried. She stepped out of the house and walked down the path. As she opened the gate, she looked at the sky. It was grey and menacing. Jenny pulled her coat tighter around her and walked on faster.

Commentary: The sentence pattern of the paragraph is:

compound; simple; compound; complex; simple; compound.

The sentence variety gives the paragraph a more varied rhythm. It makes the story more interesting to follow and is much more likely to hold the interest of the reader.

EXAMPLE

Look at the opening of this adventure story by Judith O'Neill. Notice in particular the way she varies the styles of sentences she uses to create different sentence rhythms, and to hold the reader's interest. She uses simple, compound and complex sentences, plus another style that we rarely hear about. This is the 'minor sentence' – a sentence which does not contain a verb. Minor sentences can have powerful impact if used occasionally. Notice how Judith O'Neill uses two of them to add variety to her text.

LEVEL 7
Imaginative Writing

Angels

complex → Ben woke to find himself lying on a white sandy beach under a blazing sun. His whole body ached. His blue shirt and trousers were stiff with dried salt water. His feet were bare. For a few bewildered minutes he remembered nothing, but then in a rush it all came back to him. The instant when their ship had struck a reef in the dark; wild screams as the terrified immigrants shoved their way towards the lifeboats; a sudden lurch as the ship rolled over and sank; his own leap into the sea, a cork lifebelt around his waist, cold water gurgling in his throat. And then the long, long struggle to the shore. ← minor

Ben lifted his head. There was no sign of the ship out to sea. Not even one floating mast or a sail. The beach was empty too, apart from a bundle of sodden clothes right by the water's edge. He crawled awkwardly over the hot sand till he reached the bundle. Cautiously, he poked at it. He shivered. Someone was there, inside those wet clothes! Alive or dead? He dragged the bundle away from the water and rolled it over. A thin waif of a girl opened her eyes and stared up at him.

(simple, simple, compound, complex, minor, simple, complex, simple, compound, compound)

The real test of the opening of a story is whether it makes you want to read on. A text which is written in a single sentence style is less likely to succeed. Judith O'Neill's story opening quickly establishes place and character, and surprises the reader with the discovery of the girl. Most importantly, think about how you could create a similarly varied effect if you were to vary your sentences like this.

71

LEVEL 7
Imaginative Writing

Check yourself

A finished product

At level 7 you also need to be able to create 'a finished piece of fiction'. This means more than just getting to the end of your story. It means that you have redrafted the work, so that you have thought carefully about the language choices you have made. A finished piece of fiction will feel like one where every word serves an important purpose.

Look at these opening sentences of a story, written by Jenny in Year 9. It is a first draft.

> The road stretching ahead of her was long, winding and dark and it disappeared into the distance. The girl knew that she was going to have to travel all the way along it but her heart sank at the thought of how far she had to go. She carried on walking and tried to think of things that would keep her mind off the distance she had to travel. She walked on and noticed that it was beginning to get darker. She was not sure how long it would take her to get home but she knew her mum would be waiting for her when she got there.

Would this story opening make you want to read on? Almost certainly not. Why?

- The sentence rhythms are all the same, making it feel monotonous and uncontrolled.
- The vocabulary is dull and often predictable ('winding road … her heart sank … things …').
- We learn nothing about the character or the place.
- We feel no tension – why is she on this journey? Where is she going?

At present this is a reasonable first draft, but it would not gain Level 7 for the reasons listed above. Your task is to work on it, sentence by sentence, redrafting it, cutting words, adding details, changing sentence types until you feel you have created the opening of a finished piece of fiction.

Answer and tutorial can be found on page 81.

To move beyond level 7 your imaginative writing needs to:

- be fluent and original;
- use structure to gain the reader's interest – for example, by holding back key pieces of information, or cutting between two separate storylines;
- create characters who feel real – in their words, thoughts and behaviour;
- use language that is precise, but not flashy; that adds to the story, not distracting the reader.

In other words, you will be an accomplished story writer.

Chapter 16

Variety and range

Introduction

LEVEL 7

Writing to inform and persuade

We know that narratives are a powerful way of hooking readers' attention. We use stories in jokes and gossip all the time because we know that people enjoy following narratives.

But non-fiction texts do not usually use narrative. They have to find other ways of keeping the reader's interest. In both coursework and examinations you may be asked to write a leaflet or article about a topic which does not really interest you. Your real challenge will be to make it interesting to your reader.

There are a number of ways in which you can make non-fiction writing interesting for your reader:

- Try to imagine who your reader is – imagine you are writing directly to her or him.
- Use an informal style, if appropriate.
- Use a range of language – including different styles of sentences, and varied vocabulary.

Range of language

Using a range of language is similar to what we looked at in Imaginative Writing – varying the styles of sentences you use (simple, compound and complex). But it goes beyond this. In a piece of informative writing you may feel you have to work harder than in a story to hold the reader's interest, so you need to use as many different language techniques as possible. Here are a few possibilities:

Vary your sentences

You could use these three types of sentences:

- statements (Here are the facts about good health.)
- questions (How healthy are you?)
- commands (Look at this!)

You need to

- organise your ideas in a sensible way
- interest and convince your reader
- write in a clear and interesting way
- develop some of your ideas more fully
- use a more formal style
- give examples to support your case
- begin to use words and phrases for particular effects
- structure your piece of writing to create an effect on the reader

plus . . .

- deliberately use a range of language to create particular effects in your writing
- create a finished piece of informative or persuasive writing

LEVEL 7
Writing to inform and persuade

Create visual variety

This means making the reader want to read your text by making it look easy to read. You could use:

- short paragraphs
- headlines
- subheadings
- bold print
- italics
- different font sizes
- bullet points
- boxes or panels of text
- lists of facts
- quotations.

Vary your vocabulary

Use words which your reader will understand – but try to use interesting words too. You might use some emotional words ('How much do you really care about others?'), or a more factual style ('These are the facts about AIDS …'). You might use straightforward, monosyllabic (one syllable) words ('care') or more complex, polysyllabic (more than one syllable) words ('compassion', 'thoughtfulness', 'empathy'). Interesting writing will usually contain a lively mix of words – not just predictable ones.

EXAMPLE

Opposite are the front and back covers of a leaflet produced by the Research Defence Society (RDS). The leaflet aims to inform readers about the use of animals in experiments, and to persuade them that this is fair. Notice the way the writers and designers use language variety to create a successful overall effect.

LEVEL 7
Writing to perform and persuade

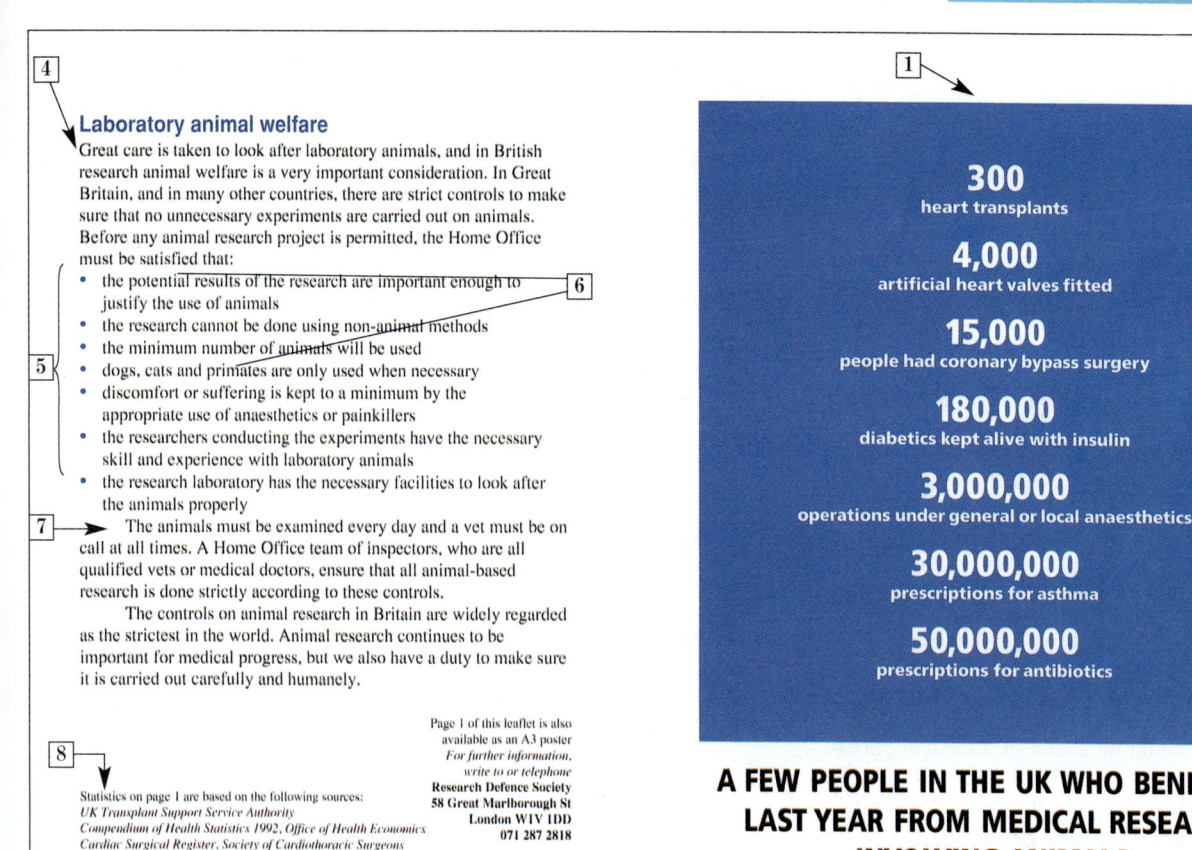

[4]
Laboratory animal welfare

Great care is taken to look after laboratory animals, and in British research animal welfare is a very important consideration. In Great Britain, and in many other countries, there are strict controls to make sure that no unnecessary experiments are carried out on animals. Before any animal research project is permitted, the Home Office must be satisfied that:

[5]
- the potential results of the research are important enough to justify the use of animals [6]
- the research cannot be done using non-animal methods
- the minimum number of animals will be used
- dogs, cats and primates are only used when necessary
- discomfort or suffering is kept to a minimum by the appropriate use of anaesthetics or painkillers
- the researchers conducting the experiments have the necessary skill and experience with laboratory animals
- the research laboratory has the necessary facilities to look after the animals properly

[7] The animals must be examined every day and a vet must be on call at all times. A Home Office team of inspectors, who are all qualified vets or medical doctors, ensure that all animal-based research is done strictly according to these controls.

The controls on animal research in Britain are widely regarded as the strictest in the world. Animal research continues to be important for medical progress, but we also have a duty to make sure it is carried out carefully and humanely.

Page 1 of this leaflet is also available as an A3 poster
For further information, write to or telephone
Research Defence Society
58 Great Marlborough St
London W1V 1DD
071 287 2818

[8]
Statistics on page 1 are based on the following sources:
UK Transplant Support Service Authority
Compendium of Health Statistics 1992, Office of Health Economics
Cardiac Surgical Register, Society of Cardiothoracic Surgeons
Diabetes in the UK 1988, British Diabetic Association

The Research Defence Society is an organisation of doctors, vets and medical researchers which informs the public about the role of animals in medical research

PRINTED ON ENVIRONMENTALLY FRIENDLY PAPER

---

[1]

300
heart transplants

4,000
artificial heart valves fitted

15,000
people had coronary bypass surgery

180,000
diabetics kept alive with insulin

3,000,000
operations under general or local anaesthetics

30,000,000
prescriptions for asthma

50,000,000
prescriptions for antibiotics

A FEW PEOPLE IN THE UK WHO BENEFITED LAST YEAR FROM MEDICAL RESEARCH INVOLVING ANIMALS.
[2]

Without animal research, the possibility of finding better treatments for serious diseases such as cancer, AIDS and multiple sclerosis would be dramatically reduced.

RDS Research Defence Society

ANIMAL RESEARCH SAVES LIVES. [3]

For further information, please write to or telephone the Research Defence Society, 58 Great Marlborough Street, London W1V 1DD. Telephone 071-287 2818.

---

[1] Panel of facts to grab our attention.

[2] Headline then comments on these facts: 'a few people' refers to the millions of people listed in the facts. This is a good way of persuading us to change our attitude.

[3] Straightforward persuasive slogan – perhaps printed rather too small to have its full effect.

[4] Emotional words to persuade us that animal experiments are fair – 'Great care'.

[5] Use of bullet points to emphasise all the checks that are used before animals are tested.

[6] Some high-level vocabulary (e.g. 'potential' and 'primates') adds to the factual feel of the leaflet.

[7] Last two paragraphs are reassuring – make us feel that standards are high and that tests are necessary.

[8] Giving the sources of information further persuades us that the leaflet contains information which is factually correct.

LEVEL 7

Writing to inform and persuade

Check yourself

Health experts tell us that we should aim to eat five sources of fruit and vegetables each day. Could you persuade someone who hardly thinks about their diet that this is possible?

Try to write a one-side leaflet which will persuade a reluctant vegetable-eater that it is time to change their diet. You might mention:

- a diet containing five portions of fruit and vegetables can reduce the risk of cancer and heart disease;
- there is a huge variety of fruit and vegetables to choose from – not just the obvious ones;
- fruit and vegetables add variety to our diet – in their colours, textures and tastes;
- fruit juice counts as one source;
- dried and semi-dried fruits count as another;
- fruit could be added to breakfast cereal.

Use the techniques outlined earlier in this chapter – particularly a variety of sentence styles – to devise a finished leaflet.

Answer and tutorial can be found on page 82.

To move beyond level 7 your persuasive writing needs to:

- capture and hold the reader's interest;
- use an ambitious range of vocabulary and sentence styles;
- use layout and design features to add clarity and interest;
- achieve its aim of persuading the reader to change his/her attitude.

LEVEL 7
Answers and Tutorials for Check Yourself

13 Reading and Understanding Fiction (page 64)

Answers

A1 The writer starts with a dramatic opening sentence. We do not know who Andrew is, or where the hall is, but the writer immediately gets us involved. Words like 'wrong', followed by 'dark wave of dread' in the next sentence create an ominous, menacing atmosphere.

The writer then creates the feeling that Andrew is isolated from other people. In the second paragraph, the woman says 'Ah, there you are'. This shows that she has been waiting for Andrew. His reaction is surprising: he 'blinked at her . . . He wanted to turn and run.' As readers, this surprises us. We are not sure why Andrew is reacting like this, and so the tension is increased.

The writer keeps using ominous language to describe an everyday house. As Andrew walks into the house, 'fear settled around him like a dark stifling blanket'. We might expect a blanket to be comforting and warm. The writer makes it threatening and dangerous. Even the staircase becomes menacing, 'rising into the shadows'.

Later Andrew sees a boy of his own age. We might expect this to be pleasant and reassuring. Instead the writer mentions 'his eyes as cold as stone'.

The writer's technique is to take an ordinary scene and to show how it has been changed by the sense of fear in Andrew's mind – but he does not tell us why Andrew should be feeling like this.

Tutorials

T1 This is a good analysis of the text. It pays close attention to the writer's language, noting the use of menacing words, and highlighting the unexplained feelings Andrew has. The response is written in a precise, controlled style, so that the answer says exactly what it needs to, without wasting words. It does not, for example, say 'I think . . .' and 'I believe': instead the answer is very tightly written, covering the points efficiently. The writer also shows an awareness of how the text plays against the expectations of the reader: 'We might expect this to be . . .'.

LEVEL 7
Answers and Tutorials for Check Yourself

Reading and Understanding Fiction (page 64)

A2 This is a very powerful opening to a ghost story. The writer tells his story quickly, with little descriptive detail, while creating a strong sense of Andrew's unease. Because we cannot explain what is worrying Andrew, we keep reading. The suspense builds as each new element of the plot is introduced: Andrew stepping into the hall; Andrew meeting Mrs Sharman; Andrew entering the room; Andrew noticing Danny.

T2 This answer briskly states whether the text is successful or not, and states why. It shows a sense of confidence in responding to the text as a whole and making a judgement about it. It also supports those comments with some direct references to the text.

To move beyond level 7, the answer might have gone into more detail on the later part of the text – for example, the portrayal of the other characters and the use of dialogue. It would have an analytical style, commenting all the time on the writer's use of language, integrating short quotations throughout to support the points that are being made.

LEVEL 7
Answers and Tutorials for Check Yourself

14 Reading and Understanding Non-fiction (page 68)

Answers

A1 The writer takes us straight to the heart of the story. There is no general introduction, such as 'I spent a day with Pc Bob Murray …'. In fact, we get no reference to the writer at all. This creates a more direct and factual tone, which works well. The writer immediately establishes the central interest of the article: we are told who, where and what.

The dramatic language – 'some of Plymouth's toughest streets' – makes us keen to read on. The writer has created a kind of drama – a lone policeman (and colleagues) out there on the mean streets. The writer tells us more about the task and its success – crime rates down and detection rates up – but this is not the core of the article.

The main technique used is to tell the day in the life story of Pc Bob Murray using time-zones. This, again, creates quite a dramatic effect because it allows readers to imagine what a typical day might be like. It also gives a very structured feel to the article, taking us step-by-step through a series of short paragraphs.

The writer's style changes in these paragraphs. He uses note-form rather than complete sentences: 'Return to station …' rather than 'He returns to the station …'. Again, this adds a kind of tension to the story, making it feel more dramatic than if it were written in conventional paragraphs.

The writer uses some of the typical techniques of journalism – for example, using labels: 'Pc Bob Murray, 34, …' and 'Pc – acting Sgt – Murray'. Both allow the writer to give information in a compressed form.

Tutorials

T1 This answer identifies the writer's techniques very effectively. Points are supported by quotations, showing close attention to the text, and the answer successfully balances points about language (e.g. the use of labelling devices) with points about structure (the way the article is constructed – background and then diary format).

The answer makes some observant points about the way the text is written – particularly in noticing that the type of sentence used in the diary section is different from the earlier sentences ('Return to station …' rather than 'He returns to the station …'). This is a sign of an increasingly confident and alert reader.

LEVEL 7

Answers and Tutorials for Check Yourself

Reading and Understanding Non-fiction (page 68)

A2 The article is successful in showing us what the reality of this Pc's life must be like. It is written in an impersonal style, so that we learn about the policeman and not the interviewee. This gives it a direct tone. The writer establishes the person, place and subject-matter very efficiently, and then uses the diary format, in note-form, to tell his story. This format helps us quickly to become involved in the Pc's routine, as well as being easy to read because the paragraphs are short and straightforward.

T2 This answer states very directly that the writer is successful, and then explains why. It builds on the points made in the answer to the first question, without seeming just to repeat points. It clearly addresses the demands of the question – to make a judgement about the text – and, in doing so, indicates a thoughtful, confident reader operating at level 7.

To move beyond level 7 the answer to Q1 might have been even better if it had begun with a sentence stating the techniques which would be outlined: 'This article uses a variety of techniques, including change of structure, labelling devices and dramatic vocabulary.' The paragraphs which followed would then each address one of those techniques, giving greater clarity to the reader. The answer might also have explored the writer's vocabulary more – informal words like 'seedy' and 'punch-ups' which help to create a sense of atmosphere.

LEVEL 7

Answers and Tutorials for Check Yourself

15 Imaginative Writing (narrative) (page 72)

Here is a rewritten version of Jenny's story. Read the tutorial to see how it has been redrafted to make a finished piece of fiction which could achieve level 7.

> The dark road stretched ahead. The girl knew that she had no choice but to travel along it. She felt a sense of gloomy anxiety as she thought how far there was to go. She walked. She looked above her and noticed the clouds gathering above the trees. She heard the wind rising in the woods. She saw the darkness of night falling around her. And on she walked, trying desperately to keep her nerve, to hold back the sense of panic that was building inside her. She tried hard not to think of the distance she had to go, and instead tried to imagine her destination – mum waiting at home, warmth, security, the safety of home. But that was a long way off.

Tutorial

This rewritten version has a real sense of atmosphere to it. We gain a sense of the girl's environment – the darkness, the trees, the wind. Although we still do not learn the name of the main character, we do start to see inside her mind. We sense her feelings of fear, her attempts to keep her mind off the worrying possibilities of the journey. We look through her eyes.

Perhaps most important is the way the sentences have been revised to give a real sense of variety. We have simple sentences:

> The road stretched ahead.
> She walked.

And we have complex sentences:

> She tried hard not to think of the distance she had to go, and instead tried to imagine her destination – mum waiting at home, warmth, security, the safety of home.

The short sentences create a powerful sense of suspense. The longer ones maintain a rhythm that makes us want to read on.

The vocabulary is precise. These are not particularly flashy words – 'gloomy', 'worrying', 'darkness' – but they are words which have a powerful emotional effect. They help us to feel the sensations that the girl herself is feeling. They also feel as if the writer has tried hard to choose the right word to create the right effect – in other words, that this is a finished piece of writing.

To move beyond level 7 the vocabulary might contain more surprises, and perhaps we would learn more about the girl's character. The writer might actually have held back a few more details to intensify the reader's feelings of suspense.

LEVEL 7
Answers and Tutorials for Check Yourself

16 Writing to inform and persuade (page 76)

Here is a sample leaflet persuading readers to eat more fruit and vegetables:

ARE YOU READY FOR A FIVE-DAY CHALLENGE?

Research shows that eating five sources of fruit and veg each day can make you healthier. You are less likely to get heart disease and cancer, and more likely to feel good.

Why?

Fruit and vegetables are good for you. But more important: they taste great. Don't just think of carrots and frozen peas. Be adventurous. Go wild with peaches, strawberries, broccoli, rhubarb, mango, sultanas ..., the list is endless.

And you'll find the lively tastes, colours and textures of fruit and veg bring new life to your diet.

How could I start?

If eating 5 sources of fruit and veg a day sounds impossible, try these tasty ideas:

- sprinkle fresh fruit on your breakfast cereal
- drink a cool glass of morning juice – it contains one portion
- remember that dried fruit counts too – prunes as a sweet snack, fruit cake as a light treat.

So don't find excuses to ignore your diet get a fruit and veg five-a-day habit.

After all, doesn't your body deserve it?

Tutorial

In your leaflet you will need to have used a variety of techniques to persuade its readers. This one has a light informal tone – 'get into the five-a-day habit . . . doesn't your body deserve . . .?' It catches the reader's attention by using questions throughout, and keeps up the sentence variety. There are simple sentences – 'Be adventurous' – and complex sentences – 'And you'll find that the lively tastes, colours and textures of fruit and veg bring new life to your diet'. The effect is to create a varied rhythm which helps to hold our interest.

The leaflet also works because it gives some specific advice to readers. It tells them in practical terms how they might manage to change their current eating habits. This is far more successful than just telling them that they need to make a change. The suggestions here should help some readers to get started.

Your leaflet should have the feeling of a finished piece of non-fiction writing. In this one, the language feels carefully-chosen, both in vocabulary, sentence structure and tone (the way the reader is addressed). A higher-level leaflet might provide more information, and make more ambitious use of layout, but if your leaflet used the kinds of techniques listed in this tutorial, then it deserves level 7.

An above level 7 leaflet would seem almost perfect. It would perhaps have been more daring – using funny, or unexpected headlines, perhaps persuading the reader by using quotations from people who think they dislike fruit and vegetables, and then showing how they have been 'converted'. The language itself might have greater variety of styles, and more visual variety: this could make it feel impossible to ignore.

Chapter 17

LEVELS 4–7

Reading and Writing about Shakespeare

This section aims to build your skills and confidence in reading and responding to Shakespeare's plays.

How to make progress

Start by looking at this chart of how students improve, level by level. It should help you to work out your own strengths and weaknesses.

Level 4 Shakespeare Response

- You probably understand the story quite well, but you may spend too much time in your written work simply retelling it.

- You are able to make a few comments about characters' thoughts and feelings but may find it difficult to maintain this. For example, if you are asked to write in role ('Imagine you are Juliet. Write a diary . . .'), you may slip out of role by mistake.

Level 5 Shakespeare Response

- You show a good understanding of the main characters' situations, and are able to express what they are thinking and feeling.

- Your writing in role is more controlled, though you may still tell the story at times.

- You are able to make a few comments about the language of the text.

LEVELS 4–7

Reading and Writing about Shakespeare

Level 6
Shakespeare Response

- Your response to character is good, and you support your ideas by mentioning some specific parts of a scene, or using quotations.
- You are able to explore a character's more complex feelings – for example, Juliet's feelings about Paris and how these change once she meets Romeo.
- You are able to write about the impact of language in a scene – why it might be in verse or prose, for example.

Level 7
Shakespeare Response

- You are able to imagine a character's thoughts and feelings very convincingly.
- You show sensitivity towards the difficult situations of some characters – for example, Juliet's fear of betraying her parents mixed with her devotion to Romeo.
- You are able to comment on the language used by different characters in a scene.

Above level 7 . . .

- You can do all of the above – understanding characters very sympathetically; exploring their complex emotions; writing skilfully in role.
- Your work also shows detailed awareness of the way language is working in the scene – supported by examples (quotations).

LEVELS 4–7

Reading and Writing about Shakespeare

EXAMPLE

Now we are going to look at what progress means in the context of one play – *Twelfth Night*. We are focusing on the *opening* scene of the play, rather than the scenes which will be set for the KS3 tests. This is so that you can understand what is going on without any previous knowledge of the play.

Act One

Scene one

A room in the Duke's palace

Enter **Duke, Curio, Lords**; Musicians *attending*.

Duke   If music be the food of love, play on;
Give me excess of it, that, surfeiting[1],
The appetite may sicken, and so die.
That strain[2] again! it had a dying fall;
O, it came o'er my ear like the sweet sound   5
That breathes upon a bank of violets,
Stealing and giving odour. Enough! no more;
'T is not so sweet now as it was before.
O spirit of love! how quick and fresh art thou,
That, notwithstanding thy capacity   10
Receiveth as the sea[3], nought enters there[4],
Of what validity and pitch soe'er,
But falls into abatement[5] and low price,
Even in a minute; so full of shapes is fancy
That it alone is high fantastical[6].   15

Curio   Will you go hunt, my lord?

Duke   What, Curio?

Curio   The hart[7].

Duke   Why, so I do, the noblest that I have.
O, when mine eyes did see Olivia first,
Methought she purged the air of pestilence[8],
That instant was I a hart,   20
And my desires, like fell and cruel hounds,
E'er since pursue me.

Enter **Valentine**.

(*To* Valentine) How now! What news from her?

Valentine   So please my lord, I be admitted;
But from her handmaid do return this answer;
The element[9] itself, till seven year's heat,   25
Shall not behold her face at ample view[10];
But, like a cloistress[11], she will veiléd walk,
And water once a day her chamber round
With eye-offending brine[12]; all this to season
A brother's dead love, which she would keep fresh   30
And lasting in her sad rememberance.

85

LEVELS 4–7
Reading and Writing about Shakespeare

DUKE O, she that hath a heart of that fine frame
To pay this debt of love but to a brother,
How will she love, when the rich golden shaft [13]
Hath killed the flock of all affections else   35
That live in her; when liver, brain, and heart,
These sovereign thrones, are all supplied, and filled
Her sweet perfections, with one self king!
Away before me to sweet beds of flowers;
Love-thoughts lie rich when canopied with bowers [14].   40

Exeunt

[1] surfeiting *being too full*
[2] strain *melody*
[3] notwithstanding ... as the sea *able to swallow up everything, like the sea*
[4] nought enters there *nothing, however valuable, can enter*
[5] falls into abatement *is lessened in value*
[6] fancy ... high fantastical *love, which is the most imaginative thing*
[7] hart *stag. The Duke Orsino hears the word as 'heart', which is a pun on the actual word.*
[8] purged the air of pestilence *purified the air*
[9] element *air*
[10] at ample view *completely*
[11] cloistress *nun*
[12] eye-offending brine *stinging tears*
[13] rich golden shaft *the golden arrows fired by Cupid, the Roman god of love, made people fall in love*
[14] canopied with bowers *nature provides shelter*

Questions

Remember that the kinds of questions you will meet in the test papers are quite open. This means that they are not traditional comprehension-style questions like these:

- Why is the Duke sad?
- Who is Curio?
- What happens in this extract?

Instead, the questions are designed to allow you to write at greater length and to give your own response to the play. Here is a typical question:

> This is the opening scene of Shakespeare's *Twelfth Night*. Duke Orsino has fallen madly in love and his lords and attendants are watching him.
>
> *Imagine what his servant Curio is thinking. Write Curio's diary of the day, focusing on this scene.*
>
> Before you begin you should think about:
> - where the scene takes place and what it might look like
> - the way the Duke is behaving and speaking
> - Curio's feelings about the Duke
> - what Curio expects to happen next.

LEVELS 4–7

Reading and Writing about Shakespeare

We look at other types of questions later in the chapter. Notice that this question encourages you to say something about:

- plot (what happens next)
- character (the Duke and Curio)
- language (the way the Duke speaks).

Notice also that there is a particular challenge in the way the question is set. You are expected to write *as if you are Curio*, in the form of a diary.

A level 4 answer might look like this:

> I was in the Duke's palace today. All the other servants and lords were there too. The Duke was behaving really strangely. He kept going on about music and love. When Curio asked him if he wanted to go hunting, the Duke said that he already was. This is a joke. Then Valentine came in and told the Duke about a woman (we do not know her name yet) who is very sad because her brother has died at sea. The Duke is really interested in the news.

This answer has strengths and weaknesses:

Strengths	Weaknesses
1. It shows a basic understanding of the storyline.	1. It lacks detail – it doesn't feel close enough to the text.
2. It shows some understanding of the Duke's character.	2. It says nothing about Curio's character, and not enough about the way the Duke is behaving and speaking.
3. It is quite clearly written.	3. It doesn't do what was asked: it isn't really a diary. The writer quickly loses the 'I' narrator, so that it feels like an essay rather than a diary.
	4. It is very brief, and says nothing about the setting and what might happen next.

Advice panel

- Use the bullet points given in the question. They will help you to structure your answer, and to make sure you have covered all the essential points.
- Think about your character – what would he be thinking?
- Set your answer out like a diary. Write the date, then a short paragraph. This will help you to keep the style right.

LEVELS 4–7

Reading and Writing about Shakespeare

Now look at a level 5 answer:

> *July 30 1603*
>
> *I really was amazed at the behaviour of Duke Orsino today. At times I thought he must have gone mad. He was going on about music and love, getting really worked up about something – or someone. Everyone else stood around watching. We could hardly believe it. Then Valentine brought news that the woman he was pining for was really upset because her brother had died. Orsino seemed quite happy about this. I can't think what he's up to, but there's certainly something going on. I can't wait to get back into the palace tomorrow!*

Notice how much better this feels – chiefly because the style is so much more like a real diary. It achieves a high level 5 for the following reasons:

Strengths	Weaknesses
1. The format of the diary works well – it feels realistic and entertaining.	1. We don't get a strong sense of the setting (the palace), which the first bullet point requires.
2. We get a good idea of Curio's character and his attitude to the Duke.	2. There isn't enough about the Duke's behaviour or, in particular, his language.
3. The answer shows a good grasp of the plot.	3. The answer could predict, in more detail, what might happen next.

Advice panel

- Be more disciplined in using the bullet points to structure your response.
- Look more closely at the language of the text – try to find a way of quoting specific words and phrases.

Here is a level 6 answer:

> *July 30 1603*
>
> *What a day! There was my master behaving like a complete nutter, going on about music and love, and not much else. I just didn't know what to make of it. We were all there, the usual crowd, in the dining room, and there was Duke Orsino just listening to music which he called 'the food of love' and asking the musicians to 'play on'. I said did he want to go 'hunt, my Lord' and he said he already was hunting. Very strange. Then Valentine came along with news about Olivia and the Duke got even more worked up – asking us to carry him off 'to sweet beds of flowers'. Talk about getting carried away!*

LEVELS 4–7

Reading and Writing about Shakespeare

The diary format again works well, though perhaps the tone is too joky. This has the makings of a very good answer.

Strengths	Weaknesses
1. The diary is very confidently written. 2. We get a strong sense of Curio's character. 3. Even more than this, we get a sense of the way Curio feels about his master – affectionate but bewildered by his current behaviour. 4. The answer uses some quotations from the text.	1. The style feels very modern, and perhaps too chatty and joky. 2. We could learn more about the Duke's character. 3. It is a bit vague about Valentine's message – we need more detail about this part of the scene. 4. The use of quotations feels very contrived or phoney – it makes the diary feel like an essay. Quotations need to be integrated more.

Advice panel

- Make your written style a little more formal.
- Focus even more on the Duke's character and Curio's feelings about it.
- Say more about what happens later in the scene – when Valentine arrives.
- Try to make the quotations integrate with the text more.
- Be more precise in predicting what might happen next.

Now read this level 7 answer:

July 30 1603
I can't imagine what was wrong with my lord today. We were all gathered about him in the palace dining hall. Rather than talking about the meal I was to bring him, the Duke said something about music being 'the food of love'. The musicians carried on playing, even though I think they were expecting to have a break for lunch. The Duke lay back in his chair, closed his eyes and started trying to describe the music. He said it was like the smell of violets. This all seemed a bit much for him because just as suddenly he called for the music to stop. He said it was enough. I asked if he wanted to go hunting and he said something about already being a hart. I decided I might as well just keep quiet. Then Valentine came in with news of Olivia. He said she was weeping and wailing at the loss of her brother. Apparently she's walking around wearing a veil all day – with 'eye-affecting brine', as Valentine put it. What a way with words! Orsino seemed strangely happy. He said 'how will she love',

89

LEVELS 4–7

Reading and Writing about Shakespeare

> *as if her strong feelings about her brother's death showed how good she was at loving someone. I can tell we are in for a right old time. I expect he's going to be sending one of us over with gifts or messages – same as usual. Here we go again. I'd better get some sleep.*

Notice how successfully this addresses all the hints suggested in the bullet points beneath the original question.

Strengths	Weaknesses
1. The style of the diary is a nice mixture – light but not too joky.	1. Some people might still find the tone too lighthearted – but it seems to work well.
2. We learn a lot about Curio – his bemused attitude to Orsino's behaviour.	
3. We also get a feeling of the Duke's character that he is someone who frequently falls in love like this. This shows the writer's confidence in interpreting the play.	
4. The use of quotations is impressive – they are quite naturally integrated into the diary.	
5. The prediction of what will happen next works well.	

To move beyond level 7…

There isn't too much to improve – but you could write in the same style, with *more* specific references to plot, characters and language. This means writing in more detail, using the same style, working more slowly through the scene so that more of its details are commented upon.

QUESTION TYPES

This section gives you advice on approaching the different types of questions which are sometimes set on Shakespeare in the KS3 tests. In general there are two types of questions – *character* and *staging* – but there are two possible approaches to the character questions, as you will see.

LEVELS 4–7

Reading and Writing about Shakespeare

Character questions

Questions in role

These questions often ask you to imagine that you are a character and to write about her or his thoughts and feelings in role. For example:

> Imagine you are Juliet. Write about your thoughts and feelings explaining why you have taken this desperate action. You could begin:
> 'I don't know if I will see Romeo again ...'. (Romeo and Juliet)
> or
> You are Peter Quince. Write about how well you think your play went.
> (A Midsummer Night's Dream)
> or
> You are Viola. Write about your confused emotions towards Orsino.
> (Twelfth Night)

Character questions sometimes ask you to write in a specific format – a diary or a letter. When they do this, you need to get the style right:

- Set your answer out on the page so that it looks like a diary or letter.

- Use an informal style for a diary, perhaps a more formal one for a letter – but think about who your audience is supposed to be.

- Really try to imagine yourself as the character – write as if you are her or him using 'I' and 'me'.

Even where you are not given a suggested format, you still need to make sure that you sound like the character – like this answer written in role as Peter Quince:

> My play certainly made the audience laugh. I just wish I hadn't been so nervous about everything, then I might have been able to relax a bit and enjoy it more. It all began with the decision that our play had been chosen to be performed ...

One final hint: it is important that you don't just retell the story from the character's point of view. Remember that the examiner is testing your ability to understand a character, so you need to keep focusing on thoughts and feelings, and not just on what happened.

LEVELS 4–7
Reading and Writing about Shakespeare

Questions out of role

A second type of character question asks you to look at characters from the outside – that is, to study them and compare then without imagining that you are a character. Here are some typical questions:

> Oberon and Theseus are important characters in this scene. What do you think of the parts of Oberon and Theseus and the parts they play in this scene?
>
> *(A Midsummer Night's Dream)*
>
> or
>
> In this scene both Brutus and Antony want to win the support of the crowd. Why do you think Antony is more successful than Brutus?
>
> *(Julius Caesar)*
>
> or
>
> In this scene Friar Lawrence tells Romeo that he is banished and tries to help him. What do you think of the advice Friar Lawrence gives to Romeo in this scene?
>
> *(Romeo and Juliet)*

These questions are still testing your understanding of the characters, but this time you are not being asked to write as if you were them. Your style therefore will be a bit more impersonal and formal. Remember the key features of a more formal style:

- Avoid using compressed words – say 'is not' rather than 'isn't'.

- Try not to use 'I' too often.

- Keep your vocabulary formal rather than chatty – say 'the play went well' or 'the play was well received' rather than 'the play was okay'.

Staging questions

Another type of question asks you about how the play might be performed on stage. Here are some typical questions:

> Your class is going to perform this scene for your Year Group. Imagine you are going to direct the scene. Explain how you want the lovers to play their parts and how you want the audience to react to the scene.
>
> *(A Midsummer Night's Dream)*
>
> or
>
> The performance of this scene is often the funniest part of *Twelfth Night*. Why do you think audiences find it so funny?
>
> or
>
> In this scene the conspirators meet to plan the murder of Caesar. Explain in detail how Shakespeare builds up a feeling of excitement and suspense for the audience in this scene.
>
> *(Julius Caesar)*

LEVELS 4–7

Reading and Writing about Shakespeare

The key to these questions is being able to imagine what the scene will look like on stage. It will help if you have acted the scene out in class or been to see a production of the play at the theatre. Remember that you should comment on the different possibilities of the theatre. You might write about:

- Where you would place the actors on stage (this is called 'blocking' a scene).
- How they should move, speak, react to other characters.
- What the scenery would be like (realistic? abstract designs?).
- The costumes – whether you would dress the actors in period outfits or use costumes from a different time, such as modern dress.
- Lighting and music effects.

Remember also that your task is to show how the scene would work for the audience, so in your answer you should keep mentioning them – like this:

> By using two spotlights on the lovers at this point, the attention of the audience will be held on Romeo and Juliet, while the other characters merge into the background.

or

> Creating a very dark setting for the conspirators to meet will contrast well with the earlier scene where we saw Caesar addressing the crowds. It will make the audience realise how secretive and scheming the conspirators are being.

General advice

Whichever type of question you are answering, you should aim to:

- remember that the scene was written to be performed, not just read – so keep writing about the audience rather than the reader;
- use the bullet points in the question to help structure your answer;
- avoid re-telling the story; keep making points about characters' thoughts, feelings and language;
- quote words directly from the play, if possible, to show an understanding of the language.

LEVELS 4–7

Reading and Writing about Shakespeare

Check yourself

Now look at this extract from the opening scene of *A Midsummer Night's Dream*. The question is in the style of the KS3 tests, but it does not require you to write in role this time. It shows the other standard format of the questions you will encounter.

Write your answer and then use the answers and tutorials on pages 96–100 to see what level you are working at, and what you need to do to make progress.

Act One

Scene one

Athens

Enter **THESEUS, HIPPOLYTA, PHILOSTRATE,** *and* **ATTENDANTS**

THESEUS Now, fair Hippolyta, our nuptial hour
Draws on apace[1]. Four happy days bring in
Another moon. But, O, methinks, how slow
This old moon wanes, she lingers my desires,
Like to a step-dame[2] or a dowager[3], 5
Long withering out[4] a young man's revenue[5].

HIPPOLYTA Four days will quickly steep themselves in night,
Four nights will quickly dream away the time;
And then the moon, like to a silver bow
New-bent in heaven, shall behold the night 10
of our solemnities[6].

THESEUS Go Philostrate,
Stir up the Athenian youth to merriments,
Awake the pert and nimble[7] spirit of mirth,
Turn melancholy[8] forth to funerals;
The pale companion is not for our pomp. 15
[*Exit* Philostrate

Hippolyta, I wooed thee with my sword,
And won thy love, doing thee injuries.
But I will wed thee in another key,
With pomp, with triumph, and with revelling

Enter **EGEUS, HERMIA, LYSANDER,** *and* **DEMETRIUS**

EGEUS Happy to be Theseus, our renowned[9] duke. 20

THESEUS Thanks good Egeus.
What's the news with thee?

EGEUS Full of vexation[10] come I, with complaint
Against my child, my daughter Hermia.
Stand forth, Demetrius. My noble lord,
This man hath my consent[11] to marry her. 25
Stand forth, Lysander. And my gracious duke,
This man hath bewitched the bosom
of my child.
Thou, thou, Lysander, thou hast given her rhymes,
And interchanged love-tokens[12] with my child.
Thous hast by moonlight at her window sung, 30
With feigning voice, verses of feigning[13] love,
And stolen impression of her fantasy
With bracelets of thy hair, rings, gauds, conceits,
Knacks, trifles, nosegays, sweetmeats[14]
– messengers
Of strong prevailment in unhardened youth[15]. 35
With cunning hast thou filched my daughter's heart,
Turned her obedience, which is due to me,
To stubborn harshness. And my gracious duke,
Be it so she will not here before your grace
Consent to marry with Demetrius, 40
I beg the ancient privilege of Athens.
As she is mine, I may dispose of her
Which shall be either to this gentlemen,
Or to her death, according to our law
Immediately provided in that case. 45

---

[1] out nuptial ... apace *our wedding day will soon be here*
[2] step-dame *stepmother*
[3] dowager *widow*
[4] withering out *wasting away*
[5] revenue *income*
[6] solemnities *celebrations*
[7] pert and nimble *lively and quick; agile*
[8] melancholy *sadness*
[9] renowned *great*
[10] vexation *anger*
[11] consent *agreement*
[12] love-tokens *gifts*
[13] feigning *pretend*
[14] sweetmeats *sweets*
[15] of strong prevailment in unhardened youth *strongly tempting to an innocent child*

LEVELS 4–7

Reading and Writing about Shakespeare

THESEUS What say you Hermia? Be advised fair maid.
To your father should be as a god;
One that composed your beauties; yea and one
To whom you are but as a form in wax
By him imprinted, and within his power   50
To leave the figure or disfigure [16] it.
Demetrius is a worthy gentleman.

HERMIA So is Lysander.

THESEUS In himself he is,
But in his kind, wanting your father's voice,
The other must be held the worthier.   55

HERMIA I would my father looked but with my eyes.

THESEUS Rather your eyes must with his judgement look.

HERMIA I do entreat [17] your grace to pardon me.
I know not by what power I am made bold,
Nor how it may concern my modesty   60
In such a prescence here to plead my thoughts.
But I beseech [18] your grace that I may know
The worst that may befall [19] me in this case,
If I refuse to wed Demetrius.

THESEUS Either to die the death, or to abjure [20]
For ever the society of men.   65
Therefore, fair Hermia, question your desires,
Know of your youth, examine well your blood,
Whether, if you yield not to your father's choice
You can endure the livery [21] of a nun,
For aye [22] to be in the shady cloister mewed,   70
To live a barren sister all your life,
Chanting faint hymns to the cold fruitless moon.
Thrice-blessed they that master so their blood,
To undergo such maiden pilgrimage.
But earthlier happy is the rose distilled,   75
Than that which withering on the virgin thorn
Grows, lives and dies in single blessedness.

[16] disfigure *destroy*
[17] entreat *beg*
[18] beseech *plead with*
[19] befall *happen to*
[20] abjure *give up*
[21] livery *costume*
[22] aye *ever*

In this scene Theseus and Hippolyta talk positively about love, while Egeus presents love as negative.
How would you direct this opening scene to show the different views of love in the scene?
In your answer you might mention:

- how Theseus and Hippolyta should speak and act
- how Egeus should speak and act
- how the lovers should speak and act
- how you would organise the scene on stage.

Remember:

- to use a formal style
- to mention the staging possibilities – blocking, setting, lighting, music and so on
- to keep mentioning the effect on the audience
- to comment as much as you can on characters' thoughts, feelings and language
- to use quotations to support your ideas.

LEVELS 4–7

Answers and Tutorials for Reading and Writing about Shakespeare

Level 4

Answer

I would direct this scene so that Theseus and Hippolyta were on stage at the beginning and they seemed very in love. When Egeus comes in he should seem really angry, shouting and bawling about his daughter. He should seem really furious. Hippolyta and Theseus would seem quite shocked by this. The lovers would come on and look a bit embarrassed by it all – except for Lysander who should seem quite cocky.

There would be a huge row on stage and this would really make the audience laugh. It would show them what a mess love causes.

Tutorial

This is the basis of a very good answer. Its real problem at the moment is that it hasn't enough detail. When the writer says that Theseus and Hippolyta should seem 'very in love', the answer needs to say how – for example, by looking into each other's eyes all the time, by touching, by ignoring people around them.

We need to learn more about how they would show that they are shocked when Egeus bursts in – how they react, whether they find it at all funny.

The answer is good at hinting that Lysander is self-confident, but again we need to know how the actor would show this.

The mention at the end of the way love causes confusion is really impressive – it shows what a good grasp of the play the writer has. But now we need to have a much more detailed, longer answer. It needs quotations, more reference to staging, and closer attention to language.

LEVELS 4–7

Answers and Tutorials for Reading and Writing about Shakespeare

Level 5

Answer

Theseus and Hippolyta would hold hands and look deeply into each other's eyes. They would speak in quite a poetic way – especially Hippolyta: for example:

'Four days will quickly steep themselves in night,
Four nights will quickly dream away the time …'

Theseus would be very gentle in his voice, and this would show how much he is in love.

I would get Egeus to charge in, so that the peace is suddenly shattered. Egeus is really furious. He should be holding tightly onto Hermia's hand, showing his control over her. The other lovers would all stand around.

I would make the setting quite cold and not very emotional, so that this would contrast with scenes in the forest.

Tutorial

Although very short, this answer shows progress. It feels much more as if the writer has a clear view of how the scene would be staged. The answer refers to the way the actors would behave and speak, and ends with an interesting idea about the setting. It uses a quotation, but doesn't really go into sufficient detail about how these words would be said 'poetically'.

To improve, the answer needs to say more about the individual characters – to start to create a sense of what each of them is like, how they would behave and act.

The answer also needs to concentrate more on the issue in the question – the way love is presented. The writer needs to emphasise the way different views of love are being shown in the scene, and say how these could be made clear in the staging.

LEVELS 4–7
Answers and Tutorials for Reading and Writing about Shakespeare

Level 6

Answer

The scene would open with Theseus and Hippolyta sitting together, perhaps on a bench or settee. Philostrate, the servant, would be standing apart watching but feeling like an outsider. This would create an impression of the way Hippolyta and Theseus are completely absorbed in each other. Their language is poetic and gentle – 'fair Hippolyta' – and their voices should be similarly soft. The audience will get an impression of deep, true love. The moon might even be shining in through a window overhead to emphasise the romantic scene.

This atmosphere needs to be shattered when Egeus arrives. Although at first he is formal and polite – 'Happy be Theseus, our renowned duke' – he quickly shows his anger. He should speak very aggressively, pointing to the two young lovers, Lysander and Demetrius, as he names them. These two, as the words say, should 'stand forth' when he is talking about them. The scene could almost look like a trial, with Egeus calling the different youngsters forward to name them.

During this Theseus should look on sternly, perhaps nodding his head in agreement. Hippolyta might have gone back to her seat, showing no interest in this argument. Hermia needs to seem furious, as if she is struggling to control her feelings. When her father says 'This man hath bewitched the bosom of my child' she could roll her eyes, or groan, to show how much she disagrees with her father.

The overall effect of this will show the audience a serious side of love contrasted with a much more lightweight, trivial view of love.

Tutorial

This is a good answer. It focuses well on the different characters, and gives some useful directions about how they should behave and speak. There is some attention to the setting of the scene – the moonlight idea shows a good understanding of the way the words of the text could be echoed in the scenery.

The answer could look more closely at the language used by Theseus and Hippolyta. At the moment it is described as 'poetic', but we could have more detail about this. The idea of making the scene suddenly seem like a trial is good, and the answer could explain a bit more about how this would actually work on stage.

We learn a little from the answer about Hermia, but there ought to be more detail about the other youngsters – for example, the way they each react to Egeus's words.

The way the answer finishes by talking about the theme of love is really impressive – it shows close attention to the exact question set.

To improve, the answer could be better organised, using the bullet points in the question to structure the response. It needs more supporting quotations and closer attention to the language of the text.

LEVELS **4–7**

Answers and Tutorials for Reading and Writing about Shakespeare

Level 7

Answer

The scene starts with a discussion of love. Theseus's words suggest how impatient he is for his marriage to Hippolyta to take place. He talks of the way time drags: 'But, O, methinks, how slow / This old moon wanes …'. The way he talks of the moon is quite poetic – people often associate love with moonlight. But I think Theseus is also trying to show that he will be a good husband. When Philostrate goes out, he says:

'Hippolyta, I wooed thee with my sword,
and I won thy love, doing thee injuries.'

This almost sounds like an apology. He is describing the way he gained Hippolyta as his wife, and it sounds as if he was violent. He now tries to explain that he will 'wed thee in another key'. He is suggesting, in other words, that he has changed, and will make a suitable husband.

For this reason, I would make Hippolyta a little distant. Although she says her formal, poetic speech – 'Four days will quickly steep themselves in night …' – I would not have her holding hands or touching Theseus. This should feel a little more formal, as if she is still wary of him. She is Queen of the Amazons and now finds herself in a strange land, about to marry a man she hardly knows. I think it would be wrong to make the love look too strong. For this reason I would also make the setting cold, full of marble pillars and tiled floors. It should look sleek, shiny, but also quite harsh and unwelcoming. This will give the audience an interesting first impression of love.

When Egeus comes on he should be polite and formal, but simmering with rage. He could say his opening words quickly – 'Happy be Theseus, our renowned duke' – to show that he is eager to get to his main news. At this point he should pull his daughter onto stage and clasp her hand all the time he is speaking. This would show the audience how possessive a father's love can be. Hermia should look sullen and angry all the time he is speaking.

Egeus would work like the director of the scene. When he says 'Stand forth, Demetrius', he could click his fingers to show that he is in control. He would do the same when he says 'Stand forth, Lysander'. Demetrius is Egeus's favourite, so I would make him behave in a very courteous way. He would be nicely dressed, with his hair carefully parted. Lysander should look more casual. I would give him a more modern haircut, perhaps, to make him seem trendy and more sexy. This would illustrate to the audience Hermia's words: 'I would my father looked but with my eyes'. The favourite of the father is not the favourite of the daughter.

When Hermia asks how she will be punished if she disobeys her father, Theseus answers: 'Either to die the death, or to abjure for ever the society of men'. He must seem cold and heartless, and Hermia and the others should seem shocked by how severe the punishment would be. At this point Hippolyta, sitting in the background, should also look up in shock – she is reminded of how cold-hearted her future husband can be.

The overall effect will be to show how dangerous and painful love can be – for people of all ages.

LEVELS 4–7

Answers and Tutorials for Reading and Writing about Shakespeare

Level 7

Tutorial

This is a very impressive answer. It uses the bullet points of the question to organise its points, so that every main heading is covered.

It has a confident style. The opening idea about Theseus and Hippolyta's love is interesting and well-supported from the text. It would mark this answer out as different from those of most other candidates and would gain the student credit.

The answer focuses well on the language, using quotations to show individual words and phrases. It mentions not only what characters say, but also how they should speak. The comments about the appearance of the lovers – especially Demetrius versus Lysander – show a good understanding of the play.

The final idea about the way love seems dangerous is extremely thoughtful, and fits with the overall theme of the play.

Above Level 7 ...

To gain a higher level, the answer could pay more attention to the individual words of characters. Egeus, for example, uses words like 'stolen' and 'bewitched' to describe the way Hermia has fallen in love. It shows the depth of his feeling that he is presenting Lysander as a thief. The way he says 'dispose of' when talking about his daughter hints that he sees her as an object or possession, rather than as an individual.

A higher-level answer might also say more about other staging techniques – lighting, movement, grouping of characters – all to show how the play might be made clear and relevant for a theatre audience.

Chapter 18

LEVELS 4–7

The Essentials of Language

INTRODUCTION

The way you write is often as important as what you write. Throughout your English work, and in other subjects, your ability to communicate clearly and precisely will be crucial to your success. In the KS3 tests you need to be able to write accurately throughout the exam papers, and in your ongoing coursework through the year.

> Clear communication has five essential ingredients:
> - **grammar** – the way we structure language into sentences and paragraphs;
> - **punctuation** – the way we use special marks and symbols to help the reader follow our ideas;
> - **vocabulary** – the words we use;
> - **spelling** – the way we write those words down;
> - **handwriting** – the way we present our writing.

This chapter is in two main sections.

- What you need to know
  This tells you what you need to know in each of the five areas of communication (grammar, punctuation, vocabulary, spelling and handwriting).
- Putting it into practice
  This shows you how writing can improve, level by level, and what you need to do to make progress.

WHAT YOU NEED TO KNOW

GRAMMAR

Grammar is the way we organise words to make sense. From around the age of one, we begin to put words together to communicate meanings. We learn that:

'this is my cup' is grammatical – it makes sense;

and

'my this cup is' is ungrammatical – it does not make sense.

LEVELS 4–7

The Essentials of Language

SENTENCES

The most important unit of meaning in written language is the sentence. Here's what you need to know about sentences:

A sentence …

- is a collection of words which makes sense
- usually tells us what someone or something (the subject) is doing (the verb) – for example:

> 'My Uncle Ernie whistles in the forest' has a subject (Uncle Ernie) and a verb (whistles). It also has other features to tell us where something is happening (in the forest – a phrase).

- can be short or long – for example:

> I agree. (I = subject; agree = verb)
>
> I completely agree with everything you have said so far this evening. (I = still the subject; agree = still the main verb)

You also need to know that there are different types of sentences:

- simple
- compound
- complex.

Simple sentences

A simple sentence gives you *one* main item of information.

> *The train was late.*
> *I walked home across the fields.*
> *Night was falling.*
> *The journey was quite nerve-wracking.*

Simple sentences are really useful. But they can also sound plodding and repetitive if used too much. It would be impossible to get to the higher National Curriculum levels if you wrote all the time in simple sentences – like this:

> *The car was blue. It was dirty. It looked old. Sam got out. He walked to the house. He knocked at the door. Kate opened the door. Sam went in …*

LEVELS 4–7
The Essentials of Language

For this reason, the National Curriculum expects students to be able to use compound and complex sentences as well. These sentence types contain more than one main idea and allow you to create writing that has greater rhythm and interest.

Compound sentences

We use compound sentences all the time, especially in spoken language. They are made up from simple sentences joined together by the **conjunctions** *and, but,* and *or*. Compound sentences can change the rhythm of your writing, making it more interesting to read – like this:

> The car was blue but it was dirty and it looked old. Sam got out and walked to the house. He knocked at the door. Kate opened the door and Sam went in …

This brief paragraph has suddenly started to become more interesting because it has greater variety – compound sentences, plus one simple sentence (He knocked at the door.).

But beware: if you use compound sentences too much, your style can become rambling and uncontrolled – like this:

> The car was blue but it was dirty and it looked old and Sam got out and walked to the house and he knocked at the door and Kate opened it and Sam went in …

To achieve the highest levels you will need to be able to write with greater variety, using other types of complex sentences.

Complex sentences

Complex sentences are made up of two or more clauses. A clause contains a verb and has a subject.

Wh– clauses

These are groups of words we add to sentences to give more detail. They usually begin with a wh– word, such as which, or who. They are also called **relative clauses**.

> The house, which looked old and decaying, stood before us.
>
> I decided to go to my auntie, who wasn't too far away.

LEVELS 4–7

The Essentials of Language

–ing clauses

These are two-part sentences where one part has an -ing verb at the start of it – like this:

> Sitting on the bridge, the lorry-driver ate his sandwiches.
>
> I walked down the street, thinking about my terrible mistake.

Subordinate

These sound difficult, but they are not. Subordinate clauses help you to create two-part sentences which can be especially useful in formal writing. Look at these examples and you will see that the adverbial clauses have been highlighted.

> Despite being told off, Jack still walked up the hill.
>
> Although she felt angry, Catherine still decided to turn up.
>
> However much the pain hurt, Sandra was determined not to show it.

Subordinate clauses give background information about when something happened, or how people feel. They always begin with words like ***however, although, despite, in spite of, before, because***. They can be placed in either the first half of the sentence (as above) or in the second half:

> Because of what had happened, John was not prepared to answer the phone.
>
> or
>
> John was not prepared to answer the phone, because of what had happened.

There are many different types of sentence possible in English, and only a few have been mentioned here. The important thing to remember is that you should use a variety of sentence structures. Too many short sentences can be dull; too many complex sentences can be confusing.

LEVELS **4–7**

The Essentials of Language

PUNCTUATION

When we speak we move our voice up and down to show our meaning. For example, we could say this sentence in two (or more) different ways – one to show we mean what we are saying, the other to show that we are being sarcastic:

> That's a really nice new shirt, Craig.

Say it a few times, sometimes sincerely (as if you really mean it), sometimes sarcastically (as if you don't). Notice how you use the pitch of your voice each time to show what your real meaning is.

In writing, punctuation has a similar role. We use it to help the reader follow the meaning of our sentences.

Capital letters and full stops

For example, we show the reader where a sentence starts and ends by using capital letters and full stops. Without these, the meaning of sentences would be difficult to follow – for example:

> the car was stuck in the morning we decided we would move it

You will almost certainly have had problems following the meaning of those words at first. Look how punctuation would help you:

> The car was stuck. In the morning we decided we would move it.

Notice that a slightly different meaning could be shown using commas:

> The car was stuck. In the morning, we decided, we would move it.

Capital letters have one other main use: to show the names of people, products and places (Viola, Sainsburys, Edinburgh).

Commas

Commas are the punctuation marks which people most frequently get wrong. Look again at the example above and notice how the commas help the reader understand meaning within the sentence, by creating an island of words from *we decided*. Here are some other examples of the way commas can help the reader to follow the meaning within sentences:

LEVELS 4–7

The Essentials of Language

- Orsino, who is in love, listens to the music.
- My strongest memory, from when I was a child, is of Mrs Samson.

Neither of these sentences actually needs the commas – but they are useful in helping the reader to follow the writer's meaning.

The other main use of commas is to separate items in a list:

- Romeo feels frustrated, angry and determined to get revenge.
- Caesar, Cassius, Brutus and Antony all have very contrasting views.

The biggest mistake people make is to think that commas can link sentences together. They can only be used *within* sentences to help clarify meanings. This, for example, is wrong:

> The lovers run into the forest, they wish to escape Egeus.

This consists of two sentences and should therefore be written like this:

> The lovers run into the forest. They wish to escape Egeus.

Semi-colons

Sometimes a full stop can feel too 'strong' between sentences. You feel that a different punctuation mark is needed, somewhere between the power of a full stop and a comma. This is where a semi-colon can be useful. It works a bit like the word 'and', linking sentences together. You could write:

> The lovers run into the forest; they wish to escape Egeus.
>
> or
>
> The play begins with music; it ends with marriage.

The semi-colon is an advanced punctuation mark. Many writers – including professional journalists – never feel the need to use it. But occasionally you may find it useful in formal writing, wherever you want to separate two parts of a sentence, and the full stop feels too strong, the comma too weak.

Colons

These are also advanced punctuation marks, and are useful when writing about literature. Think of a colon as a pair of searchlights: they point ahead to what comes next. They can therefore be especially useful in introducing longer quotations – for example:

LEVELS 4–7

The Essentials of Language

The play opens with highly poetic language from Orsino:

> If music be the food of love, play on;
>
> Give me excess of it …

Notice how the colon tells the reader that something is to follow – in this instance a quotation.

Speech marks

Speech marks are useful but fiddly. There are quite a few conventions (unwritten rules) about how they should be used. Here's a summary.

1 Speech marks are placed around the words a person says.

> 'Welcome home,' said my Auntie.

2 The first word inside the speech marks begins with a capital letter.

3 The words inside the speech marks always end with a punctuation mark (e.g. full stop, question mark [?], exclamation mark [!], or a comma).

Remember that:

- Punctuation is placed *inside* the speech marks.
- If the sentence carries on after the speech marks, then you use a small letter even after a question mark or exclamation mark – like this:

'Welcome home!' yelled my Auntie.

Apostrophes

Many people struggle to know when and where to use the apostrophe. Just look at notices in shop windows! Seen recently outside a garage:

> All your need's

A simple rule of thumb is 'is it a shortened form?' For example, 'the caretaker's broom' is short for 'the broom of the caretaker'. The broom belongs to, or is being used by, the caretaker.

LEVELS 4–7

The Essentials of Language

Here are some conventions for the use of the apostrophe:

- When something belongs to someone, or is in their possession (e.g. Donna's bag; the cat's whiskers; the popstar's Ferrari).

- When something belongs to more than one (e.g. the cats' hair; children's clothes; the popstars' records).

- When letters have been missed out (e.g. I'm (I am); won't (will not); o'clock (of the clock)).

- *Don't* use the apostrophe when there is no possession (e.g. Sainsburys; Harrods).

Probably the most common misuse of the apostrophe is in 'its'. Only use an apostrophe if you intend it as an abbreviation of 'it is' or 'it was'.

> It's a lovely day.
> The alien was on its way towards Earth. (not *it is*)

Paragraphs

From level 4 onwards you need to show you can organise your work into paragraphs. Like punctuation, this is a technique for helping the reader to follow your ideas. Just as sentences group ideas together, so paragraphs place sentences together which have a similar topic or theme.

A paragraph should contain sentences which are linked to a similar theme. In a response to a fiction text you might have:

– a paragraph about the storyline

– a paragraph about the main character

– a paragraph about other characters

– a paragraph about the setting

– a paragraph about the writer's language.

In general, paragraphs should not be too short or too long. Too short usually means fewer than three sentences, because these can feel odd. However, newspapers frequently use one-sentence paragraphs, in order to keep the reader interested. In a formal essay, or in examination conditions, you should probably aim for around three paragraphs per A4 page. This is usually the right length. Any longer and the reader can feel bogged down in a text, unclear about the overall development of the writer's ideas.

In the KS3 tests it usually makes sense to build your paragraphs around the bullet points which form part of each question. This will help you to organise your work, and to make sure that each paragraph is about a slightly different topic.

LEVELS 4–7

The Essentials of Language

VOCABULARY

Writing clearly also means choosing words with a precise meaning. It can be tempting to write the first word you think of, words which we use frequently in speech – like **get, okay, all right, really, good, nice** – but these are often too vague for most writing.

In general, as you write, ask yourself whether a word you are about to use is actually needed. Would the sentence be just as effective without it? Look at these examples:

The novel was really interesting.

The novel was okay really.

The novel was pretty good.

The words *really* and *pretty* are being used here as 'intensifiers' – they add more weight to what we are saying: the novel isn't just interesting; it is *really* interesting.

The problem with these words is that we use them frequently in everyday speech, and they can make writing feel a little informal. The sentences could probably be more precise without them, perhaps by choosing more interesting vocabulary. For example, you could say:

The novel was fascinating/gripping/enthralling/highly entertaining.

or

The novel was reasonable/quite entertaining/mediocre/disappointing/lacking suspense.

Notice that your expression becomes more precise because you are telling the reader more accurately what your feelings about the novel are.

The secret here is not to use a thesaurus. Looking up lots of fancy words is likely to make your writing style too formal, and you may use words which don't quite fit in the context. Instead, pause and think of an alternative word or phrase that you already know.

In particular, when you use two-part verbs (we call them phrasal verbs) – such as *get on, think about, pick up, hold on* – you can usually find another which will convey the same meaning in a more formal way. For example:

get on with work = continue working

get on a bus = enter/embark

think about = consider/contemplate/reflect

pick up an idea = learn easily/understand/grasp

hold on = grip/persist/persevere

109

LEVELS 4–7

The Essentials of Language

In other words, think more about the words you are using. Ask yourself:

- Are they serving a useful purpose in the sentence?
- Are they formal enough in this context?
- Is there a better word I already know which would make my meaning more precise?

SPELLING

We learn patterns of spelling when we are learning to read and write – mainly around the age of 4–7. If you find correct spelling difficult, there is no simple solution. You should:

- Keep a personal spelling dictionary, containing words you get wrong. Refer to this often.
- Try to memorise tricks for spelling certain words correctly – for example, *necessary* = 'never eat chips – eat sausage, sandwiches and raspberry yoghurt'.
- Try to spot spelling patterns in similar words – for example, all words ending in full only have one 'l' (wonderful, hopeful, and so on).

The National Curriculum does not require perfect spelling from you at most levels, but at levels 4 and 5 you are expected to be able to spell simple and common **polysyllabic** words. What does this mean?

> **Monosyllabic** words have one syllable: cheese, mouse, wait, witch.
>
> **Polysyllabic** words have more than one syllable: station (2 syllables: sta+tion); beautiful (three syllables: beau+ti+ful); disappointing (four syllables: dis+ap+point+ing); unnecessary (five syllables: un+ne+cess+ar+y).

Spelling checklist

This is a list of words commonly spelt incorrectly by students. Try to find ways of memorising any which you have difficulties with:

ie words (remember i before e except after c)
achieve
believe
relief
grief
friend
piece

-ful words
careful
faithful
helpful
successful

single -l words
almost
although
skilful
fulfil

-ly words
cruelly
coolly
finally
generally
especially

words which keep their 'e' before -ly
definitely
completely

ei words
neither
seize
weird
receive

verb/noun changes
practice (e.g. football practice)
practise (e.g. I practise a lot)
advice (e.g. here's some advice)
advise (e.g. let me advise you)
licence (I have a fishing licence)
license (You'll have to license that)

trickiest spellings
unne<u>c</u>essary
defin<u>it</u>e
sep<u>a</u>rate
hum<u>o</u>rous
acco<u>mm</u>odation
fulfil/ful<u>filled</u>
knowledg<u>e</u>able
notic<u>e</u>able
di<u>sa</u>ppointing
meter (measuring instrument)
metre (linear measurements)

When you encounter new words use the look/cover/write/check method to make sure you spell them correctly from the beginning.

LEVELS 4–7

The Essentials of Language

HANDWRITING

Just as grammar and spelling help us to communicate clearly, so should handwriting. Everyone's handwriting is different, because it mirrors our different personalities, but the National Curriculum does have certain requirements. At levels 4 and 5 your handwriting needs to be legible. This means that people can read what you have written, even under examination conditions. At level 5 it should also be fluent. This means that your handwriting has a flowing style to it – it will not feel broken up, irregular or disjointed. At higher levels your handwriting should have a clear, fluent style.

PUTTING IT INTO PRACTICE

This section shows you how language skills need to build up, level by level. After each description of what you need to do to achieve a certain level, there is a sample answer written at that level. Each example has been written in response to the same question, so that you can compare them more easily. This is the sample question, taken from a real KS3 English paper:

> **Describe a person you know who has influenced you or been important in your life.**
>
> In your answer you could:
>
> - describe what you and other people see in the person you have chosen;
> - include some memories which show what the person is like;
> - describe the effect the person has had on you.

Each sample answer has margin notes to show you why it is a level 4, 5, 6 or 7. The tutorial then explains how the language needs to improve to move the student up to the next level. Notice that the comments focus only on the language skills, not on the other features of the writing which are covered in other sections of this book.

LEVELS 4–7

The Essentials of Language

Level 4

Grammar

- Writing is mostly organised in a clear way.
- Pupils begin to choose words effectively.
- There are some grammatically complex sentences.
- Punctuation is used mostly accurately to show sentences and there is some punctuation *within* sentences.

Spelling

- Simple and common polysyllabic words are spelt correctly.

Handwriting: mostly clear and legible.

Sample answer

The person who had a big affect on me was Mrs Samson. She was my teacher in my last year at primary school and I can remember her very well. She looked middle aged but I think she was probably about 28. She had long, dark hair. I liked her because she made the work interesting. She taught us all the different subjects except PE. Mr Webb taught us that.

One of my strongest memories of Mrs Samson was when she took us on a school trip to a farming museum at Lichfield. This was great fun and we spent the day there. I remember her telling us all about the museum before we left school. On the coach she told us that we had to behave propally. The best part of the day, for me, was when we had our sandwhiches on the lawn by the river.

1 Spelling error (should be 'effect'), but most simple and common words are correctly spelt.

2 Use of compound sentences adds variety to the style.

3 Simple sentence adds variety.

4 Vocabulary is accurate, but not interesting – note repetition of 'taught'.

5 Use of paragraphs shows sense of structure.

6 Spelling errors ('properly', 'sandwiches').

113

LEVELS 4–7
The Essentials of Language

Tutorial

This is a sound piece of writing. It has some sentence variety (simple and complex), a firm grasp of punctuation, and reasonably good spelling. It uses the bullet points in the question to help structure the response – and the use of two paragraphs shows an understanding of how to organise work.

To move to a higher level it needs:

- a more interesting variety of sentences – a more varied rhythm of simple and complex sentence types;
- more precise vocabulary to make the memories come to life;
- more accurate spelling;
- a more fluent handwriting style.

Level 5

Grammar

- Writing is clearly structured.
- A wide range of vocabulary is used, though some words may not be used precisely.
- Simple and complex sentences are used within this structure, or within paragraphs.
- Punctuation, including commas and apostrophes, is used accurately.

Spelling is generally accurate – including words with complex regular patterns.

Handwriting: generally clear and legible in a fluent style.

Refer back to the question on page 112.

LEVELS **4–7**

The Essentials of Language

Sample answer

The person I remember best was Mrs Samson, my old primary schoolteacher. She taught me for two years and had quite an influence on me. I don't see her any more — I think she has moved to a new school — but I do think about her. She made lessons seem really interesting. We did quite a few projects with her and I remember really enjoying doing one about 'Roman Britain'. I spent hours drawing maps and diagrams and carefully labeling them. This was partly because I was interested in the subject but also because I wanted to please Mrs Samson.

A specially strong memory is the trip she organised to the Lichfield farming museum. She told us about it one afternoon and the whole class got really excited. We prepared for it and when the day came we got on the coach and traveled to Lichfield, which was actually quite near. We took sandwiches. I can still remember mine — ham.

1 Use of comma shows increasing grasp of grammar.

2 Use of dashes to create island of words.

3 Simple sentence followed by compound sentence – creates varied rhythm.

4 Spelling errors ('labelling', 'travelled') of two quite tricky words.

5 Improving use of vocabulary.

TUTORIAL

This is a more interesting piece of writing because the vocabulary is making it feel more vivid. It is easier to imagine everything that is being described. The answer is clearly organised, with a strong control of sentence punctuation. There is also a range of sentences, but, for a higher level, the text needs greater sentence variety. It still feels a bit plodding at times. The spelling is sound, and the handwriting more fluent.

To move to a higher level, the answer needs a more interesting mix of sentence types, and more precise vocabulary.

115

LEVELS 4–7

The Essentials of Language

Level 6

Grammar

- A range of sentence types and use of paragraphing contributes to the quality of the writing.
- A range of punctuation is used to clarify meaning.
- Vocabulary is varied.

Spelling is accurate, though there may be errors in difficult words.

Handwriting: a fluent and legible style.

Refer back to the question on page 112.

Sample answer

1 Vocabulary is very precise.

2 Complex sentences show increasing control and range of sentence types.

3 Commas used to create island of words.

4 Well organised – paragraphs are used logically.

5 Good attention to detail.

6 Simple sentence gives feeling of emphasis at the end.

> The person who sticks most vividly in my mind is Mrs Samson. She wasn't an old teacher, though she always seemed really wise. We knew that we could rely on her for answers to tricky questions. She taught us everything from English and Maths to cooking and art. In fact, she taught us everything, except PE, which was taught by Mr Webb.
>
> She once took us on a trip to an open-air farming museum at Lichfield. The whole class was really excited from the minute she told us. We had various worksheets and tasks we had to complete before we went. It didn't seem like real work.
>
> Then the big day arrived. I remember that I actually woke up earlier than normal, exilerated at the idea of a school trip. We were only going three or four miles from school, but it seemed a real adventure.
>
> I remember wishing that the coach trip would last and last. It was just long enough for John Gibson to feel sick. Then we arrived.

LEVELS 4–7

The Essentials of Language

TUTORIAL

This is an impressive piece of writing. Vocabulary and sentence variety give it a much more interesting, vivid style. The contrast between longer and shorter sentences creates an interesting rhythm as you read. Notice how the writer has slowed down the whole storyline, so that we get more details, for example, about the coach journey.

To move to a higher level, the answer needs to continue to develop the sentence variety and the ambition of vocabulary. A few more unexpected words (but not just picked from a thesaurus) could help to create an even more vivid account. The spelling could be more accurate (e.g. exhilarated).

Level 7

Grammar

- A range of grammatical features.
- An effective use of vocabulary.
- Paragraphing and punctuation make the sequence of ideas clear.

Spelling, including that of complex irregular words, is correct.

Handwriting: fluent and legible.

Refer back to the question on page 112.

Sample answer

Mrs Samson was her name and, although I haven't seen her for three or four years, she had a powerful impact upon me.

I hated the first day I was in her class. Mrs Samson terrified me. She seemed so cold, so disciplined, so unsmiling. Now, looking back, I can see that it was part of her routine, her way of getting the group as she wanted them. But at the time I worried that I couldn't stand a year in such a stifling, silent room.

1 Attention-grabbing opening sentence.

2 Lovely, controlled use of vocabulary, separated by commas.

3 Island of words allows the writer to move into the present tense – to compare how he feels now with how he felt then.

117

LEVELS 4–7

The Essentials of Language

4 Paragraphing works well – the repetition of 'silent' and 'stifling' refers back to the last sentence, keeping the flow.

5 Again, 'listened' links to last paragraph.

6 Use of dialogue further varies the rhythm of the writing.

7 Skilful sentence, linking back to the reference to 'story' in the previous paragraph.

> But it wasn't stifling or silent for long. Mrs Samson prompted us to produce our best, most creative work. She read to us, talked to us and – really importantly – listened to us. You felt she really cared about what you thought.
>
> It was because she listened that we went on the school trip. It was one hot day in June and Mrs Samson sat us all down for a daily story. 'I have an announcement,' she said, with a really serious look in her eyes. I was terrified. I thought she was going to tell us she was leaving. 'Because of all your mythering, I've organised a trip.' Mythering was one of her special words. I've never heard anyone use it since, but Mrs Samson used it all the time.
>
> We clapped and cheered, and I don't think we ever got to the story that day.

TUTORIAL

You can feel from the use of language what makes this so powerful. It is beautifully organised, moving from memories of the past to thoughts in the present really skilfully.

It has an impressive range of sentence types – and uses dialogue further to vary the rhythms. The vocabulary is very precisely chosen and helps to create a vivid scene. We also get a very strong sense of how influential this teacher was – she is powerfully presented in the writer's descriptions.

Beyond level 7

To improve beyond this level means sustaining this quality over a whole answer, keeping the vocabulary vivid and the sentences just as varied. You would be expected to achieve the following:

Grammar

- A range of grammatical features and vocabulary enables clarity and emphasis to be achieved.
- There is a clear grasp of punctuation and paragraphing.

Spelling, including irregular complex words, is correct.

Chapter 19

WHAT IS IN THE PAPER?

TEST PRACTICE

Test Techniques Paper 1

Paper 1 consists of three sections:

Section A is a test of *reading and understanding*. It usually includes a passage of narrative – part of a story which may be fiction or non-fiction. But sometimes the passage is from a newspaper, magazine or advertisement (a media text).

You will be asked two questions on this passage. Both questions test how well you understand the passage and what effect the writer is trying to achieve, but one is worth 11 marks and the shorter question is worth 6 marks.

This section is therefore worth 17 marks.

Section B is also a test of *reading and understanding*. It includes either a passage from a newspaper, magazine or advertisement (a media text), or a passage of narrative – part of a story which may be fiction or non-fiction.

You will be asked one question which tests how well you understand the passage and what effect the writer is trying to achieve. For a media text, you will be asked to explain how the passage seeks to persuade the reader.

This section is worth 11 marks.

It is important to realise that, if Section A contains a narrative, Section B will contain a media text, and vice versa. You will always be tested on both kinds of writing.

Section C is a test of *writing*. Three topics are set and you will be asked to write an essay on one of them. The three topics are:

- a story – either true or made up;
- a discussion essay – you are asked to give opinions on a subject like dangerous sports or the treatment of old people;
- a piece including description – this could be a description of a person or a place.

This section is worth 33 marks.

All three sections are loosely connected. Sections A and B give two different views of the same subject and the topics in Section C relate to this subject in some way. This means that you can use the passages in Sections A or B as a springboard for your answer to Section C.

TEST PRACTICE

Test Techniques Paper 1

ANSWERING THE QUESTIONS

Reading time

Before you can start answering the questions, you will have 15 minutes to read the question paper. During this time, you cannot start answering the questions, but you can make notes on the question paper. Obviously most of this time will be spent reading the passages in Sections A and B. To make the best use of the reading time:

- Read the question carefully *before* you read the passage on which it is set and try to work out what information the answer requires. You will then know which aspects of the passage to concentrate on as you read.

- In pencil, mark any words or phrases in the passage that look particularly relevant to your answer. You might want to quote them in your answer and, if they are marked, your eye will be guided back to them. You are less likely to forget important points in the passage if they are marked.

- Use the inside cover of the question paper to make some notes. You should jot down some ideas and quotations from the passage relating to the prompts beneath each question (see next section).

Sections A and B

Each of the questions has several prompts printed underneath it. These are suggestions about what you should include in your answer. In fact, they focus on key ideas in the passage. If you write a paragraph on each of the prompts, you will give a full answer (although its level will depend on how detailed and accurate your comments are). You are welcome to bring in other ideas which are not covered by the prompts, but these will help your answer *only if they are relevant to the question.*

Each question ends 'you should support your ideas with words and phrases from the passage'. This means you are expected to quote from the passage, but remember:

- quotations must be short – more than a sentence is a waste of your time;

- quotations must be relevant – they need to illustrate something important in the passage, such as how a character feels, what the author thinks about an incident, etc.;

- quotations must be explained – it is not enough just to quote; you need to explain the *effect* of the writer's words at that point in the passage; how do they help express what the writer intends?

Media texts usually include one or more illustrations and features of layout such as headlines, subtitles, etc. In your answer you must comment on the effect of these but only if the question or prompts ask you to. If the question or prompts don't mention illustrations or layout, you can gain no marks by writing about them.

Section C

You need to plan and write an interesting, well-written piece of between one and two sides in length. (If your handwriting is large, you may need to write a little more.) Such a piece will gain more marks than a longer, more rambling piece that is cut short for lack of time.

You need to write this piece as carefully as possible, legibly, in paragraphs, with accurate punctuation and spelling. **This is because Section C is marked on handwriting, paragraphing, punctuation and spelling as well as how interestingly written and well organised it is**. (Answers to Sections A and B are not marked on handwriting, paragraphing, punctuation and spelling. Because they are tests of reading and understanding, they are marked only on how fully you understand the passages. This does not mean that you should be careless when answering Sections A and B, of course. But it does mean that, if you have time at the end of the test to check your work, you should check your answer to Section C first.)

PLANNING YOUR TIME

You will have 1 hour 30 minutes to write your answers to Paper 1. A sensible allocation of your time would be:

Section A	30 minutes
Section B	20 minutes
Section C	35 minutes

Some schools advise pupils to answer Section C first. This is quite a good idea because:

- Section C is worth more than half the marks on the paper (33 out of 61);

- it is the only Section where answers are marked on handwriting, paragraphing, punctuation and spelling, so you need to be specially careful;

- you are at your freshest at the start of the test.

It does not matter in which order you answer the questions. Certainly you should not spend too much time on the question (Question 1 or Question 2) which is worth only 6 marks.

If possible, you should leave 5 minutes at the end of the test to check your work.

TEST PRACTICE

Test Techniques Paper 1

Finally, if you find you want to add something to an answer and there isn't enough space on that page, all you need do is write 'continued at end' at the end of the original answer, turn to the last page of the answer booklet and continue. Remember to write the appropriate question number in the margin where you continue the answer.

PRACTICE PAPER 1

The following chapter consists of a practice Paper 1 which you should try answering to help prepare yourself for your Test. This sample Paper is structured like the Paper 1 which you will meet in your Test.

Sample students' answers and examiner's comments

There are no right answers in English but there are very good answers and not so good answers. In Chapters 24–26 (pages 152–180) there are examples of students' answers at different levels. The examiner provides a commentary on each sample answer, discussing how successful it is **under the same criteria that examiners use when marking test questions**. The examiner also outlines how each sample answer could be improved to achieve a higher level.

You should try answering each question on the practice Paper before you turn to the relevant section to look at the sample answers and examiner's comments. Then you can compare your own answer with the samples given. You should then be able to decide how successful you think your own answer is and decide how it could be improved.

If you meet any particular problems when writing your answers, you can refer back to the skills sections of this Guide.

Chapter 20

TEST PRACTICE

Paper 1

Section A

*Read the following passage. Then answer question 1 **and** question 2.*

A young woman wishes to find out about her future.

I turned to *Time Out*, the local press and women's magazines. I chose three entries at random. First, a 'psychic clairvoyant' who advertised a variety of talents. Not only could he read the Tarot and the Crystal Ball, the Dice and the Sand. He could cast spells and concoct potions, he could read your handprint, teach you to predict and took party bookings. 5

I phoned and said I was interested in having a postal hand-reading. Wearily, with an edge of cockney in his voice, he said, 'Now listen, love. Are you sure you want this? I mean, I get lots of people, you know, phoning, and then they never send nothing, so it's just a waste of my time, see?'

I assured him I really did want a reading, so he said I should paint my palm red 10
and press it onto some paper, but make sure I pressed every bit of it ('It has to be accurate, see? Just paint it red, see? Red's better. Shows up more.') and send it to him.

I had to decide whether I wanted one or two hands read. 'Your right hand is the future and your left hand is the past. Now, you can say all I need is the future 15
'cause you know your past, don't you? But it's useful for you to test me, see? So you know if it's true what I say about your future.'

We agreed I would send two handprints plus a money order for £7.50 addressed to Oberon and he would reply within two days. Two weeks later, having received nothing, I phoned. "Course I remember particularly because you did yours in red,' 20
he said.

'But you said they *had* to be in red.'

'Yeah, I know. But lots of people don't care. They still do them in black you know.'

He claimed he had read mine and sent them back and couldn't think what had happened to them, but was not surprised with the Post Office being what it is. 25
Still, if I would send him a new set of prints he'd do them right away at no further cost. So I resmeared my hands with red paint and, experienced now, pressed them on a sheet of paper laid across a rolling pin.

123

Twenty-seven days later Oberon wrote to me: 'Many thanks for the palm prints you have sent me. The only problem is, they're different from the ones you sent me originally, or seem to be!' I did not take up his offer of a personal consultation at 'no further charge'.

My second choice, Mr Adam Fudge, takes a boxed and decorated display advertisement in several publications. It runs to seventeen lines and is aimed only at those of a serious disposition. I phoned and booked an evening appointment. When the day came, having consulted a street map and found that this guide to the future lived in a far-off suburb of London, I persuaded my mother to come with me. We arrived at a small terraced house and rang the bell.

After a long delay, the door inched open and clouds of Indian Rose[1] wafted out at us. A few more inches and a young, blond, bearded man was revealed. He wore a white Indian wrap and flip-flops. 'You are the six o'clock appointment?' he intoned.

'Yes,' I said, 'and this is my mother.'

He showed us through a tiny entrance-hall, and into the front room.

'You have booked for one person. Do you wish to make it a double?'

I asked what he thought best.

'It is as you wish,' he recited. 'The single sitting is £25, the double sitting is £40.'

'Oh, well,' said my mother briskly, 'I'll wait out here then.'

He turned to me. 'You have come in a car. I suggest that your mother wait in the car, not in this room. I shall leave you to think about it.' He glided out.

We whispered frantically. 'You've come this far, you may as well come in.'

'Nonsense. Why should we pay an extra £15?'

'I don't want you waiting in the car.'

'Why doesn't he want me here? What's he afraid I'll see?'

'I don't know. I don't want you leaving me in this house on my own. You're coming in.'

Mr Fudge silently reappeared. 'Have you decided?'

'Yes,' I said, 'we're both coming in.'

---

[1]Indian Rose: *a kind of incense*

'Very well. We shall go into my study.' We followed him along a narrow corridor. The study was small and dark. We sat side by side on a sofa against the wall. Mr Fudge sat at a round glass table facing us. There was silence except for an occasional gentle musical tinkling. Several incense sticks were burning.

Mr Fudge looked up. 'Have you ever been with a sensitive before?'

My mother shook her head as if to say, 'Do I look like a fool? I'm only here because I have this crazy daughter.'

I tried to make amends. 'I haven't actually been with one before, but I've read lots and lots about it and I've always wanted to.'

He sat thoughtfully, looking down at his glass table for a long long time. The incense burned and the bells tinkled and we sat very still and finally a clock struck and Mr Fudge looked up and announced, 'I cannot sit for you.'

'Oh!' we exclaimed. 'Why not?'

'There is a hostile presence. Perhaps it is your mother.' He turned to her. 'You don't want to be here, do you?'

'Well,' said my mother, 'I'll go and sit in the car. How long will you be?'

Mr Fudge was getting cross. 'I do not *know* how long I'll be. When you are dealing with *them*' – he indicated an empty space on the other side of the table – 'you must let *them* decide all things. I am a medium.' His voice rose and the whites of his eyes went red. 'I have had this gift since I was a small boy in India. I never went to school in this country. I do not *need* to sit. You are fortunate that you got this appointment. Appointments with me are rare.'

Eventually he calmed down and, reaching for his appointment book, he offered to see me on the next day, alone. Desperate to end the scene I made an appointment and we scampered off.

The medium was 'sensitive' enough to know that I would never dare to go back to his house. Next morning when my husband phoned to cancel the appointment, Adam Fudge said, 'This is no more than I foresaw.'

TEST PRACTICE

Paper 1

*Answer question 1 **and** question 2.*

1 **Do you think that Mr Fudge is more genuine than Oberon, or do you think he is just as dishonest?**

In your answer you should comment on:

* differences between how the two men speak to their clients;
* the appearance of Mr Fudge and his house;
* the two men's approach to money;
* why the young woman learns nothing about her future.

You should support your ideas with words and phrases from the passage.

11 marks

2 **Why do you think the young woman wanted to find out about her future? How might this be connected with her relationship with her mother and her husband?**

You should support your ideas with words and phrases from the passage.

6 marks

TEST PRACTICE

Paper 1

Section B: Media

In October 1997, there was much argument when two 13-year-old girls wanted to take part in a boxing match. In fact, the match was cancelled because of all the criticism.

Read the article that you have been given and answer the question.

Refer to words and phrases in the article to support your ideas.

3   **What does the writer think about women's boxing?**

In your answer you should comment on:

* the views of the newspapers and boxers quoted in the article;
* the opinion of the British Medical Association;
* how men's views affected women's Olympic sports;
* how the last sentence links with the last two paragraphs of the article and with the title.

11 marks

October 1997

Today, two young women slug it out in the first female fight approved by the Amateur Boxing Association. **Sally Weale** writes about its impact

A blow for equality?

No ordinary fight gets headlines this big. 'Who has the stomach for this fight?' in the *Daily Mail*. 'A bout of madness', the *Mirror*. The cause of the outcry? Two schoolgirls, Emma Brammer and Andrea Prime, both 13, who will today make history – of sorts – when they take part in the first female fight to be approved by the Amateur Boxing Association.

Until now, women boxers have been limited to sparring in supervised gyms. Now, after 116 years, the ABA has finally agreed to let women compete on its circuit. This evening, if the fight isn't cancelled at the eleventh hour, Brammer and Prime will climb into a ring at Kay's nightclub in Stoke-on-Trent to fight in three 90-second rounds.

Our sportswriters have never been so outraged. Here's Ian Wooldridge, full of rage in yesterday's *Daily Mail*: 'In a lifetime of sports writing, I have witnessed nobility and honour, cheating and disgusting behaviour. But never have I encountered a sports event as degrading as this.' These two schoolgirls shouldn't be 'belting the daylights out of one another for the entertainment of yobbos in a nightclub', Wooldridge says. They should be at home 'swotting up their geography'.

Few of us, I imagine, like the idea of two teenage girls slugging it out in a ring. I wouldn't want to watch it and I wouldn't want any daughter of mine to take up the sport. But neither would I want any *son* of mine to go into the ring.

The problem with boxing is that it presents danger for everyone

127

who takes part. As the British Medical Association put it yesterday, the decision to allow women in to the ring provides 'equal opportunities for eye and brain damage'.

In this case, age is clearly a factor: young bodies, male or female, are still developing, so are particularly vulnerable. If it is unacceptable for 13-year-old girls to box, how can one say that it is all right for 13-year-old *boys* to ditch their homework in favour of a bout in the ring?

Lots of people don't like boxing; many would like to see it banned. But to have men decide for women that we really don't want them to mess up their hair and get involved in such a nasty, aggressive business is a different issue. That's just plain sexist.

Throughout the history of sport, men have told women what they can and can't do, what's good or bad for their health. Women weren't allowed to compete in the Olympic marathon until 1984 – *1984*! – because men in the medical profession told them that their wombs would fall out.

In 1928, women were allowed to run in the 800m race for the first time. At the end of the event, a number of the competitors collapsed with exhaustion. Immediately, this was seized upon by organisers and doctors (all male, no doubt) as evidence that women really weren't made for such feats of endurance. From that point on, they were banned from running further than 200m in Olympic events until 1960. Women who competed over longer distances were warned that they would 'become old too soon'.

This time, we have comments like this from former world featherweight champion Howard Winstone, now father of twin girls: 'Women's boxing is not very nice. It's not natural. I am very glad my daughters were more interested in the opposite sex, rather than into boxing.'

And this from former heavyweight Henry Cooper: 'Women are made differently from men. Their entire body structure is not like a man's. Women are made for loving and not hitting.'

Pass me the gloves, Henry.

Squaring up in the square ring . . . the 13-year-old contestants in tonight's controversial match are Andrea Prime (left) and Emma Brammer

PHOTOGRAPHS: NEIL PLUMB, DAVE BAILEY

Section C

This section of the paper is a test of writing. You will be assessed on:

- *your ideas and the way you organise and express them;*
- *your ability to write clearly, using paragraphs and accurate grammar, spelling and punctuation.*

Choose **ONE** of the following.

4   EITHER
   (a)   **Write about someone who has to take a difficult decision.**
   *   You could write about yourself or someone else.
   *   You could base your writing on a real or imaginary experience.

   OR
   (b)   In every society, some people have always tried to find out about their future.
   Write about whether you think it is possible to find out about the future or whether it is impossible.
   In your answer you could:
   *   describe the various methods of telling the future and say how far you think they could work;
   *   suggest reasons why some people want to know the future;
   *   describe any experience of telling the future that you have read or heard about.

   OR
   (c)   **Describe a person who tricks or deceives other people, or who deceives themselves.**

   In your answer you could:
   *   describe the person's appearance;
   *   explain how the person tricks or deceives others, or deceives themselves;
   *   say whether they are found out and, if so, what happens.
   You could base your writing on a real or imaginary person.

33 marks

Chapter 21

TEST PRACTICE

Test Techniques Paper 2

WHAT IS IN THE PAPER?

This test lasts 1 hour 15 minutes. There is no reading time because the test is based on a Shakespeare play which you have studied beforehand.

At the start of the test, you will be given three booklets:

- a question booklet
- a 'Scenes from Shakespeare Plays' booklet containing the scenes which have been set for study
- an answer booklet.

Three plays are set each year and you will have studied one of them. Two scenes (or groups of short scenes) from each play are set for detailed study. In the question booklet, one question is set on each of the scenes (or groups of short scenes). There will therefore be two questions on the play that you have studied. Turn to these questions and decide which **one** of them you will answer.

PREPARING YOUR ANSWER

Having chosen your question, read it carefully at least twice to check what it is asking. Questions usually have 'trigger words' which are especially important: for example, How does Shakespeare make this scene tense and exciting? or What do we learn about X's character from this scene? When planning and writing your answer, you must focus on tension and excitement in the first example and on a particular character in the second. Examples of these kinds of answers are given on page 188 (excitement) and pages 181 and 195 (character).

You should now do two things before writing your answer.

- *Mark your quotations.* Go quickly through the scene in the 'Scenes from Shakespeare Plays' booklet and, in pencil, mark the quotations that look as if they will be useful in answering the question. This will remind you of important points about the scene and help you to find quotations quickly when writing your answer.

- *Use the prompts to plan your essay.* Each question will have several prompts printed beneath it. As in Paper 1, these are suggestions about what you should include in your answer. They focus on key ideas in the passage and, if you write a paragraph on each of the prompts, you will give a full answer (although its level will depend on how detailed and accurate your comments are). By all means bring in other ideas which are not covered by the prompts, but these will help your answer *only if they are relevant to the question.*

TEST PRACTICE

Test Techniques Paper 2

On the inside front cover of your answer booklet, you should jot down some thoughts and quotations *for each of the prompts*. This will give you a ready-made framework for answering the question. It is not enough just to explain what happens in the scene. There will be a particular question about the scene and the prompts will help you to focus your knowledge of the scene on answering the question.

It is worth spending 10 minutes on this planning before you start writing your answer. You will then be able to answer more confidently, knowing what you are going to write and what quotations you are going to use.

ANSWERING THE QUESTION

Your answer will receive two marks:

- for Understanding and Response (up to 22 marks)
- for Written expression (up to 16 marks)

so you need to know how to gain the best marks in each category.

Understanding and Response

This mark is given for how well you understand the scene (understanding) and for making comments which show your own ideas and feelings about the scene (response). You therefore need to:

- explain everything that happens in the scene that is relevant to the question;
- support what you write with frequent short quotations;
- give your opinion, with reasons, if the question asks for this.

Quotation is very important. In fact, **you cannot achieve Levels 6 or 7 unless you quote from, or at least refer to, Shakespeare's words.** (Reference is where you explain what a character says, rather than quote it. 'Juliet wonders why Romeo is called Romeo' is a reference. 'Romeo, Romeo, wherefore art thou Romeo?' is a quotation. It is usually easier to quote, and quotation tends to receive higher marks than reference.)

Your answer should therefore include frequent quotations; but remember:

- *quotes must be short* – more than two lines is usually too much; you will gain more marks with three two-line quotations than with one of six lines.
- *quotes must be relevant* – they need to illustrate something significant in the scene, such as how a character feels, what attitude he or she is expressing, etc.

131

TEST PRACTICE

Test Techniques Paper 2

- *quotes must be explained* – it is not enough just to quote; you need to explain the effect of Shakespeare's words at that point in the scene; how do they help express what Shakespeare intends?

You do not have to write out quotations in lines, as they appear in Shakespeare's text, but you should put quotation marks at the beginning and end of each one.

Written expression

This mark is given for how well you express your ideas in writing. This includes handwriting, paragraphing, grammar, punctuation and spelling, as well as the range of words you use and how well organised your answer is. This is similar to Paper 1, Section C, except that a separate mark is given.

You therefore need to write this piece as carefully as possible, legibly, in paragraphs, with accurate punctuation and spelling.

TWO SPECIAL KINDS OF QUESTION

Role-play questions — character

Each year, Paper 2 includes at least one question which asks you to write about the scene as if you are one of the characters in it. Pupils have been asked to give the Nurse's view of her taking messages between Romeo and Juliet, and Sir Toby Belch's reactions to watching Malvolio being tricked by the letter. Of course, when you take the test, there may not be a role-play question on the play that you have studied, but it is a possibility for which you should be prepared.

When answering this kind of question, you are expected to adopt the role and write the whole answer as if it is spoken by the character specified. You gain credit for writing in a style suitable to how the character speaks. For example, the Nurse would speak in the down-to-earth language of a working woman who has been insulted for trying to appear 'posh' but who is very fond of Juliet, while Sir Toby would start off furious at Malvolio's comments, then be delighted when the trick works so well.

You are also expected to quote from or refer to Shakespeare's language in your answer. This may seem difficult when you are writing in role as a character and in modern English, but it can be done in two ways. First, when referring to something another character says, quote it in Shakespeare's words. For example, Sir Toby's anger towards Malvolio can be shown by him quoting some of Malvolio's comments and Sir Toby's reply in the original language. For example, Sir Toby should say: 'When he imagined being married to Olivia, I wanted to hit him in the eye'. But for a higher mark you could write: 'When he said "Having been three months married to her", I wished I had "a stone-bow to hit him in the eye!"'

Second, when describing something dramatic in role – Juliet begging her father not to make her marry Paris, for example, or Lady Macbeth pressurising Macbeth into killing Duncan – you can either adapt Shakespeare's words or slip them in as brief quotations. Instead of Lady Macbeth saying 'I wish I had killed our baby rather than go back on my word like he had', she could say: 'I told him I would have "plucked my nipple from his boneless gums And dashed the brains out" rather than go back on my word like he had' (see sample answer on page 181).

Role-play questions – director

The paper may also include a question which asks you to imagine that you are directing the scene on stage and instructing the actors how to perform their roles. Again, when you take the test, there may not be such a question on the play that you have studied (or at all), but it is a possibility for which it is worth being prepared.

The question is really asking you to explain why the characters behave as they do in the scene. It is not necessary to maintain the tone of a theatrical director. Guided by the prompts, you should focus on explaining the characters' motives and how these are shown by what they say and do. For example, when Macbeth calls the Witches 'you secret, black and midnight hags', you would need to explain the disgust in his voice but also that he is no longer afraid of the Witches and he knows where to find them.

As with character role-play questions, you need to quote from and refer to Shakespeare's language. This is not difficult because you are directing a group of actors and can explain what feelings they should express in particular lines. You can write your answer either *about* the actors ('As Macbeth comes in, he stares at the Witches and says…') or as if you are speaking *to* the actors ('Macbeth, when you come in I want you to stare at the Witches and say…').

Altogether, you need to focus on *the meaning of the language of the scene* set for study. You would gain little credit for writing about other aspects of stage production, such as scenery, lighting and costumes. Although a real stage-director would be concerned with these matters, they are not important in the test.

TEST PRACTICE

Test Techniques Paper 2

THE 2000 SCENES

The Shakespeare scenes set for the 2000 tests are:

Macbeth

- Act 1, Scenes 6 and 7
- Act 4, Scene 1

Romeo and Juliet

- Act 1, Scene 5
- Act 3, Scene 5, line 64 ('Ho, daughter, are you up?') to the end

Twelfth Night

- Act 1, Scene 5, line 81 ('Madam, there is at the gate a young gentleman') to the end
- Act 2, Scene 5

THE 2001 SCENES

Two scenes will be the same as in 2000:

Macbeth

- Act 4, Scene 1 (probably)

Twelfth Night

- Act 1, Scene 5, line 81 ('Madam, there is at the gate a young gentleman') to the end

Another, new scene will be set for each of these plays and *Romeo and Juliet* will be replaced with *Henry V* from which two scenes will be set.

The new scenes will be published by the Qualifications and Curriculum Authority in September 2000 and all schools will be notified then.

PRACTICE PAPER 2

Chapter 22 contains examiner's hints on *all* the scenes that will be set for the 2000 exam. Read this through carefully, then try answering Practice Paper 2 (Chapter 23). This sample Paper is structured exactly as the Paper 2 which you will meeet in your Test. There is a question on each of the two set scenes from each play.

TEST PRACTICE
Test Techniques Paper 2

It obviously makes sense for you to answer the question on the scene from the play that you have been studying. In order to do this, you will need to refer to the relevant scene in a copy of *Macbeth*, *Romeo and Juliet* or *Twelfth Night*. In the Test, you will be provided with a separate booklet which contains the set scenes from the three plays.

Sample Student's Answers
[Examiner's] Comments

[...] but there are very good [...]
[...] 27, 28 and 29 give examples [...]
[...] *Romeo and Juliet* and *Twelfth* [...]
[...] a commentary on each [...]
[...] useful it is **under the same** [...]
[...] **marking test questions**. The [...]
[...] sample answer could be improved to [...]

[...] on the practice Paper before [...]
[...] at the sample students' [...]
[...] then you can compare your own [...]
[...] should then be able to decide how [...]
[...] is and also decide how [...]

[...] when writing your answer,
[...] 22.

Paper 2

Chapter 22

EXAMINER'S HINTS

MACBETH ACT 1 SCENES 6 AND 7

Two scenes have been set and the question will be on both of them. As the only character who appears in both scenes is Lady Macbeth, the question will be about her.

You must write about both scenes in your answer.

Points to revise

In Scene 6 Lady Macbeth is welcoming Duncan to the castle. She curtseys to him and speaks very politely, thanking him for the honours he has given to them. We know she is being hypocritical because, in the previous scene, she has prayed to the powers of darkness ('you murthering ministers') to give her strength to bring about Duncan's death.

In Scene 7 we see her real character. Macbeth has decided not to go ahead with the plan to kill Duncan and she makes him change his mind by:

– sneering at him ('Was the hope drunk/Wherein you dress'd yourself?');

– saying he doesn't love her ('From this time/Such I account your love');

– calling him a coward ('Art thou afeard/To be the same in thine own act and valour/As thou art in desire?');

– saying that he is less than a man ('When you durst do it, then you were a man');

– saying that, if she had sworn something as important as he had, she would have killed her baby ('pluck'd my nipple from his boneless gums/And dash'd the brains out') rather than gone back on it. This last speech shows the terrible ruthlessness of her character. It is also a savage attack on Macbeth's manhood; she is saying she would rather kill their child than keep it with such a pathetic father as he has turned out.

Macbeth gives in under this pressure and Lady Macbeth quickly comes up with the plan to get Duncan's guards drunk, use their daggers for the murder, smear them with Duncan's blood and blame them for the murder. Macbeth immediately agrees.

Taken together, the two scenes show that Lady Macbeth is **hypocritical** towards Duncan and completely **ruthless** towards her husband. She cruelly puts increasing pressure on him, making him feel that their relationship is finished unless he gives in to her, which he soon does. At this point in the play, she is stronger than him.

Possible questions

A straight question is given on page 146.

There could also be a character role-play question on Lady Macbeth and you could practise the question. **Imagine you are Lady Macbeth. Write down your thoughts and feelings at the end of these scenes.** Remember to write about both scenes.

A director role-play is unlikely because there are two scenes and the question has to cover both of them. Directing two scenes would be too complicated.

MACBETH ACT 4 SCENE 1

This is the scene where Macbeth visits the Witches to find out about his future. At first sight, the scene is dominated by the Witches: they chant the spell at the beginning and they create the various apparitions. Looking closer, we see that **the scene centres on Macbeth**. He begins by demanding to know his future and ends by realising that his children will not become kings after him so he may as well be a murderous dictator.

Questions will therefore be set on Macbeth, not on the Witches.

Points to revise

Remember that Hecate's arrival [lines 39–43] and the First Witch's speech [lines 125–132], with the songs that they introduce, were not written by Shakespeare. They were added later to create a musical version of the scene.

Unlike the beginning of the play where the Witches lie in wait for Macbeth, he now knows where to find them. He is willing to track down and meet with the local representatives of the powers of darkness which shows how far he has committed himself to evil. The Witches know someone wicked is coming – 'By the pricking of my thumbs,/Something wicked this way comes' – and they probably know it is Macbeth.

Macbeth does not treat the Witches with respect. He sneers at them – 'How now, you secret, black and midnight hags' – and demands that they tell him what he wants to know, even if it causes the destruction of the world [lines 51–59]. This shows how desperate he is.

The Witches call up three apparitions:

– an armed head (a head wearing a metal helmet) which warns Macbeth against Macduff. In fact, the apparition is a trick. At the end of the play Macduff beheads Macbeth and brings in his 'armed head'.

> **EXAMINER'S HINTS**
>
> **Paper 2**

– a bloody child which says 'none of woman born/Shall harm Macbeth'. This makes Macbeth more confident, but again it is a trick. Macduff was 'from his mother's womb/Untimely ripp'd' (born by caesarian section) and so was covered in blood at birth.

– a child crowned with a tree is his hand which tells Macbeth that he 'shall never vanquish'd be until/Great Birnam wood to high Dunsinane hill/Shall come against him'. This makes Macbeth feel he is completely safe but, again, it is a trick. Near the end of the play, Malcolm orders his men to cut down branches in Birnam wood to disguise the size of the army as it marches towards Macbeth's castle.

Macbeth is reassured by the apparitions, but he still wants to know whether Banquo's children will become kings as the Witches said at the beginning of the play. He forces the Witches to answer and they create a last apparition – a show of eight kings followed by Banquo who 'points at them for his'. Macbeth curses the Witches – 'Infected be the air on which they ride/And damn'd all those that trust them!' – **which is ironic because he trusts them himself**.

Lennox brings news that Macduff has fled to England and Macbeth decides to hesitate no longer: 'From this moment,/The very firstlings of my heart shall be/The firstlings of my hand'. He will seize Macduff's castle and 'give to th' edge o' the sword/His wife, his babes, and all unfortunate souls/That trace him in his line'. He will massacre Macduff's family even though he knows it is pointless. It is an act of **terrible revenge** on Macduff for fleeing to England. It is also an **act of spite**, doing to Macduff what he failed to do to Banquo (that is, kill his children).

This scene shows a further stage in Macbeth's decline towards being completely evil. He is now no longer a murderer of individuals (Duncan and Banquo) but a vicious tyrant who is willing to massacre whole families including women and children.

Possible questions

A director role-play question is given on page 147. This focuses on Macbeth because he is the central character in the scene. A more general director question, such as how to direct the scene to make it tense and exciting, is unlikely because pupils would be tempted to write about stage effects (lighting, sound, how the apparitions are created) which would gain few marks.

There could be a straight question on Macbeth and you could practise the question **How do Macbeth's reactions change during the scene and what does this show about his character?**

There could also be a character role-play question on Macbeth and you could practise the question **Imagine you are Macbeth. Write down your thoughts and feelings at the end of this scene.**

EXAMINER'S HINTS

Paper 2

ROMEO AND JULIET
ACT 1 SCENE 5

This scene is full of action, but it works in a series of close-ups: the servants bustling about; Capulet encouraging his guests to dance; Romeo seeing Juliet for the first time; Tybalt wanting to attack Romeo and being stopped by Capulet; Romeo and Juliet talking and kissing; and finally Juliet using the Nurse to find out who Romeo is.

There is no central character who takes part in the whole scene (as Juliet does in the other set scene), so the question will be on the scene as a whole. For example: How does Shakespeare make the scene tense and exciting? or, How do the various characters add to the drama of the scene?

Points to revise

The servants bustling about their work open the scene in a lively way, giving the impression of an important social occasion.

Capulet and his family greet the guests. He is in a cheerful mood and encourages the ladies to dance by threatening to say they have corns if they don't: 'She that makes dainty/I'll swear she hath corns'. Note: only the younger people wore masks. The idea was to enjoy yourself by dancing and chatting intimately with someone to whom you hadn't been introduced by your family. Capulet refers to this [lines 21–24].

Most of the guests dance because Capulet orders the tables to be turned up against the wall to make more space [line 27]. He then chats to his cousin about how long it is since their last masked ball and our attention moves to...

Romeo who sees Juliet and is struck by her beauty: 'O she doth teach the torches to burn bright'. Another dance is in progress so he decides to wait till it's over, then go and talk to her: 'The measure done, I'll watch her place of stand/And touching hers, make blessed my rude hand'.

Tybalt recognises Romeo's voice and immediately sends for his rapier so that he can hopefully kill him: 'To strike him dead I hold it not a sin'. (As guests in Capulet's house, the young men would have left their weapons at the door.) Capulet tells Tybalt to leave Romeo alone, partly because he is 'a virtuous and well-govern'd youth' and partly because he doesn't want the party upset: 'You'll make a mutiny among my guests'. When Tybalt tries to argue, we see the sudden rage that Capulet also turns on Juliet in the other set scene. He calls Tybalt 'goodman boy' and 'a princox', meaning an insolent youth, and forces Tybalt to back down. Tybalt exits muttering that he will attack Romeo later [lines 90/91].

Romeo and Juliet talk for the first time. Their speeches form a romantic sonnet which ends in a kiss. After four more rhyming lines they kiss again and Juliet is called away to her mother.

139

EXAMINER'S HINTS

Paper 2

Romeo asks the Nurse who the girl is and learns that she is Capulet's daughter. He realises at once how dangerous this is: 'My life is my foe's debt' (my life is in debt to my family's enemy). The party ends and, to avoid suspicion, Juliet asks the Nurse the names of three young men including Romeo. When she finds out who he is, she too realises how dangerous it is: 'My only love sprung from my only hate' (I love a man whom my family hates).

This scene gives hints about what will happen later in the play. Romeo and Juliet are in love, but they know this must be kept secret from their families. Tybalt is going to find Romeo and punish him for gatecrashing the party.

Possible questions

A straight question is given on page 148.

A character role-play question is very unlikely because all the main characters – Capulet, Tybalt, Romeo, Juliet, Nurse – only speak at certain times in the scene and Shakespeare gives no clue about what they thought during the rest of the scene.

Although there is plenty of action, a director role-play question is also unlikely. There is so much happening that it would be difficult to direct the whole scene, yet each of the 'close-ups' is too short to sustain a full answer. There are also practical difficulties like realising that only certain characters wear masks, that the tables are turned up [line 27] and that there is a second dance which is not mentioned in the stage directions [see line 49].

ROMEO AND JULIET ACT 3 SCENE 5, LINES 64 TO THE END

The part of the scene that is set begins after the Nurse brings news that Juliet's mother, Lady Capulet, is coming and Romeo leaves Juliet to go away into exile in Mantua.

Juliet is the only character who is on stage for the whole of the scene, so the question is almost certain to be about her.

Points to revise

Juliet is under great and increasing pressure during the rest of the scene. You need to cover all four stages of this pressure in your answer.

EXAMINER'S HINTS
Paper 2

Lady Capulet is bitter about Tybalt's death and wants revenge on Romeo. Juliet doesn't want to hear Romeo being abused, but she can't disagree with her mother openly so she speaks with double meanings – saying things that mean one thing to her mother and something else to herself. Your copy of the play will explain these. For a higher level, you need to quote and explain *two examples* of Juliet's use of double meanings.

Lady Capulet also brings news of their decision that Juliet will marry Paris. Juliet rejects this ('Now by St Peter's Church, and Peter too,/ He shall not make me there a joyful bride') because she is already married to Romeo.

Lord Capulet is quite sympathetic to Juliet when he comes in. He thinks she is weeping about Tybalt's death and gently mocks her: 'How now, a conduit, girl? What, still in tears? Evermore showering?' But he quickly becomes angry when he hears that Juliet is refusing to marry Paris. He threatens to drag her to the wedding on a hurdle; he shouts abuse at her ('Out, you green-sickness carrion! Out, you baggage!'); he wants to hit her ('my fingers itch'); and he ends by telling her to accept the marriage or else he will throw her out ('Beg! Starve! Die in the streets!/For by my soul I'll ne'er acknowledge thee').

Juliet begs her mother for help, but her mother coldly rejects her.

The Nurse. Juliet turns to the Nurse for advice, believing she will help her as she always has in the past. But the Nurse advises her to forget Romeo and marry Paris: 'I think it best you married with the County./O he's a lovely gentleman./Romeo's a dishclout to him'. Juliet checks that the Nurse means what she says – 'Speakest thou from thy heart?' – then dismisses her sarcastically: 'Well, thou hast comforted me marvellous much'. Juliet says she will go to Friar Laurence for confession.

Juliet alone. Juliet knows she cannot rely on the Nurse any more. She will go to the Friar for advice and, if there is no alternative, she will kill herself: 'If all else fail, myself have power to die.'

Throughout the scene, Juliet has been put under increasing emotional pressure. In turn, she has been left by Romeo; heard him abused by her mother; been abused and threatened by her father; been rejected by her mother; and had the Nurse side with her parents against her. She is alone, trapped and in a desperate emotional state. If the Friar cannot help her, she sees suicide as the only way out.

Possible questions

A character role-play question is given on page 149, but the question can also be straight as it was in 1999: **What are the pressures that Juliet is under and how does she react to them in this scene?**

A director role-play question is unlikely because the scene is quite static. There are only four characters and they mostly stand and talk to each other.

141

EXAMINER'S HINTS
Paper 2

TWELFTH NIGHT ACT 1 SCENE 5, LINES 81 TO THE END

The part of the scene that is set begins when Maria brings Olivia news that a young gentleman wishes to speak to her. Olivia is in mourning for her father's and brother's deaths and refuses to see him, but eventually she becomes curious and agrees to receive him. She is attracted to the young man, Cesario (who is Viola in disguise), and falls in love with him.

Olivia is the only character who is on stage for the whole of the scene, so the question is almost certain to be about her. The important part of the scene is where Olivia changes from rejecting men to falling in love with Cesario (Viola), so the question will focus on this.

Points to revise

Maria brings news that a young gentleman wishes to speak to Olivia, mentioning that he is attractive: 'T'is a fair young man'. Olivia tells Malvolio to get rid of him if he is from Orsino: 'I am sick or not at home – what you will to dismiss it'

Malvolio brings back news that the visitor refuses to go away: 'he says he'll stand at your door like a sheriff's post...but he'll speak with you' Olivia is intrigued by his persistence and asks what the man is like. Among some sneering comments, Malvolio says that he is between a man and a boy and that he is good looking: 'He is very well-favoured' Olivia is **beginning to be interested** in him and agrees to see him.

As she is in mourning, Olivia covers her face with a veil, as does Maria. This was proper behaviour when a person in deep mourning received someone outside the family. Viola cannot tell which is the lady of the house. She begins her speech on behalf of Orsino, then interrupts herself because she does not want to waste it: 'I would be loath to cast away my speech'

Olivia admits that she is lady of the house, but tells Viola to cut the speech short: 'Come to what is important in it. I forgive you the praise'. Maria tries to usher Viola out ('Will you hoist sail, sir? Here lies your way.'), but Viola refuses cheekily ('No, good swabber, I am to hull here a little longer') and persuades Olivia to hear her alone.

When they are alone, she persuades Olivia to lift her veil and show her face. Viola then starts her speech praising Olivia's face on behalf of Orsino, saying it would be cruel to take such a face to the grave 'and leave the world no copy'. Olivia mockingly replies that she will have some copies made. Viola goes on with the speech of praise and Olivia

> EXAMINER'S HINTS
>
> Paper 2

rejects Orsino again: 'But yet I cannot love him./He might have took his answer long ago'

Viola then starts talking in her own words and says that, if she loved Olivia like Orsino does, she would not give up. She would 'make me a willow cabin at your gate' and call to her till she gave in. Olivia is **attracted by Viola's passion** and murmurs 'You might do much' (you might succeed). She checks that Viola is a gentleman, i.e. of the same class as herself although he is a messenger, which hints at her **growing interest**. She sends Viola back to Orsino, but invites her back to tell her how he takes her refusal.

Alone, Olivia admits that she is attracted to Cesario (Viola). She wishes it was Viola, not Orsino, who was in love with her ('Unless the master were the man') and suddenly realises that she has fallen in love: 'Even so quickly may one catch the plague? Methinks I feel this youth's perfections...creep in at my eyes.' She calls Malvolio and tells him to return a ring that Viola has left. This is untrue; it is a trick to get Cesario (Viola) to return tomorrow.

Olivia ends the scene **confused**. She is attracted to Cesario by many things: his good looks, his humour, his passion, his refusal to take no for an answer. She is surprised at the suddenness of her feelings, but she also fears she may be making a fool of herself: 'I do I know not what, and fear to find/Mine eye too great a flatterer for my mind' (I don't know what I'm doing and I'm afraid I'm being led astray by his appearance).

Possible questions

A straight question is given on page 150.

A character role-play question is quite likely and it would be set on Olivia rather than Viola because Olivia's feelings during the scene are more complicated. Viola is simply doing her job. You could practise: **Imagine you are Olivia. Write your thoughts and feelings at the end of this scene.**

A director role-play question is unlikely because the scene is quite static. Sir Toby staggers in and out half drunk and Malvolio walks in and out pompously, but for the main part – the conversation between Olivia and Viola – the characters mostly stand or sit and talk to each other.

EXAMINER'S HINTS

Paper 2

TWELFTH NIGHT ACT 2 SCENE 5

This is one of the funniest scenes in the play and the question is certain to involve humour. It is important to realise that the humour arises in two stages, as explained below.

Points to revise

Three characters want revenge on Malvolio: Sir Toby because Malvolio reports his drinking to Olivia; Fabian because he reported him to Olivia for bear-baiting; and Maria because he is a pompous idiot with no sense of humour who tries to make himself seem more important than he is. As always, Sir Andrew just tags along with Sir Toby.

The humour begins when Maria reports that Malvolio is coming and drops the letter in his path, telling the others to hide in the box tree. For the rest of the scene, the humour develops in two stages. First, Malvolio comes in and talks to himself, imagining being married to Olivia. Note: his second sentence – 'Maria once told me she did affect me' – means that Maria told him that Olivia was keen on him. Maria has been planning this trick for some time!

Each of Malvolio's comments provokes an outraged reaction, usually from Sir Toby, and Fabian struggles to keep him quiet enough not to give the game away. Examples:

– at first Sir Andrew wants to attack Malvolio as a rival for Olivia's affection and Sir Toby tells him contemptuously to be quiet: 'Peace, peace';

– but when Malvolio starts describing married life with Olivia, this is too much for Sir Toby and he immediately wants to punish Malvolio: 'O for a stone-bow to hit him in the eye!';

– Malvolio imagines sending servants for Sir Toby who 'curtsies' to him. He imagines looking coldly at Sir Toby – 'with an austere regard of control' – and telling him: 'You must amend your drunkenness'. Toby's reaction is increasingly violent, including a wish to smack Malvolio in the mouth: 'And does not Toby take you a blow o'the lips then?' Fabian only just manages to keep him quiet enough;

– Malvolio then mentions 'a foolish knight' and Sir Andrew instantly recognises himself.

At this point Malvolio sees the letter and the second stage of the humour begins. The main points are:

– Malvolio assumes that M.O.A.I. refers to his name, although the letters are in the wrong order;

- the letter asks him to wear yellow stockings and to be cross-gartered. Malvolio persuades himself that Olivia likes these, though yellow stockings are inappropriate in a house of mourning and both yellow stockings and cross-garters were unfashionable when the play was written;

- the postscript asks him to smile a lot – 'thy smiles become thee well'. In fact, Malvolio has not smiled at all in the play until now. He has no sense of humour and his face is ghastly as he practises smiling before going off happily to put on his yellow stockings and cross-garters.

The others are delighted by the success of the trick. Maria knows that Olivia will be appalled at Malvolio grinning at her in yellow stockings and cross-garters, and Sir Toby realises that, when Malvolio becomes aware that he has been fooled, he will go mad: 'thou hast put him in such a dream that when the image of it leaves him, he must run mad'. This hints at Malvolio being locked up as a madman later in the play.

Possible questions

A straight question is given on page 151.

A character role-play question (on Sir Toby) was set in 1999 and is unlikely to be set again.

A director role-play question is quite likely because the scene has plenty of action. The question could focus on Malvolio who starts by acting as if he is Olivia's husband and then becomes more and more excited as he reads the letter. Or it could focus on how humour is created by Malvolio and the others. You could practise: **Imagine you are going to direct this scene for a class performance. Explain how you want your actors to make the scene funny for the audience.**

Chapter 23

TEST PRACTICE

Paper 2

If you have studied 'Macbeth', do either task 1 or 2.

Macbeth

Act 1 Scenes 6 and 7

> ### TASK 1
>
> In these scenes, Duncan arrives at the Macbeths' castle and they plan to murder him.
>
> **What do you learn about Lady Macbeth's character from these two scenes?**

Before you begin to write, you should think about:

* the way Lady Macbeth speaks to Duncan when welcoming him;
* how she persuades Macbeth to murder Duncan;
* how she plans the murder.

Read the task again before you begin to write your answer.

> In the test, the scenes will be given to you in a booklet. To answer this task, refer to your copy of the play.

TEST PRACTICE

Paper 2

If you have studied 'Macbeth', do either task 1 or 2.

Macbeth

Act 4 Scene 1

TASK 2

In this scene, Macbeth visits the Witches to find out about his future.

Imagine you are going to direct this scene for a class performance. Explain how you want the pupil acting the part of Macbeth to show his responses to the Witches and the apparitions.

Before you begin to write, you should decide what advice to give the pupil about:

* how Macbeth speaks to the Witches;

* how Macbeth reacts to the three apparitions;

* Macbeth's state of mind after seeing the kings;

* how Macbeth reacts to Macduff's flight to England and what this shows about how he will behave in the future.

Read the task again before you begin to write your answer.

In the test, the scenes will be given to you in a booklet. To answer the task, refer to your copy of the play.

147

TEST PRACTICE

Paper 2

If you have studied 'Romeo and Juliet', do either task 3 or 4.

Romeo and Juliet

Act 1 Scene 5

> **TASK 3**
>
> In this scene, Romeo and Juliet meet for the first time at Capulet's party.
>
> **How do Capulet, Tybalt, Romeo and Juliet contribute to making this scene exciting?**

Before you begin to write, you should think about:

* how Capulet speaks and behaves at the beginning of the scene;
* how Tybalt reacts to Romeo and to Capulet;
* how Romeo and Juliet speak and behave towards each other;
* the hints in the scene about what may happen in the future.

Read the task again before you begin to write your answer.

> In the test, the scenes will be given to you in a booklet. To answer the task, refer to your copy of the play.

TEST PRACTICE

Paper 2

If you have studied 'Romeo and Juliet', do either task 3 or 4.

Romeo and Juliet

Act 3 Scene 5, lines 64 to the end of the scene

> ### TASK 4
>
> In this scene, Juliet is in a very difficult situation.
>
> **Imagine you are Juliet. Write your thoughts and feelings at the end of the scene.**
>
> You could begin: *I've never felt so desperate. I can't believe how my parents and the Nurse have treated me.*

Before you begin to write, you should decide what Juliet thinks and feels about:

* how her difficult situation has come about;
* how she has managed to hide her real feelings from her mother;
* how she reacts to her parents' pressure to marry Paris;
* her feelings about the Nurse's change of opinion.

Remember to write as if you are Juliet.

Read the task again before you begin to write your answer.

> In the test, the scenes will be given to you in a booklet. To answer the task, refer to your copy of the play.

149

TEST PRACTICE
Paper 2

If you have studied 'Twelfth Night', do either task 5 or 6.

Twelfth Night

Act 1 Scene 5, lines 81 to the end of the scene

TASK 5

In this scene, Cesario (who is Viola in disguise) comes to Olivia with a message from Orsino.

Explain how Olivia's attitude to Cesario changes during the scene.

Before you begin to write, you should think about:

* Olivia's reaction to hearing about Orsino's messenger;

* how Cesario (Viola) speaks to Olivia;

* how Olivia's reactions to Cesario change during their conversation;

* Olivia's thoughts and actions after Cesario leaves.

Read the task again before you begin to write your answer.

In the test, the scenes will be given to you in a booklet. To answer the task, refer to your copy of the play.

TEST PRACTICE

Paper 2

If you have studied 'Twelfth Night', do either task 5 or 6.

Twelfth Night

Act 2 Scene 5

TASK 6

In this scene, Malvolio finds a letter. It seems to be from Olivia, but in fact it has been written by Maria.

What do you learn about Malvolio in this scene and how does his character add to the humour of the scene?

Before you begin to write, you should think about:

* why Maria and Sir Toby want to make a fool of Malvolio;

* the way Malvolio imagines and describes his life as Olivia's husband;

* how Malvolio persuades himself that the letter is meant for him;

* how he is going to make a fool of himself in front of Olivia.

Read the task again before you begin to write your answer.

In the test, the scenes will be given to you in a booklet. To answer the task, refer to your copy of the play.

Chapter 24

ANSWERS AND EXAMINER'S COMMENTS

Paper 1: Section A Narrative

Sample student's answer: 1

1 Mr Fudge was born and raised in India, where-as Oberon has a Cockney accent. Oberon speaks to his customers in an unproffesional way referring to them as "love" and being negative about them, "Are you sure you want this?" This would put off a client as they would not be sure about his proffesionalism. Oberon charges £7.50 for his services which is sent with the handprints needed for the reading.

   Mr Fudge speaks to his customers in an extremely proffesional way asking them their every wish "Do you wish to make it double?" "It is as you wish." This gives the clients a sense of profesionalism. Mr Fudge appears in front of his customers in Indian garments and flip-flops, his house smells of incense, which is very traditional and gives a feeling of the mystic. Mr Fudge deals with money as a shop would, giving special offers if you buy two items at the same time. He makes a double session cheaper than two single sessions, charging £40 for a double and £25 for a single. But at least mr Fudge will tell his customers' fortunes face to face, where-as Oberon just takes their money and sends nothing.

   The young woman only learnt that she would not go back to Mr Fudge's house for a second appointment.

   I think that they are both fakes but Mr Fudge is just better at it.

2 The young woman does not have a good relationship with her mother. Her mother thinks she is a "crazy daughter" and is only there because she feels she has to be. This could be the reason that the young woman wants to find out about her future, because she feels unstable in her family.

152

ANSWERS AND EXAMINER'S COMMENTS

Paper 1: Section A Narrative

Examiner's comments

How successful is this answer?

Q 1 *Know what the characters in a text are like*
The answer makes several important points about Oberon and Mr Fudge. Oberon speaks with a cockney accent, calls his clients 'love' and is negative towards them. On the other hand, Mr Fudge was raised in India. He speaks politely to his clients and appears to them in Indian garments and flip-flops. His house smells of incense.

Begins to read beneath the surface
The answer makes the good point that Oberon's casual way of speaking is 'unprofessional' and would tend to put clients off. By contrast, Mr Fudge's way of speaking is described as 'professional' and his appearance, with the incense, is well described as 'very traditional and gives a feeling of the mystic'. (*Note:* although 'professional' is misspelt three times, this does not affect the answer's level; see page 121.)

Show an overall understanding of the text
The question focuses on dishonesty. The answer does not explain Oberon's dishonesty at first, just mentioning that he charges £7.50 for a handprint reading. However, Mr Fudge's keenness to make money is dealt with well by comparing him to a shop 'giving special offers if you buy two items at the same time'. His willingness to meet his clients is then contrasted with Oberon who 'just takes their money and sends nothing' – a good, brief summary of the difference between them. The answer ends with a sentence that answers the question, but gives no explanation for the student's opinion.

Note the effect of some words or phrases
The answer refers closely to some parts of the text, quoting both Oberon and Mr Fudge as they speak to the young woman and saying whether they are being 'professional'. The second quotation ('Are you sure you want this?') is rightly described as negative towards the client.

Level: there is enough evidence under all four criteria for this answer to achieve Level 5.

How could you do better?

Q 1 *Know what the characters in a text are like*
Begins to read beneath the surface
A better answer would give some more detail about Oberon's attitude and his dishonesty. It would mention that he speaks in a very casual way, with not only 'love' but 'yeah' and, very often, 'see?'; also that he seems bored and negative. He says a lot of people never send anything, 'so it's just a waste of my time, see?' [line 9].

You should then explain his dishonesty: how he takes the money but sends nothing, blaming the Post Office when the woman phones him weeks later. His dishonesty is also shown when he says he remembers her prints because they were red when he told her to do them in red and, later, when he says the second prints were different from the first.

On Mr Fudge, you should mention some of the other things he does to impress clients: the seventeen-line advertisement 'aimed only at those of a "serious" disposition' [lines 34/35]; the fact that he says he grew up in India and wears Indian garments although, being blond, he is probably not Indian himself; his mysterious manner ('He glided out' – line 49; he 'silently reappeared' – line 55); the 'occasional gentle musical tinkling' in his house [line 60]; his claim to be a 'sensitive' [line 61].

Show an overall understanding of the text
The question asks you to assess how honest the two men are and you need to give your opinion of each one *backed up by reasons*. A good answer would make the following points:

- Oberon is obviously a fake who is in the fortune telling business just for the money. He takes the woman's money, sends nothing and tells lies to excuse himself. He advertises a large number of fortune telling skills [lines 3–5] which suggests that he is out to make money in as many ways as possible.
- Mr Fudge has all the trappings of a serious fortune teller and it is more difficult to tell whether he is just a cleverer 'con man' than Oberon or whether he genuinely believes in his

153

ANSWERS AND EXAMINER'S COMMENTS

Paper 1: Section A
Narrative

powers. His appearance, his manner, his Indian childhood, the incense, the musical tinkling could all be part of an elaborate set-up to impress his clients. He is also keen to make extra money from double bookings.

- He refuses to tell the women's fortunes and becomes enraged. This could mean that he could not cope with the mother's hostility and needs gullible clients if he is to perform. On the other hand, if he just wanted the money, he could put on an act and tell them anything. By sending them away, he loses £25 or £40, which a complete 'con man' would not do.

Comment on the writer's use of some words or phrases

As shown above, a good answer quotes examples of how Oberon and Mr Fudge speak to their clients, and refers to their advertisements explaining what these show about the two men's attitude to fortune telling.

Q2 This question asks you to read beneath the surface of the text and think about why the young woman wanted to know her future. There could be several reasons, but the question also asks you to think about her relationships with her mother and husband. How might these have some bearing on her wish to know her future?

The answer points out that the young woman does not seem to have a good relationship with her mother. The mother thinks her daughter's wish to know her future is a waste of time and the answer quotes the phrase ('crazy daughter') which expresses this attitude most clearly.

The answer suggests that the woman wants to find out about her future because 'she feels unstable in her family'. This is well put – 'unstable' suggests stress and lack of control – but the idea is not explained.

Level: the understanding shown by this short answer, together with the well-chosen quotation, means that it achieves Level 5.

Q2 Questions like this are 'open' and credit is given for different answers provided they are believable interpretations of the text.

A better answer would think more deeply about why the young woman wants to know her future. It would mention the woman's husband and the fact that she relied on him to cancel her appointment with Mr Fudge. She seems to have a weaker personality than either her mother or her husband. She may feel helpless in her life and, as a passive person, wants to know what the future will do to her, rather than trying to create a future for herself. Alternatively, she may be unhappy and is looking for a comforting view of the future.

Either of these explanations would lift the answer into Level 6. To mention both of them as possibilities would achieve Level 7.

ANSWERS AND EXAMINER'S COMMENTS

Paper 1: Section A Narrative

Sample student's answer: 2

1. I think that Mr Fudge is no more genuine than Oberon. He may *seem* convincing, but I do not believe he can actually read the future, since he did not do so for the young woman.

There are a lot of differences between Oberon and Mr Adam Fudge. Oberon speaks with 'an edge of cockney in his voice' which suggests that he is nothing more than an average everyday person out to make some money. He speaks 'wearily' as if he is tired and bored, and he goes on about people wasting his time. He speaks in a slangy way with words like 'love' and 'yeah', which doesn't sound professional or mysterious.

Oberon is a complete 'con' in the way he treats the young woman. He tells her to smear her hands with red paint and, when she phones him, says he remembers them because they were red! He blames the post for the first reading going astray, then blames the woman, saying the second set of prints were different.

I think Oberon is a straightforward 'con artist'. He just keeps the money and probably tears up the handprints, reckoning that people are too stupid or vulnerable to pursue him. When the young woman contacts him again, he still doesn't send a reading. He isn't dedicated to being a 'psychic clairvoyant', as Mr Fudge is to being a 'sensitive'. Oberon's advertisement offers a lot of different kinds of fortune telling, which probably means he isn't any good at any of them. He also offers 'party bookings' which suggests that he is an entertainer really.

Mr Fudge's advert runs to 17 lines (which must be expensive) and is 'aimed only at those of a serious disposition'. He seems to be a genuine fortune teller at first, with his 'white Indian wrap and slip-slops', the 'clouds of Indian Rose' incense and the 'occasional musical tinkling'. This sets up the atmosphere of a traditional fortune teller. He speaks politely to his clients, 'It is as you wish. Have you decided?' He tells them that 'I have had this gift since I was a small boy in India' and 'Appointments with me are rare'.

This is impressive but then some things are doubtful. He is a young man and fortune tellers are usually older. Perhaps he has a beard to make him look older. He is blond and Indians are never blond, although he could have grown up in India as the child of European parents. He is also willing to make extra money by offering a double sitting, which seems greedy. And if appointments with him are rare, how come he could offer another appointment the next day?

On the other hand, he is upset by the mother not believing in him. If he was a 'con artist' like Oberon, he could just pretend to tell their fortunes, or he could send the mother to wait in the car and make up a fortune for the daughter. But he gets angry because of the mother's hostility and refuses to sit for them, even though he loses £25 or £40.

I can't decide whether Mr Fudge is as dishonest as Oberon. He looks a fake, but he didn't make some easy money by lying to the woman and her mother. At least he's not out to make 'a fast buck' like Oberon.

The young woman learns nothing about her future except 'never to go back to mediums or palm readers'.

2. The young woman's relationship with her mother seemed quite rocky, —'I'm only here because I have this crazy daught'! — she was only there because her daughter was, and she held some resentment towards her daughter for it.

Her relationship with her husband seems to be a 'big brother' type, since she made him cancel the appointment for her. With rocky relationships like this, she began to look to her future for some comfort.

155

ANSWERS AND EXAMINER'S COMMENTS

Paper 1: Section A Narrative

How successful is this answer?

Q1 *Be aware of what the writer is trying to achieve*

The whole answer relates to the question of the two fortune tellers' honesty. In the text, the writer does not actually say that they are dishonest. She simply retells what happened when she consulted them and leaves the readers to make up their own mind about whether either of them were genuine.

The answer describes Oberon's way of speaking and his treatment of the young woman, then expresses an overall opinion of him: 'I think Oberon is a straightforward "con artist". He just keeps the money and probably tears up the handprints, reckoning people are too stupid or vulnerable to pursue him' [lines 12–13]. This is a convincing interpretation which is supported by perceptive comments on his advertisement [lines 15–17].

The answer deals fully with Mr Fudge, mentioning first all the reasons why 'he seems to be a genuine fortune teller at first' [line 19], then many of the doubts that the writer raises in our minds [lines 24–29]. The answer then deals with the two possible interpretations of Mr Fudge's refusal to tell the woman's fortune [lines 30–33] and comes to the conclusion that it is impossible to decide whether Mr Fudge is as dishonest as Oberon: 'He looks a fake, but he didn't make some easy money by lying to the woman and her mother.'

This is a fair conclusion and could well reflect the writer's own uncertainty about Mr Fudge. Unfortunately this conclusion does not quite fit together with the first paragraph of the answer. Evidently the student changed her mind a little as she wrote the answer.

Comment on the writer's use of words and phrases

The answer selects a good range of quotations and references and, in almost every case, their significance is briefly explained.

Examiner's comments

Comment on the writer's technique
Say how successful you think the writer has been

The whole answer shows an awareness of the writer's technique, but it is not discussed directly. The text is written in a clear journalistic style and is not intended to create any strong feelings in the reader. Rather, it presents us with two character sketches on which we are asked to make up our own minds. The question focuses on interpretation of character, not on technique or success in creating a particular effect, so these criteria are not very relevant on this occasion.

Level: the answer clearly achieves Level 7.

How could you do better?

Q1 The answer is already full and convincing. It could be further improved (and so achieve Above Level 7) if the student came to a decision, with a supporting reason, about whether Mr Fudge was more genuine than Oberon. It could be argued that Mr Fudge is a serious 'con man'. He is probably trying to make a living out of future telling and needs people to believe that he is absolutely serious so that he has lots of clients. His success depends on convincing his clients that he is genuine and he would rather not take the risk of sitting for someone (in this case, the mother) who would dismiss what he said as nonsense.

ANSWERS AND EXAMINER'S COMMENTS

**Paper 1: Section A
Narrative**

How successful is this answer?

Q2 The woman's relationship with her mother is seen as uneasy and stressful ('rocky'). The answer points out that the mother resents having to accompany her daughter and quotes the dismissive sentence which expresses this: 'I'm only here because I have this crazy daughter'. The answer also notes that she seems to be under her husband's influence – he is described as 'big brother'. It ends with the perceptive suggestion that 'With rocky relationships like this, she began to look to her future for some comfort'.

Level: the slightly fuller account of the relationship with her mother, together with a perceptive comment about the husband and a plausible reason for looking to the future, lift this answer to Level 6.

How could you do better?

Q2 A further point, which would lift the answer to Level 7, is that (as mentioned under *How could you do better? Q2* on page 154) the young woman seems to have a weaker personality than either her mother or her husband. She may feel helpless in her life and, as a passive person, wants to know what the future will do to her, rather than trying to create a future for herself.

Chapter 25

ANSWERS AND EXAMINER'S COMMENTS

Paper 1: Section B Media

Sample student's answer: 1

The author (Sally Weale) takes a lot of opinions from different people. I think she feels as the British Medical Association does – the decision to allow women into the ring provides "equal opportunities for eye and brain damage".

She is keen to point out that "men decide for women... that's just plain sexist". She has almost a whole column on men deciding what women can and can't do in sport; for example, women "were banned from running further than 200m in Olympic events up to 1960".

Sally is showing the brutality of the sport... I would even say she is announcing that she doesn't like the sport.

I think that over all Sally Weale doesn't like boxing as a sport, dislikes girls boxing but hates most of all the sexism that surrounds women and sports.

ANSWERS AND EXAMINER'S COMMENTS

Paper 1: Section B Media

Examiner's comments

How successful is this answer?

Be able to locate ideas and information in the text
This is a short answer, but it locates several important points:

- the view of the British Medical Association
- the writer's complaint about sexism
- the treatment of women in the Olympics.

Be aware of the purpose of the text
Show an overall understanding of the text
The answer shows clear understanding of the writer's purpose and the overall effect of the article. It points out that the writer 'feels as the British Medical Association does' that to allow women's boxing is to provide 'equal opportunities for eye and brain damage'.

The final paragraph gives a brief but accurate description of the writer's opinion, that she dislikes boxing including girls' boxing, 'but hates most of all the sexism that surrounds women and sports'.

Note the effect of some words and phrases
The answer does not do this.

Note the effect of features like layout
This was not asked for in the question or the prompts.

Level: this answer just achieves Level 5.

How could you do better?

Be able to locate ideas and information in the text
The answer does not mention the views of the newspapers and boxers that the article quotes. It mentions women Olympic runners being limited to 200 metres, but not the reason for this. And it does not mention the writer's view that *boys* should not go in for boxing. You need to deal with each of these points.

Note the effect of some words and phrases
The headlines in the *Daily Mail* and the *Mirror* [first paragraph] suggest that the girls' boxing match is sickening ('Who has the stomach for this fight?') and mad. In the third paragraph the journalist Ian Wooldridge says that, 'In my lifetime of sports writing . . . I have never encountered a sports event as degrading as this', which is a powerful attack on it. His description of the two schoolgirls 'belting the daylights out of one another for the entertainment of yobbos in a nightclub' takes the attack further. It is hard to disagree with him until you realise that this is what male boxers do also.

Wooldridge goes on to say that girls should be at home 'swotting up their geography'. The writer of the article obviously feels that this is a sexist attitude, like the comments of Howard Winstone: 'I am very glad that my daughters are more interested in the opposite sex and cooking and cleaning, rather than into boxing' [paragraph 10] and by Henry Cooper: 'Women are made for loving and not hitting' [paragraph 11]. The writer's last comment – 'Pass me the gloves, Henry' – suggest that she is so angry that she pretends to want to punch Henry Cooper!

The fourth prompt asks how the last sentence of the article links with the last two paragraphs and with the title. You need to mention that 'Pass me the gloves, Henry' is angry but not really serious. Sally Weale doesn't really want to punch Henry Cooper. The last sentence suggests that women punching people is as silly as male boxers saying they shouldn't be allowed to box.

Note the effect of features like layout
A media question might ask you to comment on layout. If it did in this case, you would need to comment on the headline (big and attention-grabbing) and on the photos of the two 13 year old girls. They wear headguards (as shown in one of the photos), but they have no other protection. They also wear shirts and singlets like male boxers and punch each other with leather gloves. This makes them look serious about boxing but also vulnerable.

159

ANSWERS AND EXAMINER'S COMMENTS

Paper 1: Section B
Media

Sample student's answer: 2

The writer, Sally Weale, obviously thinks that if men are allowed to take part in boxing, then so should women. She has taken a lot of quotes from other writers and former boxers who all think it would be wrong for "two schoolgirls to be belting the daylights out of one another for the entertainment of yobbos in a nightclub." (Ian Wooldridge, Daily Mail)

● The writer includes what the British Medical Association says about it. They say that to allow women into the ring provides "equal opportunities for eye and brain damage." So they think boxing is just as dangerous for men and women.

She thinks that it has taken too long for men to realise that women also want to compete in sports. Such as boxing. She was disgusted that it had taken until 1984 for women to be able to run in the Olympic marathon and that in 1928, after the first female 800 metre race, that women would not be allowed to compete in races over 200 metres until 1960.

● Former heavyweight Henry Cooper said; "Women are made differently from men. Their entire body structure is not like a man's. Women are made for loving and not hitting." She was obviously angry at the last comment from Henry Cooper, saying: "Pass me the gloves, Henry." She is pretending she would like to punch him for being sexist and this is how the last sentence links with the title. Punching people isn't "a blow for equality."

The writer says, "I wouldn't want any daughter of mine to take up the sport, but neither would I want any son of mine to go in the ring." Really she doesn't like the idea of boxing, but if men can do it, so can women. That is what I think her attitude is.

ANSWERS AND EXAMINER'S COMMENTS

Paper 1: Section B Media

Examiner's comments

How successful is this answer?

Be able to locate ideas and information in the text
This answer follows the prompts printed under the question and locates most of the necessary information, though not in the same order as the prompts. The answer deals with the restrictions on women's Olympic events first, then turns to the writers and boxers quoted, the BMA and the effect of the photos. This is perfectly acceptable; the prompts can be used in any order.

Show an overall understanding of the text
Be aware of what the writer is trying to achieve
The answer shows a convincing understanding of the writer's purpose. The first sentence accurately summarises Sally Weale's opinion and this is returned to and expanded in the last paragraph which is a good brief summary.

Comment on the writer's use of some words or phrases
The answer quotes Ian Wooldridge, but does not comment on his views. It does not quote Howard Winstone. However, it quotes Henry Cooper and comments, 'She (the writer) was obviously outraged and insulted by the last comment of Henry Cooper, saying "Pass me the gloves, Henry"'. The answer has grasped that the writer is enraged by such sexist remarks that she is pretending she would like to punch Henry Cooper. The link between this and the title is then briefly explained.

Comment on the effect of layout, etc.
The question does not require this.

Level: this answer achieves a strong Level 6.

How could you do better?

Comment on the writer's technique
For Level 7, you would need to comment on some of the ways in which the writer organises and sets out her case. You should comment on as many of these as possible:

- The writer doesn't disagree with Ian Wooldridge's disgust at the idea of two schoolgirls 'belting the daylights out of one another for the entertainment of yobbos in a nightclub'. Instead, she answers it by saying that boys shouldn't box either and quoting the BMA that women's boxing provides 'equal opportunities for eye and brain damage'.
- The writer's central point is that 'to have men decide for women that we really don't want to mess up our hair and get involved in such a nasty, aggressive business is . . . just plain sexist' [paragraph 7]. Her irritation is shown through sarcasm, pretending that men think women don't really want to box in case they mess up their hair!
- The writer's outrage at women not being allowed to compete in the marathon is shown by the repetition of 1984 in italics with an exclamation mark [paragraph 8].
- This outrage is continued in a more mocking way as the writer gives the ridiculous reasons why women were not allowed to compete in long distance events: 'their wombs would fall out' [paragraph 8], 'women weren't really made for such feats of endurance' and 'they would "become old too soon"' [paragraph 9].
- The sexist comment by Ian Wooldridge ('They should be at home "swotting up their geography"') is taken up at the end of the article by similar comments from Howard Winstone and Henry Cooper. The writer suggests her anger by ironically calling for boxing gloves.

Say how successful you think the writer has been
This is a matter for your own opinion. Has Sally Weale persuaded you that sexism in sport is worse for women than being allowed to box? *Remember: you are asked for your opinion on the article,* **not** *for your own opinion of women's boxing.*

161

Chapter 26

Paper 1: Section C Writing

ANSWERS AND EXAMINER'S COMMENTS

Topic A

Sample student's answer: 1

1 It was a cold, blistering winters day in Keswick and as Bruce woke he was confronted with the nights remains, homework he hadn't finished,
5 morsels of pizza and in the middle of the floor his dog, Rover.

  Bruce rose to find the house empty it was Sunday and his dad was at work, he realised promptly that he had overslept and Rover hadn't been
10 out since yesterday afternoon. Bruce quickly dressed himself in anything he could find, skipped breakfast and headed for the door, Rover
15 trailing behind.

  As they approach the lake Bruce let Rover off the lead to run in the field as the sheep had been taken in. Bruce sat down
20 and got out his end of year report he had in his jacket pocket, he just started when he heard an overwhelming, crack!

  As he turned he saw Rover's
25 head and paws scrambeling on the ice he had fell threw and was only just hanging on.

  Bruce had to think quickly he had

162

heard reports of stories on the news about dog owners dying in cold water in an atempt to save there pet. But however is adrenaline took over and he found himself sprinting towards the lakeside shouting "Rover, hang on boy, I'm coming".

As he caregully skid across the ice Rover seemed to sink even more, as he aproached the hole and Rover he steaded himself and in several moves he had Rover by the collar.

He had got Rover out but the extra weight of his dog started to crack the ice beneath him, all he could do is walk steadely across back to the field and hope for the best.

At last he reached the edge of the lake, and with one final leap he and Rover were safe. But Bruce knew that Rover wasn't safe yet he still was freezing cold and he could die before he got to the vet, Bruce rapped him in his jacket which suprisingly remained dry and ran to the vet whispering words of comfort in Rovers ear.

ANSWERS AND EXAMINER'S COMMENTS

Paper 1: Section C Writing

How successful is this answer?

Think of a story that will interest your readers
This is an action story in which Bruce saves his dog from drowning in an icy lake. Rescue stories always interest readers because we want to find out if the person (or animal, as in this case) is saved. The story is realistic and fairly believable.

Organise the story to keep your readers interested
The story is written with a good sense of pace. Each paragraph moves the story on: in the first, Bruce wakes up; in the second, he dresses and takes Rover out; by the end of the third, he hears the ice crack; and so on. There are no unnecessary details.

Write it in an interesting way
Most of the story is written in a simple, direct style, but there are some imaginative touches on the first page: the description of Bruce waking up to be 'confronted with the nights remains, homework he hadn't finished, morsols of pizza and in the middle of the floor his dog, Rover' [lines 3–6]; the realistic point that Rover could be let off the lead 'as the sheep had been taken in' [lines 18/19]; and the fact that Bruce doesn't watch the dog (he reads his school report!) so that the 'overwhelming crack!' as the ice gives way [line 23] comes as a shock.

In one way, the story is interestingly structured. It is set in Keswick, a town near Derwentwater in the Lake District, on a cold winter's day, so it is not surprising that there is ice on the lake even though this is not stated before Rover falls through it.

Use some interesting words or phrases
The story uses some interesting words such as 'confronted' [line 3], 'trailing' [line 15 – more descriptive than 'walking'], 'overwhelming' [line 23], 'sprinting' [line 33 – more descriptive than 'running'] and 'steadied himself' [line 39]. On the other hand, 'blistering' [line 1] is probably misused as it is normally used for great *heat*. The end of the story – 'whispering words of comfort in Rover's ear' – leads it to a pleasant, warm conclusion.

Include conversation and description
The story does not do this.

Keep your readers' interest right to the end
The readers' interest is kept to the end by the risk of the ice cracking and both boy and dog falling through it.

Examiner's comments

However, the story does not relate very closely to Topic A. The 'difficult decision' is supposed to be whether or not Bruce should risk his own life to save his dog's. This is dealt with very briefly at lines 28–31, then forgotten as Bruce's 'adrenaline took over'.

Writing correctly
Sentence structure: Most of the sentences are straightforward, but the story avoids the monotony of 'and then . . . and then' by beginning some sentences with 'As he . . .', 'All he could do was . . .' and 'At last . . .' which create variety. The first paragraph consists of a single sentence which is complex although not properly punctuated.

Punctuation: This is erratic. Some sentences have both capital letter and full stop, but many do not. On the other hand, commas are often used correctly within sentences and speech marks are correctly used [lines 34/35], as is the exclamation mark in line 23. There should be a colon after 'remains' in line 4 to introduce a list.

Paragraphing: The paragraphs are well judged, each taking the story on the next important event.

Spelling: This is the weakest aspect of the answer. Several common words are misspelt, such as *morsols* (morsels), *skipted* (skipped), *feild* [field] and *srambeling* [scrambling]. Slips like 'he had fell threw' [line 26] and 'he carefully skid across the ice' [line 36] add to the sense of poor control.

Handwriting: Although not very neat, this is legible and fluent.

Level: this is essentially a strong Level 5 answer which is pulled down by lack of focus on the topic, and erratic spelling and punctuation, so that it just achieves Level 5.

How could you do better?

Write it in an interesting way
At present, the rescue is not very interesting to read. Essentially the boy runs across the ice, hauls the dog out and carries it back to the shore. The story would be more interesting, *and would focus better on the topic*, if Bruce hesitated before going to save the dog. He could remember in more detail a newspaper account of an owner being drowned trying to save their dog and this could affect him, making him hesitate. His heart could pound and perhaps he could feel sick, until Rover's desperate barks make him take action.

Suspense would be further increased if Bruce moved cautiously out over the ice, while it creaks ominously under him. You could describe his mixed feelings of fear and determination as he edges nearer and nearer Rover until he can grab him.

Include conversation and description
Bruce could talk to himself a few times as he moves out across the ice ('Don't let it break. Please God don't let it break!') and he could call to the dog once or twice more. This would add to the drama and suspense.

A brief description of the empty white misty expanse of ice would emphasise the boy's isolation – there is no-one around to help him.

Spelling and punctuation
These need improving, especially punctuation at the beginning and end of sentences. If possible, *you should read the story through aloud in your head*. If this is done, the need for full stops at the ends of sentences will tend to show up, as will mistakes like 'he carefully skid across the ice'.

ANSWERS AND EXAMINER'S COMMENTS

Paper 1: Section C Writing

Sample student's answer: 2

1   Simone let out an exasperated sigh and went over the events of last night in her head. She knew what she had seen. In the night club on Saturday, she saw Kevin as he casually dropped
5   the contaminated Ecstasy tablet in Kate's can of beer. He did not know she had seen him do it. Now Kate was lying in a hospital. Would Kate ever get out of the coma? Would she live to see her 21st birthday next week?
10 Simone was wondering as she was lying down in her room if she should tell anyone what she saw. Kevin was her boyfriend. How could she tell on her own boyfriend? After all he had been through a lot lately. His father had died in a car accident and
15 how would his mother cope with Kevin facing a jail sentence? The image of poor Kate lying there, white as a ghost with tube attaching her to a life support machine, drifted into Simone's mind. What was she going to do?
20 Simone lifted herself off her bed and walked to the kitchen downstairs to help herself to a glass of cool water. She tucked a strand of her uncombed brown hair behind her ear and sat on a kitchen stool. In the corner of her eye she
25 could see the telephone. It was almost as if it were saying to her, "Phone the police. Think of Kate. An innocent girl in hospital. Almost dead." She moved closer to the telephone and placed a shaking hand on the receiver. She forced her hand
30 to pick it up and lift it up to her ear. She quickly put it down with a hand slam. No, she could not tell the police it was Kevin. She had to be loyal to her own boyfriend. After all, Kate would

probably pull through ... wouldn't she?
    She put her head in her arms and cried. Should she, shouldn't she, should she ...? She wished she had not seen what she had. Then she would not have to face this terrible decision. She would either have to betray her long-term boyfriend or betray a friend. An innocent victim of drug abuse. Kate did not deserve to die. A happy, lively and pretty young girl. She had everything going for her. And now this. On the other hand, what about Kevin's mother? Hadn't she been through enough already? Still, Kevin did deserve going to prison. Kate might die any moment now.
    Simone wiped a tear out of her eye and played with a button on her nightshirt. She held her breath, got out of the chair and walked over to the telephone. She knew what she had to do and this time she was going to do it.

ANSWERS AND EXAMINER'S COMMENTS

Paper 1: Section C Writing

How successful is this answer?

Think of a story that will interest your readers
Organise it to keep your readers interested

This is a powerfully dramatic story which (unlike the previous one) focuses directly on a difficult decision: should Simone tell the police about Kevin putting a contaminated ecstasy tablet in Kate's drink? The readers want to know what decision Simone will make and the story keeps our interest by not revealing this until the very end.

The story is carefully planned to make the decision difficult for Simone and therefore keep the readers' interest. Kate is in a coma and may die. Kevin is not only Simone's boyfriend; his father has died in an accident and Simone is worried about how his mother will cope with her son being in jail.

Write it to keep your readers' interest right to the end

After the bare events have been set out in lines 1–6, the story moves between Simone's thoughts and her actions. Her thoughts are often written as questions: 'Would Kate ever get out of the coma?' [lines 7/8], 'How could she tell on her own boyfriend?' [lines 12/13]. These questions are a good way of expressing Simone's uncertainty and her endless self-questioning.

Her actions create a simple but dramatic storyline. After running over the events in her head, Simone gets up and goes to the kitchen for a glass of water. There she sees the telephone 'in the corner of her eye'. She goes slowly to it and picks up the receiver, but then slams it down. After thinking some more and weeping, she decides to make the phone call. This storyline is completely believable and also full of suspense.

Use interesting words and phrases
Include conversation and description

Most of the story is written in simple direct language. This style is varied occasionally with brief descriptions: of Kate 'white as a ghost with tube attaching her to a life support machine' [lines 17/18] and of Simone's absent-minded actions as she tries to make her decision – 'She tucked a strand of her uncombed brown hair behind her ear' [lines 22/23] and 'played with a button on her nightshirt' [line 49].

Examiner's comments

There is good dramatic description of her trying to make the first phone call [lines 28–31]. Most dramatic of all is her feeling that the phone is speaking to her: 'Phone the police. Think of Kate. An innocent girl in hospital. Almost dead.' [lines 26/27] The short phrases add to the sense of drama.

Create characters that your readers believe in and feel for

Simone's character comes across to us strongly and we feel for her in her predicament. Unfortunately the characters of Kevin and Kate are not so well created. We know nothing about Kevin except that he is Simone's long-term boyfriend and has lost his father. We are told nothing of her feelings for him before the ecstasy incident. Similarly, Kate is a friend, but we are told nothing about her relationship with Simone. The comments about her – 'An innocent victim of drug abuse . . . A happy, lively and pretty young girl' [lines 40–42] – are very vague.

Writing correctly

The story has a variety of sentence structures, both simple and more complex. Spelling and punctuation are correct. Paragraphing is appropriate. Handwriting is clear and legible.

Level: this answer achieves mid Level 6.

How could you do better?

Create characters that your readers believe in and feel for

The story would be even more successful if the characters of Kevin and Kate, and Simone's earlier feelings about them, were expressed more fully. This could be done by Simone remembering happier times, in contrast with her present misery. She could remember when she started going out with Kevin, why she liked him and an occasion when she was particularly happy with him. She could also remember when she got to know Kate and a happy occasion when they did something or went somewhere together. These memories should include a little conversation to help bring them to life.

ANSWERS AND EXAMINER'S COMMENTS

Paper 1: Section C Writing

These memories could then be contrasted with the recent memory of Kate collapsing at the night club, perhaps struggling to breathe, and the ambulance arriving.

Use words and phrases for particular effects

The highest skill in writing stories is the ability to create pictures and feelings in the reader's mind. You can do this by creating images that have this effect. When Simone visualises Kate lying in the hospital, she could get a lump in her throat. You could emphasise the choking feeling she experiences with something like 'there was a lump in her throat big enough to dam a river'.

People sometimes drum their fingers when they are nervous. You could use this: 'Simone kept drumming her fingers on the kitchen table; it was a way of stopping her having to use them to phone.' Then you could build up the tension further: 'It felt like her fingers were tapping on the inside of her skull. She had to stop.'

You could increase the sense of drama further by trying an extended image: 'Thoughts <u>poured</u> through Simone's head like a savage rushing <u>waterfall</u>. She pulled out a main thought from the <u>flood</u>: did she think more of Kevin than Kate?'

It is by working on your language skills in this way that you will come to write finished pieces of narrative in which every word counts towards the overall effect.

ANSWERS AND EXAMINER'S COMMENTS
Paper 1: Section C Writing

Topic B

Sample student's answer: 1

1. There are many ways of telling the future. Several of these ways are from the aid of tarot cards, palm reading, crystal ball gazing, star signs and in some forms from a seance. All of which, if they come true, is from coincedence.

5. Tarot cards are a set of cards which are dealt out and are supposed to be personal.

Palm reading and crystal ball gazing is very popular. It is performed mainly by gypsies at fairs. Each person has a different palm so everyone has a different future to be told.

10. The most popular form of fortune telling is looking at the star signs. Star signs are found in virtually every newspaper and magazine. There are also many star sign readers such as Mystic Meg.

There are also many reasons for why people want to
15. find out the future.

Some are to make decisions such as whether or not to make a business venture. Another reason is because they wonder what will happen to themselves.

I don't see how any of the ways of 'telling the future'
20. could work.

Tarot cards. How could a set of cards know a person's future? They are just peices of cardboard or plastic with pictures on them.

Palm reading. The lines on the palm come from how the
25. foetus holds its hands in the womb. What has this got to do with a person's future?

Crystal ball gazing. The gypsy can say anything and no-one knows if it's true.

Star signs. All the newspapers and magazines say
30. different things for the same star sign, so how do we know which is true?

I don't think the future is able to be found out about because it hasn't happened yet. You can plan your future how you want it to be but you cannot take it for
35. granted.

ANSWERS AND EXAMINER'S COMMENTS

Paper 1: Section C Writing

Examiner's comments

How successful is this answer?

Organise your ideas in a sensible way

The answer is set out in quite a sensible way. It lists five methods of future telling, says a little about four of them and gives two reasons why people want to know the future. It then gives reasons why these methods cannot work and ends with a general opinion about fortune telling.

Interest and convince your readers
Develop some of your ideas more fully

The first part of the answer is not very interesting or convincing. The descriptions of the methods of fortune telling are brief and very general. To say that tarot cards 'are dealt out and are supposed to be personal' [lines 5/6] tells us very little about them.

The answer becomes more convincing towards the end, when the student criticises the various methods of fortune telling. The student makes some good points such as that tarot cards are 'just pieces of cardboard or plastic with pictures on them' [lines 22/23] and that the lines on the palm are formed in the womb. Here, the student's ideas are developed a little more fully.

Write in a clear and interesting way
Use a more formal style

The style of writing is clear, though not very interesting. Most of the answer is written in a reasonably formal style, setting out the facts as the student sees them. Informal language appears towards the end with the student's opinions ('I don't see . . .'; 'I don't think . . .') and with the rhetorical questions, such as 'What has this got to do with a person's future?'

Give examples to support your case

The answer does not do this.

Write correctly

The answer is grammatically correct apart from 'Palm reading and crystal ball gazing is very popular' [line 7]. It is correctly spelt apart from *coincedence* (coincidence) [line 4] and *peices* (pieces) [line 22] and is accurately punctuated. The paragraphing is less confident, however, and becomes little more than a list at lines 21–31.

Level: this answer just achieves Level 5.

How could you do better?

Organise your ideas in a sensible way

It would be better to deal with each of the methods of fortune telling fully before moving on to the next. For example, you could explain what tarot cards are, then say why you think they can or cannot tell the future.

Interest and convince your readers
Develop some of your ideas more fully

Your readers will be particularly interested in your views on a range of fortune-telling methods, so you should choose several different methods and discuss them in some detail. For example, if you choose star signs (the zodiac), you could mention that there are 12 signs, each named after a constellation; that this method of future telling is very old; and that proper horoscopes are worked out from the position of the stars and planets when a person is born. The horoscopes published in newspapers and magazines are just for entertainment, but you should give your opinion on whether a proper birth horoscope could tell the person's future. You should also try to discuss the difficult question of whether the future is fixed (and can therefore be foretold) or whether it changes (and we can therefore influence it).

Write in a clear and interesting way
Use a more formal style

The answer needs little improvement in this respect, but try to avoid using rhetorical questions; for example, 'How could a set of cards know a person's future?' [lines 21/22]. Instead of asking a question, give the answer ('In my opinion, a set of cards cannot know a person's future'). Rhetorical questions are more suited to personal persuasion, like a speech, rather than a discussion essay.

Give examples to support your case

The answer would be strengthened with one or two examples of actual fortune telling, of people who have had their future told. You should choose examples that support your case. If you believe that fortune telling is possible, give examples of successful telling of a person's future. If you do not, give examples where fortune telling failed.

Write correctly

Only the paragraphing needs improvement. If each method of fortune telling were discussed in one paragraph, this would give the essay shape.

ANSWERS AND EXAMINER'S COMMENTS

Paper 1: Section C Writing

Sample student's answer: 2

Many people nowadays say that they do not believe in fortune telling. But still every newspaper and every magazine publishes columns of horoscopes, Mystic Meg claims a corner in the National Lottery Programme and palm reading seems to be more popular than ever before. So, can one really find out about one's future?

I think that it is impossible to predict one's future. From the person's past and personality, the path they will walk can often be guessed. But to tell someone's future by knowing only their birthday or lines on their palm is, I believe, impossible. A person's palm can probably show how hard a life the person has been living by their degree of roughness and how healthy a life the person is going to lead by their complexion, but other than that it is difficult to believe that a palm could be read into the whole future of a human being. Horoscopes tell the future by the movement of planets which I also think is unreliable as unless one of those planets is going to collide with Earth and cause the 'end of the world' for humans, the movement of planets does not affect our lives at all. Reading tea leaves is another method of telling the future and another that I cannot trust. The dispersion of tea leaves after one has drunk the tea could maybe show how a person drinks their tea and therefore maybe the person's character, but I cannot believe that anything more than that could be learnt from this method of fortune-telling.

The future has to be set out in order for it to be foreseen, but I do not like to think that it is so. We make decisions leading to our future everyday and many things happen by sheer chance. Therefore I do not believe that our future is fixed for fortune-tellers to tell. It would be very sad indeed if the big chances of happiness in life, such as health, love and success in career, were unchangeable and one was not able to be happy in life even if one tried just because he/she was born to be so.

People have always wanted to know about their future and looked towards the supernatural for their satisfaction. The foundation of this interest in future happenings has been curiosity in their future, anxiety about their future and sometimes confusion when decision making. Horoscopes in magazines serve as mere entertainment, while more serious consultations with fortune-tellers can help people who seek advice about life's problems.

In my case, the reason for wanting to know about my future was curiosity about what I could learn. I had my fortune told by a fortune-telling machine. I typed in my birth date and the machine produced a piece of A4 paper with my fortune written on it. It told my health, love, success and financial prospects in life. For me, it was just fun and I can hardly remember what its contents were, but I recall being rather disappointed at their vagueness.

Fortune-telling can be fun, but I believe it is impossible to rely on it as its methods cannot be trusted and the future is not fixed for it to be read.

ANSWERS AND EXAMINER'S COMMENTS

Paper 1: Section C Writing

Examiner's comments

How successful is this answer?

Organise your ideas in a sensible way
Interest and convince your readers

The answer is well organised. After an introductory paragraph, three methods of fortune telling are discussed: palm reading, horoscopes and reading tea leaves. In each case, the student explains why he or she believes they do not work. The student goes on to explain a personal view that the future cannot be foretold, then mentions several reasons why people want to know their future. A useful distinction is drawn between horoscopes in magazines which are 'entertainment' and 'more serious consultations with fortune tellers' who can give advice about life's problems. The student ends with a personal example of fortune-telling entertainment and a summarising paragraph.

The answer is interesting all the way through. It covers various aspects of fortune telling and, by its careful and serious approach, gives a convincing account of the student's viewpoint.

Develop your ideas more fully

Each of the three fortune-telling methods is criticised on practical grounds. For example, a person's palms can show 'how hard a life the person has been living by their degree of roughness' and how healthy the person is 'by their complexion' [lines 14–17], but that is all. Similarly, the answer not only points out that 'the future has to be set out for it to be foreseen', but also comments how sad it would be if one could not change one's future [lines 33–44]. In each case, a simple idea is developed in an interesting way.

Give examples to support your case

The example of the fortune-telling machine is well chosen to mock the idea of telling the future. From a person's birth date, a computer should be able to calculate a proper horoscope. But we know that fortune-telling machines in amusement arcades and fairgrounds are not properly programmed computers. They are just for entertainment. As the student comments, 'it was just fun'.

Use a formal impersonal style
Deliberately use a variety of sentences and range of language to create particular effects in your writing

Most of the answer is written in a formal impersonal style. Even when the student gives a personal opinion, using 'I', it is expressed formally. 'I think that it is impossible to predict one's future' [lines 8/9] is entirely formal, while 'I don't think anyone can tell their future' would be informal. The frequent use of 'one' instead of 'you' is a sure sign of a formal style.

The language used is correct throughout and perhaps a little 'heavy'. However, it does not seek to create any particular effects. The one unusual touch is the word 'dispersion' [line 27] which is a more scientific word for spreading out than 'dispersal' and is perhaps more appropriate to tea leaves.

Write correctly

The answer is correct in grammar, spelling and punctuation. It would be slightly improved if the long second paragraph were divided into three – one for each of the three methods of fortune telling.

Level: this answer achieves mid Level 7.

How could you do better?

Some more methods of fortune telling could be discussed and further examples of fortune-telling experiences could be given. However, the best way of achieving a higher mark would be to discuss the fact that many people seem to go to fortune tellers even though they know logically that the future cannot be foretold. This discussion would build on the comment that 'more serious consultations with fortune tellers can help people who seek advice about life's problems' [lines 52–54].

Perhaps some people do not expect to be told their actual future – that they will get married in two years' time or win a lot of money before they are 30. Rather, they want to find out about their personality and be told what they could achieve if they try hard or avoid certain influences. Perhaps the genuine fortune tellers are like advisers or counsellors. They know no more about the future than anyone else, but they are quick to understand people's personalities and can help to calm their anxieties by advising on how to face the future.

A discussion along these lines would raise the answer to a strong Level 7 or Above Level 7.

Topic C

Sample student's answer: 1

ANSWERS AND EXAMINER'S COMMENTS

Paper 1: Section C Writing

1 Amelia was waiting for Sainsbury to open. She loved going to Sainsburys. She would often dream of the shelves piled high with sweets, the huge cake counter with white iced buns with cherries on top, but
5 best of all which came into all her dreams was the giant chest freezers filled with ice cream. Pink ice cream, brown ice cream, ice cream with bits in, ice cream with nuts in and huge tubs of multicoloured ice-cream.
10 Amelia had finished her morning job as a lollipop lady seeing the children across the road to school For her morning snack she always went to the same place. She got there early and waited outside the shop until the doors opened.
15 At ten o'clock she burst through the doors and into the empty supermarket. She ran as fast as her legs could take her, with her heart pounding and her hair flying. When Amelia finally reached the ice cream section, she grabbed
20 the ice cream she wanted and started to make her way to the checkout.
   Amelia had not got half way to the checkout before she turned and ran all the way back again and swapped the Wallis strawberry and vanilla swirl
25 for the Sainsbury's version. She knew the Wallis ice cream tasted better, but it was expensive and if she saved some money she could have more tomorrow. She got to the checkout puffing and panting. She paid for the ice cream and squeezed through the checkout
30 with difficulty. Soon she was walking down the streets eating her ice cream. It was lovely.
   "Best of all," she said to herself, "Its fat free. I'm just born to be big. Ice cream has got nothing to do with it."

175

ANSWERS AND EXAMINER'S COMMENTS

Paper 1: Section C Writing

Examiner's comments

How successful is this answer?

Think of a story that will interest your readers
This story takes the idea of self-deception and describes an adult who is obsessed with eating ice cream, but believes it does not affect her size. Obsessions are always interesting to read about, though they are often difficult to write about convincingly. In fact, the story is realistic and believable.

Organise the story to keep your readers interested
The story is written with a good sense of pace. Each paragraph moves the story on. The first paragraph establishes Amelia's fascination with ice cream and the others tell her story clearly. There are no unnecessary details.

Write it in an interesting way
The story starts interestingly: the idea of someone liking a supermarket so much that she is waiting for it to open is unusual. The rest of the first paragraph describes Amelia's dreams of sweet food, building up to 'the giant chest freezers filled with ice cream' which 'came into all her dreams' [lines 5/6]. The next sentence consists entirely of types of ice cream. A sense of dream-like obsession is created very effectively.

The obsession is continued in the next two paragraphs. Amelia goes to the supermarket every day, she arrives early, she runs to the ice cream section and she changes an expensive ice cream for a cheaper one so that she can have more tomorrow. All this adds to the sense of obsession.

The fact that she is overweight is not revealed until the last paragraph: she 'squeezed through the checkout with difficulty' [lines 29–30]. It is sometimes a very good idea to reveal an important fact not at the beginning of the story but later on, when it will surprise the reader more. This is what happens here. The fact of Amelia's size leads directly on to her self-deception.

Use some interesting words or phrases
The story is written simply, without any particularly interesting language. However, in the first paragraph some describing words help to create a sense of excess: 'shelves piled <u>high</u> with sweets, the <u>huge</u> cake counter, the <u>giant</u> chest freezers.'

Include conversation and description
There is no conversation apart from what Amelia says to herself. The ice creams are described, but Amelia is not.

Keep your readers' interest right to the end
Knowing that the topic is deception or self-deception, the reader wants to know who is deceiving whom. We have to wait to the very end to find out, which keeps our interest.

Writing correctly
Sentence structure: The sentences are simple and straightforward, but the story avoids the monotony of beginning every sentence with 'Amelia' or 'She' by sometimes starting with 'For her morning snack' [line 12] and 'At ten o'clock' [line 15]. The sentence consisting of a list of ice creams [lines 6–9] also introduces variety.
Punctuation: This is generally correct, including the speech punctuation at the end.
Paragraphing: The paragraphs are well judged, each taking the story on to the next important event.
Spelling: This is correct.
Handwriting: This is legible and fluent.

Level: the originality of this story and its surprise ending make this a strong Level 5.

How could you do better?

Write it in an interesting way
After the highly original first paragraph, the rest of the story is written in a rather flat style. You could make it more interesting by:

- describing how Amelia passes her time while waiting for the supermarket to open. Does she press her nose to the glass, perhaps, trying to see the ice cream section? Does she run over the various kinds of ice cream in her mind, trying to choose which one to buy? Does she talk to passers-by or ignore them?
- describing how the person opening the supermarket reacts to her; after all, she is there every day. The person could greet her in a friendly or sarcastic way. Does Amelia reply or just charge silently into the store?
- think of a better word than 'ran' [lines 16 and 23] which captures the fact that she is overweight;
- think of a more original phrase than 'puffing and panting' [line 28].

ANSWERS AND EXAMINER'S COMMENTS
Paper 1: Section C Writing

Include conversation and description

The person opening the supermarket could speak to Amelia in a friendly, patronising or sarcastic way. Amelia could reply if the person is friendly or talk to herself about the person if they are patronising or sarcastic. (Some store employees would be sympathetic about her obsession, while others might see her as a figure of fun.) A little conversation would add variety to the story.

A description of an overweight person needs to be sensitive. Obesity is a disability and a critical or mocking description of someone who is obese would not be acceptable. It would also be better to keep the fact that Amelia is overweight for the end of the story, as at present. It would be possible to describe her features and her eager expression without revealing that she is overweight.

ANSWERS AND EXAMINER'S COMMENTS

Paper 1: Section C Writing

Sample student's answer: 2

1. The shining sports car purred along the farm tracks leading to Albert's house. The man in the car was dressed in a spotless suit. He had his hair slicked back and his expensive sunglasses covered his shifty eyes.

5. He parked his car outside Albert's farm house, opened his car door and slithered out. He brushed an imaginary speck of dust from his trouser leg and knocked on the gradually rotting door. He was sneering at how poor and rundown the place was. The door swung open to reveal an elderly man dressed in tatty jeans and a tartan shirt. His white beard covered most of his weathered face. The business man just managed to hide his contempt.

10. "What can I do for you?" wheezed Albert.

"I'm from Magnacorp Developers," said the man with a wry smile on his face. "We wrote to you, remember, about selling your house." Albert stroked his beard and the man put his hand in his pocket. The hand returned holding a chequebook. "Money is no problem, we will buy your house off you including your land."

15. Albert looked down at a man who was hiding behind his money. "This is my home. I've lived here all my life and I'm not going to move."

"Eighty thousand, Mr Cooper, eighty thousand pounds," the man hissed softly. He was secretly laughing inside. He was going to get the land he needed to build his theme park on and it would only cost him a third of what he expected to pay.

20. "No way", said Albert bluntly. "I like my peace and quiet."

The man sneered as he played his trump card. "There won't be much peace and quiet when they build the motorway through here." Albert's mouth sagged open. "Look, I'll show you the plans." He walked swiftly to his car and brought out the Ministry of Transport plans. Sure enough, the motorway was planned to pass right through

25. Albert's farm. Albert had to sit down. "I didn't know about this," he muttered, his face looked ill now. "Nobody told me."

"Don't you read the papers?" asked the businessman with a smirk.

"No, I just like my peace."

"Well, eighty thousand pounds will let you move somewhere nice and quiet," said the

30. man soothingly. "Here's the cheque. Now just sign this contract." Albert signed with a trembling hand.

The man drove off grinning. Another isolated old idiot conned into selling his land cheap. There wasn't going to be any motorway, but his draughtsman friend was brilliant at drawing Ministry of Transport type plans!

178

ANSWERS AND EXAMINER'S COMMENTS

Paper 1: Section C Writing

Examiner's comments

How successful is this answer?

Think of a story that will interest your readers
Organise it to keep your readers interested

This is a cleverly planned story which keeps the readers guessing. We know that the topic is deception and we want to know who is deceiving whom, but the story doesn't reveal the deception until the very last sentence and this keeps our interest.

The story is organised in an interesting way. It sets an unscrupulous businessman against a poor old farmer. The businessman is described unpleasantly all through the story, so we hope and expect that he will fail. But, in fact, he succeeds in tricking the old farmer, which gives a sour cynical feeling to the story at the end.

Write it to keep your readers' interest right to the end
The interest of the story lies in the way the two characters are described. The businessman, who is never named, is rich. He has a 'shining sports car', 'a spotless suit' and 'expensive sunglasses'. His hair is slicked back and he is vain about his appearance: 'He brushed an imaginary speck of dust from his trouser leg' [line 5]. By contrast, Albert Cooper lives on a 'poor and rundown farm' in a house with a 'gradually rotting door'. He is elderly, dressed in 'tatty jeans and a tartan shirt', and he wheezes.

The businessman is described negatively throughout. He has 'shifty eyes' [line 3]. He 'slithered' out of his car [line 4] and later he 'hissed softly' [line 17], both like a snake. He 'sneers' at Albert's farm [line 6] and regards Albert with 'contempt' [line 9]. He 'laughs secretly inside' when he is about to trick Albert [line 18], he 'smirks' as he does so [line 27] and he drives away 'grinning' [line 32].

Albert is full of confidence at first. He looks down at 'a man who was hiding behind his money' [line 15], suggesting his contempt for someone who is concerned only with money. He dismisses the man's offer 'bluntly' [line 20]. But when he is told about the motorway, his mouth sags open [line 22], he has to sit down [line 25], he looks ill [line 26] and he signs the contract 'with a trembling hand' [lines 30/31]. The businessman has won.

Use words and phrases for particular effects
Include conversation and description
The story uses words deliberately to describe the two characters and to dramatise their conversation. These are quoted above. The businessman is described throughout as rich, shifty, snake-like and enjoying his trickery. Albert is described as poor and dignified ('Albert looked down at a man who was hiding behind his money' – line 15], but he is reduced to helplessness by the businessman's deception.

Much of the story is carried by conversation which is quite realistic. Each speech is set in a context which tells us how it was spoken and, sometimes, what its effect was. For example:

'No way', said Albert bluntly. 'I like my peace and quiet.'
The man sneered as he played his trump card. 'There won't be much peace when they build the motorway through here.' Albert's mouth sagged open.
[lines 20–22]

Create characters that your readers believe in and feel for
The characters are a little stereotypical – the unscrupulous businessman and the gullible old countryman – but the businessman is presented so negatively that we want Albert to 'win' and we are saddened when he is tricked and defeated.

Writing correctly
The story has a variety of sentence structures, both simple and more complex. Spelling and punctuation are correct. Paragraphing is appropriate. Handwriting is clear and legible.

Level: this answer achieves mid Level 7.

ANSWERS AND EXAMINER'S COMMENTS

Paper 1: Section C Writing

How could you do better?

The story would even more effective if the two men were described more fully. After all, the topic reads *Describe a person who tricks or deceives other people* . . . . The description would include the appearance of both men and the way they talk to each other. The descriptions would further emphasise the businessman's wealth and sliminess and Albert's poverty and bluff honesty.

The story would gain further impact if the setting was described. The poverty of the farm could be emphasised (sagging roofs, broken fences, overgrown hedges, etc.), but it could lie in a beautiful valley, with the sun setting over the beech woods, for example, and fish breaking the surface of the river below an old sandstone bridge. This would make the idea of building a theme park there [lines 18/19] seem particularly sad.

Finally, the highest skill in writing stories is the ability to create pictures and feelings in the reader's mind. You can do this by creating images that have this effect. It is by working on your language skills in this way that you will come to write finished pieces of narrative in which every word counts towards the overall effect.

Chapter 27

Task 1
Sample student's answer

Paper 2: Macbeth

ANSWERS AND EXAMINER'S COMMENTS

1. King Duncan has come to visit Macbeth at his castle. He says how to nice the castle looks and how clean and the air is. Lady Macbeth appears and curtseys to him, and she says he is very welcome. She flatters and shows him into the castle. Duncan wants to know where Macbeth is. He thought he hurried home so quickly because he loved Macbeth Lady Macbeth, but the audience knows it is because they have to talk about what the witches said and about killing Duncan.

2. Scene 7 is later that night when they are having a feast for Duncan. Macbeth thinks about the reasons why he shouldn't kill Duncan. "He's here in double trust: first, as I am kinsman and his subject, strong both against the deed". He decides not to kill him.

3. Then Lady Macbeth comes and persuades Macbeth to do the murder. She calls him a coward. "When you durst do it, then you were a man". She says he is going back on his word, saying that if she had sworn to do something she would do it. "I would, while it was smiling in my face, have plucked my nipple from his boneless gums and dashed the brains out, had I so sworn as you have done to this".

4. Macbeth can't take this kind of pressure. Lady Macbeth is the only person apart from the witches who knows about his weak points. She is so tough that Macbeth starts thinking about the murder again. She comes up with the plan to get the guards drunk and she speaks as if the murder would be easy. "What cannot you and I perform upon the unguarded Duncan?" She feels nothing could go wrong and Macbeth agrees. He thinks she planned it just like a man. "For thy undaunted mettle should compose nothing but males".

5. From this scene we learn how cruel Lady Macbeth can be, also how persuasive she is.

181

ANSWERS AND EXAMINER'S COMMENTS

Paper 2: Macbeth

How successful is this answer?

Understanding and Response

Show a good understanding of the characters' situation
The answer shows awareness of how Lady Macbeth behaves differently in the two scenes. In the first, she curtseys and welcomes Duncan to the castle. In the second, she persuades Macbeth to change his mind and go ahead with Duncan's murder.

The answer mentions the background briefly at the end of the first paragraph. Duncan thought Macbeth hurried home because he loved his wife, but really it is because they have to talk about what the Witches said and about killing Duncan.

Explain what the characters are thinking and feeling
The answer mentions that Macbeth is thinking of reasons why he shouldn't kill Duncan. It goes on to explain some of the things that Lady Macbeth says to him to persuade him to change his mind, but without mentioning her feelings as she says them or Macbeth's reactions to them.

Refer to the text to support your explanations
The answer does this well. It quotes three important things that Lady Macbeth says, in each case explaining what the quotation means. For example, she calls him a coward: 'When you durst do it, then you were a man'. The answer also gives two important quotations from Macbeth, first saying why he doesn't want to kill Duncan and, second, admiring Lady Macbeth for planning the murder like a man.

Start to give your own opinion
The answer does not say much about Lady Macbeth's character, which is what the question asks about. The best comment is the beginning of the fourth paragraph: Macbeth can't take this kind of pressure. Lady Macbeth is the only person apart from the Witches who knows about his weak points. She is so tough that Macbeth starts thinking about the murder again. The end of the answer gives a brief summary: we learn how cruel Lady Macbeth can be, also how persuasive she is.

Level for Understanding and Response: this answer achieves a strong Level 5.

Examiner's comments

How could you do better?

Show a good understanding of the characters' situation
A better answer would bring out Lady Macbeth's hypocrisy in Scene 6. She behaves very humbly to Duncan and thanks him for 'those honours deep and broad wherewith Your Majesty loads our house'. In fact, she is already plotting Duncan's murder. We know this from the previous scene when she has started thinking about the murder and hinting about it to Macbeth [text lines 38–54, 60/61 and 66–70].

Explain what the characters are thinking and feeling
In Scene 7, you should emphasise Macbeth's decision not to go ahead with the murder: Duncan has honoured him by giving him a new title and visiting his house, and everyone is full of admiration for Macbeth [text lines 31–34]. Lady Macbeth sets about reversing his decision and you should explain her feelings as she puts various pressures on him. As well as the ones in the sample student's answer, you should mention:

- how she sneers at him for changing his mind ('Was the hope drunk wherein you dress'd yourself?');
- she says he doesn't love her ('From this time such I account your love');
- she calls him a coward ('Art thou afeard to be the same in thine own act and valour as thou art in desire?');
- she says that he is less than a man ('When you durst do it, then you were a man');
- her speech about killing her baby ('pluck'd my nipple from his boneless gums/And dash'd the brains out') shows the terrible ruthlessness of her character. It is also a savage attack on Macbeth's manhood; she is saying she would rather kill their child than keep it with such a pathetic father as he has turned out.

Macbeth gives in under this pressure and Lady Macbeth quickly comes up with the plan to get Duncan's guards drunk, use their daggers for the murder, smear them with Duncan's blood and blame them for the murder. Macbeth immediately agrees and admires her for thinking like a man: 'Bring forth men-children only! For thy undaunted mettle should compose Nothing but males'.

ANSWERS AND EXAMINER'S COMMENTS

Paper 2: Macbeth

How successful is this answer?

Written Expression

The ideas in the answer are expressed clearly and simply. The answer is appropriately paragraphed and accurately punctuated. The quotations are correctly put in speech marks, but they are written as separate sentences, not connected with the sentence that introduces them. One capital letter is missed. The handwriting is legible though not always easy to read.

Level for Written Expression: this answer achieves mid Level 5.

How could you do better?

Refer to the text to support your explanations
Each of the points mentioned above should be accompanied by a quotation from the text which helps to make it clear.

Start to give your own opinion
Taken together, the two scenes show that Lady Macbeth is hypocritical towards Duncan and completely ruthless towards Macbeth. She cruelly puts increasing pressure on him, making him feel that their relationship is finished unless he gives in to her, which he soon does. At this point in the play, she is stronger than him.

ANSWERS AND EXAMINER'S COMMENTS

Paper 2: Macbeth

Task 2
Sample student's answer

1. When he comes in, Macbeth shouldn't act surprised at seeing the Witches and their cauldron. He has come looking for them because he wants information from them. He just stares at them in an interested sort of way and says "How now, you secret, black and midnight hags! What is't you do?" They try to act scary and say "A deed without a name", but he isn't scared. He turns the word "conjure" back on them because it means cast a spell and he sort of casts a spell on them. He shouts at them to tell him what he wants to know "even till destruction sicken". He doesn't care what damage is caused so long as he finds out what he wants to know.

2. When the Witches offer to get their "masters" to tell him, Macbeth is confident and almost snaps "Call 'em. Let me see 'em". When the first apparition appears, he tries to question it. Later he asks it "But one word more", but the apparitions only tell him things, they don't answer questions.

3. As the apparition give their messages, Macbeth becomes more and more confident. He probably walks up and down chuckling and rubbing his hands. The first one warns him about Macduff, the second says "none of woman born shall harm Macbeth" and the third says he's safe until Birnam Wood comes to Dunsinane. Of course, all three come true in a way, but he doesn't know this. He thinks he's completely safe.

4. But he still wants to know one more thing. "shall Banquo's issue ever reign in this kingdom?" The Witches try to put him off, but he "conjures" them again by threatening them. "Deny me this and an eternal curse fall on you!" So they give in and produce the line of kings with

Banquo following them. Macbeth's confidence completely goes now. He staggers back trying to cover his eyes, "Thy crown does sear mine eye-balls. I see him cowering away and ending up on his knees in a corner shrieking "Horrible sight!"

5. The apparitions and the Witches have gone and it's quiet while he pulls himself together. All his confidence is gone and he is left depressed and bitter. He calls in Lennox and finds out that Macduff has fled to England. He decides there is no point in being nice any more because his children won't reign after him. So he may as well be as vicious as he likes and, for starters, he'll have Macduff's family killed. This is a punishment for Macduff - and a warning to anyone else.

6. He probably takes a last look behind him before he goes out, wishing he hadn't asked to see the last apparition, "But no more sights!"

ANSWERS AND EXAMINER'S COMMENTS

Paper 2: Macbeth

Examiner's comments

How successful is this answer?

Understanding and Response

Show a good understanding of how the scene develops

The answer covers all the main developments in the scene: Macbeth's lack of fear for the Witches, his growing confidence as the first three apparitions speak, his distress at the 'show of kings' and his bitterness at the end when he decides to have Macduff's family killed. Each development is explained with some indication of how Macbeth would act.

Explain some of the characters' more complex thoughts and feelings

The task centres on Macbeth and the answer rightly concentrates on him, not spending much time on the Witches. In each paragraph, the answer indicates how Macbeth would act at that moment. Examples are:

- he 'shouldn't act surprised at seeing the Witches and their cauldron' because he has come looking for them. He isn't scared of them; 'he just stares at them in an interested sort of way'. 'He shouts at them to tell him what he wants to know' [paragraph 1];
- as he becomes more and more confident, 'he probably walks up and down chuckling and rubbing his hands' [paragraph 3];
- when he sees the kings, I see him cowering away and ending up on his knees in a corner shrieking 'Horrible sight!' [paragraph 4];
- as he leaves, he probably takes a last look behind him before he goes out, wishing he hadn't asked to see the last apparition [paragraph 6].

Refer to the text to support your explanations

The answer uses a good range of quotations, from single words ('conjure', 'masters') to whole lines. Most of the quotations are short, but well-chosen. Several uses of quotation show very good understanding of the text:

- Macbeth's word 'conjure' [text line 49] is used to explain his power over the Witches (he sort of casts a spell on them) in paragraph 1 and again in paragraph 4;
- Macbeth is said to snap his instruction 'Call'em. Let me see'em' which well explains this very short way of speaking [paragraph 2];
- when he sees the kings, he staggers back trying to cover his eyes, 'Thy crown does sear mine eye-balls'. The direction to the actor is explained by Shakespeare's words [paragraph 4];
- Macbeth's feeling when he says 'But no more sights!' is explained by the last sentence.

Give a thoughtful response to the question

In a director role-play question like this, a thoughtful response is shown by the way you write as the director. This means that you have to show understanding of the character and his feelings all the way through the answer, as this answer does. In straightforward questions, you can show your thoughtfulness at the end of the answer when you can sum up your opinions (for example, see the student answers to Tasks 3, 5 and 6). But this is not suitable for a character role-play answer.

Level for Understanding and Response: this answer achieves a strong Level 6.

Written Expression

The answer is paragraphed and punctuated appropriately, spelt correctly and written legibly. There is some effective use of language, such as 'chuckling and rubbing his hands' [paragraph 3] and he is left 'depressed and bitter' [paragraph 5]. Most of the language is simple and straightforward, though it sometimes lacks precision as in 'He just stares at them in an interested sort of way' [paragraph 1] and 'there is no point in being nice any more' and 'for starters' [paragraph 5].

Level for Written Expression: this answer achieves mid Level 6.

How could you do better?

Remember: a director role-play question has to strike a balance between showing understanding of the scene and writing about it as a director. This means that you have to explain how and why the character acts as he does as the scene progresses.

You can also write as if you are speaking to the actors, such as: 'Macbeth, when you come in you're not surprised at seeing the Witches and their cauldron. You've come looking for them because you want information from them, etc.' This is an equally good way of answering.

ANSWERS AND EXAMINER'S COMMENTS

Paper 2: Macbeth

For a Level 7 answer, you could:

- explain how Macbeth's attitude changes from ordering the Witches about to listening carefully, perhaps humbly, to the apparitions.
- mention the helpless anger with which he curses the Witches after they have disappeared – 'Infected be the air whereon they ride and damn'd all those that trust them' [text lines 137/138] – without realising that he is also cursing himself.
- suggest that he speaks the lines about having Macduff's family killed very coldly to express how dead he feels inside.

Chapter 28

ANSWERS AND EXAMINER'S COMMENTS

Paper 2: Romeo and Juliet

Task 3
Sample student's answer

1. At the start of the scene Capulet is in a jolly mood. He is trying to get everyone to dance and if any of the ladies refuse, he will say they have corns. This works because when he calls for the first dance – "foot it girls" – everyone seems to dance. He has to tell the servants to make more room by turning the tables up against the walls and quench the fire because the room is too hot.

2. This starts the scene in an exciting way. Everyone is joining in the dance and enjoying themselves. Capulet chats to his cousin about how long it was since their last party and he tries to make himself seem younger by saying it was only twenty-five years, not thirty.

3. Suddenly Romeo sees Juliet and falls in love with her beauty – "O she doth teach the torches to burn bright." He says "I ne'er saw true beauty till this night." This shows that he has fallen in love with Juliet at first sight and fallen out of love with Rosaline. He decides to wait till the dance is over – "The measure done" – then he talked to her. But Tybalt hears his voice and recognises it. He knows it is a Montague and he immediately wants to fight him – "Fetch me my rapier, boy". This makes the scene exciting because we want to know what happens next.

4. Capulet at this point asks what's wrong and stops Tybalt from fighting Romeo because he doesn't want his party to be spoiled – "You'll make a mutiny among my guests". Tybalt tries to argue, but Capulet gets angry with him and he has no chance. Tybalt goes away saying Romeo's intrusion "Now seeming sweet shall convert to bitterest gall". By this he means he will get Romeo later. This part

188

is exciting because it looks as if there is going to be a fight at the party. Capulet stops this, but Shakespeare puts across that Tybalt will fight with Romeo later because he intruded at the party.

5   Romeo and Juliet talk for the first time. He describes her hands as a "holy shrine" and that his lips are "two blushing pilgrims". He means that pilgrims kiss holy shrines and he wants to kiss her hand. They flirt with each other saying things like "palm to palm is holy palmers kiss." But Romeo wants to kiss her on the lips - "then dear saint, let lips do what hands do." She agrees and they kiss on the lips which was unknown for a first meeting in those days. They kiss again and Juliet says "You kiss by the book" which means you kiss like an expert. This is exciting because you feel they really want to see each other again.

6   Juliet then has to go and speak to her mother and Romeo asks the Nurse who she is. When the nurse tells him she is the Capulets' daughter, he knows there is trouble ahead - "O dear account. My life is my foe's debt." Later Juliet finds out that Romeo is a Montague and she also realises there is trouble ahead - "That I must love a loathed enemy."

7   This is exciting because both Romeo and Juliet are in love with each other, but they know their love is dangerous because their families hate each other. If their families find out, they will be unable to see each other. But you feel they will meet again. It is also exciting that Tybalt says he will get revenge on Romeo for gatecrashing the party. It makes me feel there is going to be trouble ahead.

ANSWERS AND EXAMINER'S COMMENTS

Paper 2: Romeo and Juliet

How successful is this answer?

Understanding and Response

Show a good understanding of how the scene develops

The answer follows the main events of the scene, explaining how the four characters in the question – Capulet, Tybalt, Romeo and Juliet – are involved in these events. The question asks how these characters help to make the scene exciting and the answer deals with this very well. After each event, the answer comments on how the characters have made the scene exciting:

- after describing how Capulet has persuaded people to dance so successfully that the servants have to quench the fire and turn the tables up, the answer comments: 'This starts the scene in an exciting way. Everyone is joining in the dance and enjoying themselves' [paragraphs 1 and 2].
- when Tybalt hears Romeo's voice and sends for his rapier, the answer explains: 'This makes the scene exciting because we want to know what happens next' [paragraph 3].
- when Capulet stops Tybalt from fighting Romeo at the party, the answer comments: 'This part is exciting because it looks as if there is going to be a fight at the party. Capulet stops this, but Shakespeare puts across that Tybalt will fight with Romeo later because he intruded at the party' [paragraph 4].
- when Romeo and Juliet talk and kiss, the answer adds: 'This is exciting because you feel they really want to see each other again' [paragraph 5].

Finally, the last paragraph summarises the two ways in which the audience is left in suspense at the end of the scene. Will Romeo and Juliet meet again when their families hate each other? Will Tybalt get revenge on Romeo for gatecrashing the party?

Explain some of the characters' more complex thoughts and feelings

The task centres on how the scene is made exciting, not on the characters' more complex thoughts and feelings. However, the answer makes two quite subtle points about the characters:

- Capulet tries to make himself seem younger by saying it was only twenty-five years, not thirty, since their last party [paragraph 2].

Examiner's comments

- 'Romeo and Juliet kiss on the lips which was unknown for a first meeting in those days' [paragraph 5]. An even better answer would point out that this shows how totally they fall in love with each other at their first meeting.

Refer to the text to support your explanations

The answer frequently uses quotations to illustrate the points that are made. They are all short – some are only two or three words – showing that the student has understood that brief quotations are sufficient.

Give a thoughtful response to the question

The answer explains how all the main events of the scene make it exciting and the final paragraph gives a good summary.

Level for Understanding and Response: this answer achieves a strong Level 6.

Written Expression

The answer is paragraphed and punctuated appropriately, spelt correctly and written legibly. The quotations are both accurately punctuated and confidently integrated into the answer. The language is clear and direct, but lapses into repetition at the end where the phrase 'trouble ahead' is used three times in paragraphs 6 and 7.

Level for Written Expression: this answer achieves mid Level 6.

ANSWERS AND EXAMINER'S COMMENTS

Paper 2: Romeo and Juliet

How could you do better?

For a Level 7 answer, you would need to comment on some of the following:

- why some of the guests are wearing masks (see Examiner's comments on page 139) and how this adds to the excitement.
- Tybalt actually wants to kill Romeo there and then: 'To strike him dead I hold it not a sin'. This adds to the excitement, showing how dangerous Tybalt is.
- Capulet's sudden anger at being crossed by Tybalt shows how violent he is beneath his friendly appearance. This adds to the tension because we realise how furious, and therefore dangerous, he would be if he found out about Juliet loving someone he didn't approve of. We see this rage, of course, in the scene set for Task 4.
- The fact that Juliet was willing to allow Romeo to kiss her on the lips (twice) at their first meeting shows how totally she has fallen in love him at their first meeting. In those days, the man was only allowed to kiss the lady's hand until they knew each other very well. We know his feelings from his speech about her beauty – 'O she doth teach the torches to burn bright' – but we can tell her feelings at this point only from how she speaks and behaves with him. Letting him kiss her on the lips is a sure indication of her feelings. This adds to the excitement because we realise that they both feel the same for each other. (Note: when Juliet says 'you kiss by the book' (you kiss like an expert), this cannot be mocking or sarcastic because she has almost certainly never been kissed on the lips before. She means that he kisses very well.)
- Romeo's and Juliet's comments when they find out who each other is – 'O dear account. My life is my foe's debt' and 'That I must love a loathed enemy' – show that they both realise that their love is very dangerous. If Tybalt wants to kill Romeo for gatecrashing the party, how will he and all the Capulets feel about him kissing Juliet?

ANSWERS AND EXAMINER'S COMMENTS

Paper 2: Romeo and Juliet

Task 4
Sample student's answer

1. I've never felt so desperate. I can't believe how my parents and the Nurse have treated me. I've just spent my wedding night with Romeo. I did this though I knew he'd killed my cousin Tybalt, because my love for Romeo is more important than my family's feelings about Tybalt. We were talking at the window about whether the day was dawning when the Nurse hurried in to tell me my Mother was coming. Romeo quickly went down the ladder and suddenly I had a terrible feeling the next time I'll see him he'll be dead, "as one dead in the bottom of a tomb". I don't know what made me think that — it was horrible!

2. My mother was coming to my bedroom. I wondered "What unaccustomed 'cause procures her hither?" Did she suspect something? I don't see her very often. We've never been close; in fact, the Nurse has always been like a mother to me. I didn't want to be questioned by her, so I pretended to cry about Tybalt. My parents hate Romeo so I've got to keep our love a secret.

3. As I thought, my mother assumed I was crying for Tybalt and I went along with it. "Yet let me weep for such a feeling loss". When Mother talked about the loss of a "friend" meaning Tybalt, I agreed but inside I meant Romeo. My mother then spoke about a "villain". I didn't know who she was talking about, but when she said it was Romeo, I was so shocked that I cried out, "Villain and he be many miles asunder. God pardon him. I do with all my heart."

4. As soon as I said it I knew it was the wrong thing to say, so I covered it up with "And yet no man like he doth grieve my heart". I meant it one way and she took it the other way.

5. She called Romeo a "traitor murderer" and I realised my family will want to kill him for revenge. I said "Would none but I might venge my cousin's death" to make her think I'm on their side, but I meant I want to go to Romeo, but not kill him. My mother then talked about sending someone to poison Romeo and I was so appalled that I gave my real feelings away again, "Indeed I never shall be satisfied with Romeo till I behold him", meaning till I see him.

ANSWERS AND EXAMINER'S COMMENTS

Paper 2: Romeo and Juliet

6 | She started looking suspicious, so I covered it up at the last minute by adding "dead" and pretended I meant something different by going on "dead — is my poor heart so for a kinsman vex'd". For a second time, I nearly gave my real feelings away, but then I covered up really well. I talked about giving Romeo poison, but I would "temper it" so it would only send him to sleep.

7 | My mother then said she has good news, but when she told me I was going to marry Paris on Thursday, I couldn't believe it! I felt I was becoming hysterical. I said it's too quick and, in any case, I'd rather marry Romeo who they hate. This was clever double talk and I felt I was in control again.

8 | Then my father came in. I started crying again and this made him talk nicely to me at first, trying to joke me out of it. But when he heard I wouldn't marry Paris, he started getting cross. I'm frightened of him when he gets in a temper and I can't trick him with words like I can my mother. I tried to tell him I wasn't proud — "Not proud you have, but thankful that you have" — but this just made him more angry. He started yelling at me. All I could do is kneel and plead with him, but it made no difference. He went on and on and said if I won't marry Paris, he will throw me out on the streets: "And you be mine I'll give you to her friend. And you be not, hang! Beg! Starve! Die in the streets!"

9 | He stormed off and I turned to my mother for help — "O sweet he mother, cast me not away" — but she just coldly turned away and left.

10 | I was left with the Nurse and I turned to her for comfort and advice, like I always do: "Comfort me, counsel me." Then came the big surprise. The Nurse told me to forget Romeo and marry Paris! She says Romeo will never be a real husband and Paris is "a lovely gentleman. Romeo's a dishclout to him". The old hypocrite — she was saying how lovely Romeo was earlier! I was shocked by this — "Speakest thou from thy heart?" — and when she says yes, I break up with her. She has let me down when I really needed her. I talked to her coldly and sent her away with a message for my mother. I will never trust her again now.

11 | Now I'm completely alone. I'll go to the Friar to see if he can help me. If not, I feel so desperate, I'll kill myself! "If all else fail, myself have power to die".

193

ANSWERS AND EXAMINER'S COMMENTS

Paper 2: Romeo and Juliet

Examiner's comments

How successful is this answer?

Understanding and Response

Show a full understanding of how the scene develops

The answer shows a full understanding of how Juliet's desperate situation develops. In the first paragraph, it briefly outlines the background – spending her wedding night with Romeo, the fact that he has killed Tybalt, his quick departure and her sudden premonition of seeing him dead. Remember: although the first part of the scene is not set for study, the first prompt (how her difficult situation has come about) shows the need to mention a little of the background.

The rest of the answer works clearly through all the important points in the scene – Juliet's deceiving of her mother with double meanings, her reaction to being made to marry Paris, her father's rage, the Nurse's surprising advice – leading to Juliet being left completely alone and thinking about suicide.

Explain the characters' more complex thoughts and feelings

The question requires the answer to be written from Juliet's viewpoint and it does this all the way through. In each paragraph, the answer gives her thoughts or feelings about the point being mentioned. Examples are:

- on spending the night with Romeo, 'I did this though I knew he'd killed my cousin Tybalt, because my love for Romeo is more important than my family's feelings about Tybalt' [paragraph 1];
- on her mother's sudden arrival at her bedroom, 'Did she suspect something? We've never been close; in fact, the Nurse has always been like a mother to me' [paragraph 2];
- on being told about marrying Paris, 'I felt I was becoming hysterical. I said it's too quick and, in any case, I'd rather marry Romeo who they hate. This was clever double talk and I felt I was in control again' [paragraph 7];
- on her father, 'I'm frightened of him when he gets in a temper and I can't trick him with words like I can my mother' [paragraph 8].

These are the more obvious examples. You should read through the answer again, picking out all the places where it mentions Juliet's thoughts and feelings. There are examples in each paragraph.

Support your ideas by detailed reference to the text

Each point in the answer is supported by a well-chosen quotation. Note that these are sometimes short, like 'traitor murderer' in paragraph 5 and 'temper it' in paragraph 6. You only need to quote as much as is necessary to support the point you are making.

Give a sensitive response to the question

In a character role-play question like this, sensitive response is shown in the way you write as the character. This means that you have to show understanding of the character and her feelings all the way through the answer, as this answer does. In straightforward questions, you can show your sensitivity at the end of the answer when you can sum up your opinions (for example, see the student answer to Tasks 3, 5 and 6). But this is not suitable for a character role-play answer.

Level for Understanding and Response: this answer is sufficiently detailed and sensitive to Juliet's feelings to achieve above Level 7.

Written Expression

The answer is written confidently and clearly, and it is well organised. It is written in an appropriate style for Juliet with exclamations like 'it was horrible!' [paragraph 1] and 'The old hypocrite – she was saying how lovely Romeo was earlier!' [paragraph 10]. The answer is well punctuated, correctly spelt and written in a fluent legible style.

Level for Written Expression: this answer achieves above Level 7.

How could you do better?

The answer could only be improved by adding details such as how Juliet's father feels like hitting her – 'my fingers itch' [text line 164] – and Juliet's sarcasm when she sends the Nurse away – 'Well, thou hast comforted me marvellous much' [text line 230]. The answer already achieves the highest mark, so these are details.

Chapter 29

Task 5
Sample student's answer

ANSWERS AND EXAMINER'S COMMENTS

Paper 2: Twelfth Night

1. In the first scene, Olivia has sent back Orsino's messenger with the message that she refuses to see him because she is mourning her father and brother. Maria brings news that a young gentleman wished to speak to Olivia, mentioning that he is attractive: "T'is a fair young man". Olivia tells Malvolio to get rid of him if he is from Orsino: "I am sick or not at home - what you will to dismiss it".

2. Malvolio brings back news that the visitor refuses to go away: "he says he'll stand at your door like a sheriff's post.... but he'll speak with you". Olivia is intrigued by his persistence and asks what the man is like. Among some sneering comments, Malvolio says that he is between a man and a boy and that he is good looking: "He is very well-favoured". Olivia is beginning to be interested in him and agrees to see him.

3. As she is in mourning, Olivia covers her face with a veil, and Maria does too. This was the proper thing to do when a person in deep mourning received someone outside the family. Viola cannot tell which is the lady of the house. She begins her speech on behalf of Orsino, then interrupts herself because she does not want to waste it: "I would be loath to cast away my speech".

4. Olivia admits that she is the lady of the house, but tells Viola to cut the speech short: "Come to what is important in it. I forgive you the praise". Maria tries to usher Viola out ("Will you hoist sail, sir? Here lies your way."), but Viola refuses cheekily ("No, good swabber, I am to hull her a little longer") and persuades Olivia to hear her alone.

5. When they are alone, she persuades Olivia to lift her veil and show her face. Viola then starts her speech praising Olivia's face on behalf of

195

ANSWERS AND EXAMINER'S COMMENTS

Paper 2: Twelfth Night

Orsino, Orsino, saying it would be cruel to take such a face to "the grave" and leaves the world "no copy". Olivia mockingly replies that she will have some copies made. Viola goes on with the speech of praise and Olivia rejects Orsino again: "But yet I cannot love him. He might have took his answer long ago".

6. Viola then starts talking in her own words and says that, if she loved Olivia like Orsino does, she would "make me a willow cabin at your gate" and call to her till she gave in. Olivia is attracted by Viola's passion and murmurs "You might do much" (you might succeed). She checks that Viola is a gentleman, i.e. of the same class as herself although he is a messenger, which hints at her growing interest. She sends Viola back to Orsino, but invites her back to tell her how he takes her refusal.

7. When she is alone, Olivia admits that she is attracted to Cesario (Viola). She wishes it was Viola, not Orsino, who was in love with her ("Unless the master were the man") and suddenly realises that she has fallen in love: "Even so quickly may one catch the plague? Methinks I feel this youth's perfections........ creep in at my eyes." She calls Malvolio and tells him to return a ring that Viola has left. This is untrue; it is a trick to get Cesario (Viola) to return tomorrow.

8. Olivia ends the scene confused. She is attracted to Cesario by many things: his good looks, his humour, his passion, his refusal to take no for an answer. She is surprised at the suddenness of her feelings, but she also fears she may be making a fool of herself: "I do I know not what, and fear to find mine eye too great a flatter for my mind." She means, I don't know what I'm afraid I'm being led astray be his appearance.

196

ANSWERS AND EXAMINER'S COMMENTS

Paper 2: Twelfth Night

Examiner's comments

How successful is this answer?

Understanding and Response

Show a full understanding of how the scene develops
The answer shows a full understanding of how Olivia's interest in Cesario (Viola) develops. The first part of the scene is not set for study and it is unnecessary to mention it as it has nothing to do with Olivia's interest in Cesario. The answer works clearly through all the important points in the scene that is set: Maria's and Malvolio's messages about the visitor; Olivia's decision to see him; Cesario's persistence in persuading Olivia to see him alone and to lift her veil; Cesario's passionate way of speaking and Olivia's sudden falling in love with him.

Explain the characters' more complex thoughts and feelings
The question is about Olivia's attitude to Cesario (Viola) and, at several points, the answer gives Olivia's thoughts or feelings about him (her):

- on Malvolio's description of him, Olivia is intrigued by his persistence. Hearing again that he is very good-looking, she is beginning to be interested in him and agrees to see him [paragraph 2];
- when Viola talks in her own words (not those she has learned) about how she would not give up if she loved someone, Olivia is attracted by Viola's passion and murmurs 'You might do much' (you might succeed) [paragraph 6].

There are good accounts of Olivia falling in love [paragraph 7] and of her confused feelings [paragraph 8].

Support your ideas by detailed reference to the text
Each point in the answer is supported by a well-chosen quotation.

Give a sensitive response to the question
The last three paragraphs show a sensitive understanding of how Olivia is falling in love and paragraph 2 explains how she becomes interested in Cesario (Viola) at the beginning. But the rest of the answer, though accurate and quite full, reads like a straightforward account of the scene. These paragraphs do not focus closely enough on Olivia's feelings.

Level for Understanding and Response: because of its lack of focus on Olivia in parts, this answer just achieves Level 7.

Written Expression
The answer is written confidently and clearly. It is well organised, showing skill in integrating well-chosen quotations and in summary: 'She is attracted to Cesario by many things: his good looks, his humour, his passion, his refusal to take no for an answer' [paragraph 8]. The answer is well punctuated, correctly spelt and written in a fluent legible style.

Level for Written Expression: this answer achieves above Level 7.

How could you do better?

The answer could be improved for Understanding and Response by focusing more closely on Olivia's feelings when Cesario is present. For example:

- how she is amused at first by Viola's admitting that she has learned her speech from Orsino: 'Are you a comedian?' (i.e. actor) [text line 151];
- how she shows her lack of interest in Orsino's message by telling Viola to cut it short: 'Come to what is important in't; I forgive you the praise' [text line 159] and 'If you be not mad, be gone; if you have reason, be brief' [text lines 163/164];
- how she is attracted enough by Cesario to agree to see him alone;
- how she describes her face not as beautiful but as long-lasting – 'T'is in grain, sir, t'will endure wind and weather' [text line 194] – and talks about it mockingly in prose while Viola is trying to praise it in verse;
- finally, how Olivia speaks verse for the first time in the scene when she rejects Orsino: 'Your lord does know my mind. I cannot love him' to 'He might have took his answer long ago' [text lines 212–218 – you only need to quote the first and last lines]. This shows she is serious and her seriousness continues when she talks with Viola for the rest of the scene.

197

ANSWERS AND EXAMINER'S COMMENTS

Paper 2: Twelfth Night

Task 6
Sample student's answer

1. Maria and Sir Toby want to make a fool of Malvolio because he's pompous and always criticises them. He told Sir Toby if he didn't stop getting drunk, Olivia would throw him out. He is a Puritan who doesn't like other people having fun.

2. Malvolio thinks Olivia likes him and he imagines being married to her. "To be Count Malvolio!" He imagines getting up and putting on an expensive gown ("in my branched velvet gown") and sending for Sir Toby. He imagines Sir Toby "curtseying" to him, then he tells him "You must amend your drunkenness" and stop going round with "a foolish knight". This is Sir Andrew.

3. Sir Toby, Sir Andrew and Fabian are hiding and listening to him. At first Sir Andrew wants to attack him and Sir Toby tells him to be quiet. But soon Sir Toby gets so cross that he wants to attack Malvolio. "O for a stone-bow to hit him in the eye" and "And does not Toby take you a blow o' the lips then?" (which means he wants to smack him in the mouth) and Fabian has to keep trying to keep Toby quiet in case Malvolio hears them.

4. Now Malvolio sees the letter on the ground. Maria can imitate Olivia's writing and he thinks the letter is from her. He opens it and reads a poem which includes "I may command where I adore" and "M.O.A.I." Because he thinks Olivia likes him, he thinks this refers to him and "M.O.A.I." stands for his name. The letters are not in the right order, but he still thinks the letter is for him. The rest of the letter encourages this idea – "Some are born great, some achieve greatness and some have greatness thrust upon 'em".

5. It tells him to wear yellow stockings and be cross-gartered and he remembers Olivia liked him looking like this. It also tells him to smile at her a lot and he says he will. The others are happy he is tricked so completely, particularly when Maria tells them Olivia hates yellow stockings and cross-garters and she won't like him smiling at her.

6. We learn Malvolio has a fantasy about being married to Olivia and using this to lord it over Sir Toby and the others. This makes him fall for the letter trick easily. It's funny to see a pompous man going to make a real fool of himself. It's funny too when Sir Andrew shouts at Malvolio and has to be kept quiet by Sir Toby who starts shouting at him and has to be kept quiet by Fabian

ANSWERS AND EXAMINER'S COMMENTS

Paper 2: Twelfth Night

Examiner's comments

How successful is this answer?

Understanding and Response

Show a good understanding of how the scene develops
The answer uses the prompts for its structure. After a short introduction explaining why Maria and Sir Toby want to make a fool of Malvolio, the next four paragraphs cover all the main events of the scene, guided by the prompts. The last paragraph directly answers the question in the task.

Explain some of the characters' more complex thoughts and feelings
The task centres on Malvolio and the answer makes some good points about his character. 'He is a Puritan who doesn't like other people having fun' [paragraph 1]. He imagines being rich – 'putting on an expensive gown' – and being superior to Sir Toby who 'curtseys' to him [paragraph 2]. When he reads the letter, the answer points out that 'Because he thinks Olivia likes him, he thinks this refers to him' and that, although the letters M.O.A.I. are not in the right order, he thinks they stand for his name' [paragraph 4]. The answer does not refer to Malvolio's self-deception or wishful thinking, but this is clearly understood.

Refer to the text to support your explanations
The answer uses a good range of quotations, from single words ('curtseying') to short phrases ('in my branched velvet gown', 'a foolish knight') to whole lines. The student understands that familiarity with the text can be shown with short quotations. The answer also explains two quotations – putting on an expensive gown ('in my branched velvet gown') and 'And does not Toby take you a blow o' the lips then?' (which means he wants to smack him in the mouth) – and this shows good understanding of the text.

Give a thoughtful response to the question
The final paragraph answers the question directly and, without this, the answer would not achieve Level 6. The paragraph explains briefly but clearly that it is his fantasy of marrying Olivia that makes him fall for the letter trick so easily. It also explains, in general terms, what is funny about the scene, although the different reasons for Sir Andrew's and Sir Toby's abuse of Malvolio are not explained.

Level for Understanding and Response: this answer achieves mid Level 6.

Written Expression

The answer is paragraphed and punctuated appropriately, spelt correctly and written legibly. There is some effective use of language, such as 'pompous' [paragraph 1], 'fantasy' and 'to lord it over' [last paragraph]. However, most of the language is simple and it sometimes lapses into repetitiveness such as 'Fabian has to keep trying to keep Toby quiet' [paragraph 3] and 'he remembers Olivia liked him looking like this' [paragraph 5].

Level for Written Expression: this answer achieves low Level 6.

How could you do better?

For a Level 7 answer, you would need to do several of the following:

- write more fully about Malvolio's fantasy of marriage to Olivia, giving examples of his ridiculous pomposity such as 'after a demure travel of regard, telling them I know my place as I would they should do theirs' [text lines 44–46] or 'quenching my familiar smile with an austere regard of control' [text lines 54/55] and his exaggerated idea of his importance: 'Seven of my people, with an obedient start, make out for him' [text lines 49/50];
- explain that Sir Andrew shouts insults at Malvolio because he is a rival for Olivia's affections and is restrained by Sir Toby who then shouts worse insults when he realises that Malvolio, a servant, wants to become his superior (and cut off the generosity of Olivia on whom Sir Toby is sponging);
- mention the comic effect of Sir Andrew and Sir Toby shouting abuse and having to be restrained again and again; or possibly shouting quietly, so that Malvolio does not hear them;
- explain how the letter asks him to wear yellow stockings and to be cross-gartered. Malvolio persuades himself that Olivia likes these, though yellow stockings are inappropriate in a house of mourning and both yellow stockings and cross-garters were unfashionable when the play was written.

Two other points are mentioned in the Examiner's hints on page 145.

ACKNOWLEDGEMENTS

Published by Collins Educational
An *imprint of* HarperCollins*Publishers* Ltd
77-85 Fulham Palace Road
London W6 8JB

www.**Collins**Education.com
On-line support for schools and colleges

© HarperCollins*Publishers* Ltd

First published 2000
Reprinted 2000
ISBN 0 00 323544 0

Geoff Barton and Laurie Smith assert the moral right to be identified as the authors of this work.

All rights reserved. No part of this publication may be reproduced, stored in a retrieval system, or transmitted in any form or by any means, electronic, mechanical, photocopying, recording or otherwise, without either the prior permission of the Publisher or a licence permitting restricted copying in the United Kingdom issued by the Copyright Licensing.Agency Ltd, 90 Tottenham Court Road, London W1P 9HE. This book is sold subject to the condition that it shall not by way of trade or otherwise be lent, hired out or otherwise circulated without the Publisher's prior consent.

British Library Cataloguing in Publication Data
A catalogue record for this book is available from the British Library.

Edited by Steve Attmore
Production by Kathryn Botterill
Cover design by BCG Communications
Book design by Rupert Purcell and produced by Gecko Limited
Index compiled by Drusilla Calvert
Printed and bound in the UK by Scotprint

Acknowledgements
The Authors and Publishers are grateful to the following for permission to reproduce copyright material: David Higham Associates for permission to reproduce *The Last Act* by Roald Dahl, published by Penguin; Extract from *Odour of Chrysanthemums* reproduced with kind permission of Lawrence Pollinger Limited and the estate of Frieda Lawrence Ravagli; Health Education Authority for *Smoking: the facts* and *Getting Active. Getting Fit leaflets*; The Gallery Press, Ireland, for permission to reproduce an extract from *The Potato Gatherers* by Brian Friel from Selected Stories, published in 1994.

Photographs
Neville Chadwick Photography (page 149 left); Smith Davies Press (page 149 right).

Illustrations
Sally Artz, Richard Deverell, Hilary Evans, Gecko Ltd, Madeleine Hardy, Dai Owen, Mike Parsons, Dave Poole, Liz Roberts, Martin Sanders and Nick Ward.

Every effort has been made to contact the holders of copyright material, but if any have been inadvertently overlooked, the Publishers will be pleased to make the necessary arrangements at the first opportunity.

You might also like to visit
www.**fire**and**water**.com
The book lover's website